GEMBA KAIZEN

OTHER McGRAW-HILL BOOKS BY MASAAKI IMAI

KAIZEN: THE KEY TO JAPAN'S COMPETITIVE SUCCESS

GEMBA KAIZEN

A COMMONSENSE, LOW-COST APPROACH TO MANAGEMENT

MASAAKI IMAI

McGraw-Hill
New York   San Francisco   Washington, D.C.   Auckland   Bogotá
Caracas   Lisbon   London   Madrid   Mexico City   Milan
Montreal   New Delhi   San Juan   Singapore
Sydney   Tokyo   Toronto

Library of Congress Cataloging-in-Publication Data

Imai, Masaaki.
  Gemba kaizen : a commonsense, low-cost approach to management /
Masaaki Imai.
      p.   cm.
  Includes index.
  ISBN 0-07-031446-2
  1. Industrial management.   2. Service industries—Management.
I. Title.
HD31.I43   1997
658.5—dc21   96-52406
                                                             CIP

McGraw-Hill

*A Division of The **McGraw·Hill** Companies*

8 9 10 FGRFGR 0 5 4 3 2 1 0

ISBN 0-07-031446-2

*The sponsoring editor for this book was Philip Ruppel, the editing
supervisor was Jane Palmieri, and the production supervisor was
Pamela Pelton. It was set in Fairfield by Victoria Khavkina of
McGraw-Hill's Professional Book Group composition unit.*

 This book is printed on recycled, acid-free paper
containing a minimum of 50% recycled, de-inked fiber.

CONTENTS

FOREWORD

I was in Tokyo's Hotel Okura in 1986 when I first ran across Masaaki Imai's book, *Kaizen: The Key to Japan's Competitive Success*. For many years, I had been intrigued by why the Japanese were so very advanced in manufacturing. My curiosity about this began with my interest in photography. Back in the 1960s, the Japanese had begun making cameras that were better than those made by the European community. And they were about one-half the cost. That fascinated me. Moreover, this was just one example of the many superior products that were beginning to come out of Japan in the late 1960s and early 1970s. I wondered whether it was due to a cultural reaction to World War II or to some secret process the Japanese were using.

In search of the answer, I read a lot of books about Japanese business practices and talked to a number of Japanese executives. When I read about *kaizen*, I quickly realized I was approaching the key to their success. I also thought *kaizen*, which had worked so well in manufacturing, might have applications for the business of servicing mutual fund shareholders. I brought the concept home and started to introduce it to some of the senior management in our company. The timing couldn't have been better because, in October 1987, the United States stock market took a severe downturn. In an environment where we had little control over current investment returns, we began to focus instead on improving our service to build customer loyalty. And *kaizen*—the spirit that whatever you're doing, you can do better—gave us the foundation we needed to work as a team in setting and reaching higher service standards. It also helped us successfully weather a rough patch in our investment business.

Over the past ten years, we've continued our focus on *kaizen*, and we've seen many gains as a result. Yet we know that there is—and will always be—room for improvement, both in the services we deliver to customers and in how we apply the concept of *kaizen* to our business. That's where *gemba kaizen* comes in. It's a practical guide to implementing *kaizen* in any business, be it manufacturing or service. And anyone—employees and senior management alike—can benefit. For example, the author tells us about the many little ways that individuals can practice *kaizen* every day, whether by eliminating waste, reorganizing their workstations, or finding better ways to do their jobs. Few of these steps require approval from on high or large expenditures. They simply involve attention to details and commonsense ways of working smarter. But, taken together, they can make a big difference in terms of improved quality, lower costs, and enhanced timeliness.

I especially like Masaaki Imai's emphasis on measurement and standards. Objective measurements are the best way to determine where you need improvement and whether or not you've improved. In itself, measurement is a very simple concept. Yet, sometimes finding the right standard isn't easy. In the service business, we've found that measuring output quality is often less tangible than it is in a manufacturing operation. On a production line, you know you're in big trouble if the product you're making is supposed to last ten years but breaks down in ten minutes. It's less clear-cut when you're continually providing a service. However, the search for the right standards has helped teach us about our weakness. And it has also helped us focus on finding the best-known way to do a particular process.

With practice, as Imai demonstrates in his case studies, *kaizen,* or continual improvement, can become a way of life. It's an attitude, a spirit that prevails at all times in the company. It's not something that you can expect to implement overnight or turn on when sales start declining. But once *kaizen* does take hold, employees and managers alike begin to recognize that part of their job—as important as doing the work—is learning how to improve the way they do it. Imai points out that this approach makes work much more challenging and interesting. I agree. There's a continual dialogue between management and employees as they work together to help set and meet standards and then develop new and better standards. Improvement has no end.

Over the years, we've seen many strategies for management success come and go. In my experience, *kaizen* is different. It's not a fad. It helps us focus in a very basic way on how we do our work. The process of doing our work becomes an end in itself as well as a means of gratification. For me, that's where the real joy comes. In today's highly competitive business environment, companies that want to be leaders in their fields have to ask continually, "How can we do the job better tomorrow than we're doing it today? In *Gemba Kaizen*, Masaaki Imai gives us the tools to do just that.

Edward C. Johnson, III
CHAIRMAN AND CHIEF EXECUTIVE OFFICER
FIDELITY INVESTMENTS

PREFACE

My previous book, *Kaizen: The Key to Japan's Competitive Success* (McGraw-Hill, 1986), explained major components of *kaizen*, such as total quality control, total productive maintenance, just-in-time management, quality circles, and suggestion systems, as well as various *kaizen* principles and concepts.

Gemba Kaizen introduces a new word to Western management culture. *Gemba* means workplace, and this book explains how to use a commonsense, low-cost approach to managing the workplace—the place where value is added—whether that place be the production line, the underwriting department, or the accounting office. This is not a book of theory, but a book of action. Its ultimate message is that, no matter how much knowledge the reader may gain, it is of no use if it is not put into practice daily. *Gemba Kaizen* provides, not more theoretical knowledge, but a simple frame of reference to use in solving problems. To that purpose, it provides many checklists, examples, and case studies.

THE COMMONSENSE, LOW-COST APPROACH TO IMPROVEMENT

Today's managers often try to apply sophisticated tools and technologies to deal with problems that can be solved with a commonsense, low-cost approach. They need to unlearn the habit of trying ever-more sophisticated technologies to solve everyday problems.

Putting common sense into practice is the subject of this

book. It is for everybody: managers, engineers, supervisors, and rank-and-file employees. Along with putting common sense into practice, *Gemba Kaizen* deals with the roles of managers and the need to develop a learning organization. I believe that one of the roles of top management should be to challenge all managers to attain ever higher goals. In turn, first-line supervisors need to challenge workers to do a better job all the time. Unfortunately, many managers today have long ceased to play such a role.

Another problem besetting most companies today is the tendency to place too much emphasis on *teaching* knowledge, while disregarding group *learning* of fundamental values derived from common sense, self-discipline, order, and economy. Good management should strive to lead the company to learn these values while achieving "lean management."

There are two approaches to problem solving. The first involves innovation—applying the latest high-cost technology, such as state-of-the-art computers and other tools, and investing a great deal of money. The second uses commonsense tools, checklists, and techniques that do not cost much money. This approach is called *kaizen*. *Kaizen* involves *everybody*—starting with the CEO in the organization—planning and working together for success. This book will show how *kaizen* can achieve significant improvement as an essential building block that prepares the company for truly rewarding accomplishments.

HOUSEKEEPING, *MUDA* ELIMINATION, AND STANDARDIZATION

Everyone in the company must work together to follow three ground rules for practicing *kaizen* in *gemba*:

1. housekeeping
2. *muda* elimination
3. standardization

Housekeeping is an indispensable ingredient of good management. Through good housekeeping, employees acquire and practice self-discipline. Employees without self-discipline make it impossible to provide products or services of good quality to the customer.

In Japanese, the word *muda* means waste. Any activity that does not add value is *muda*. People in *gemba* either add value or do not add value. This is also true for other resources, such as machines and materials. Suppose a company's employees are adding nine parts *muda* for every one part value. Their productivity can be doubled by reducing *muda* to eight parts and increasing the added value to two parts. *Muda* elimination can be the most cost-effective way to improve productivity and reduce operating costs. *Kaizen* emphasizes the elimination of *muda* in *gemba* rather than the increasing of investment in the hope of adding value.

A simple example illustrates the cost benefits of *kaizen*. Suppose that operators assembling a household appliance are standing in front of their workstations to put certain parts into the main unit. The parts for assembly are kept in a large container behind the operators. The action of turning around to pick up a part takes an operator five seconds, while actual assembly time is only two seconds.

Now let's assume the parts are placed in front of the operator. The operator simply extends his or her arms forward to pick up a part—an action that takes only a second. The operators can use the time saved to concentrate on the (value-adding) assembly. A simple change in the location of the parts—eliminating the *muda* involved in the action of reaching behind—has yielded a four-second time gain that translates into a three-fold increase in productivity!

Such small improvements in many processes gradually accumulate, leading to significant quality improvement, cost benefits, and productivity improvements. Applying such an approach throughout all management activities, especially at top management levels, gradually achieves a just-in-time, lean management system. By contrast, an innovation-minded manager might be inclined to buy a device that would enable operators to perform their assembly task much faster. But this would not eliminate the *muda* of turning around to pick up the pieces from behind. Furthermore, buying a new device costs money, while eliminating *muda* costs nothing.

The third ground rule of *kaizen* practices in *gemba* is standardization. Standards may be defined as the best way to do the job. For products or services created as a result of a series of processes, a certain standard must be maintained at each process in order to assure quality. Maintaining standards is a way of assuring quality at each process and preventing the recurrence of errors.

As a general rule of thumb, introducing good housekeeping in *gemba* reduces the failure rate by 50 percent, and standardization further reduces the failure rate by 50 percent of the new figure. Yet many managers elect to introduce statistical process control and control charts in *gemba* without making efforts to clean house, eliminate *muda*, or standardize.

Peter Teufel, managing partner of the Kaizen Institute, reports that one of his clients was about to buy additional machines to handle an increase in business. When Teufel found that the utilization ratio of existing equipment was 38 percent, he recommended that management increase the ratio by implementing *kaizen* instead of buying new machines. The company saved 15 million deutsche marks without compromising quality or delivery.

Innovation-minded managers tend to resort to buying new machines or hiring more people, especially when business prospects are bright. On the other hand, *kaizen*-minded managers have learned to consider using existing human and other resources to improve productivity.

Supporting these rules of *kaizen* is the foundation of the house of *gemba*—namely, the use of such human-related activities as learning together, teamwork, morale enhancement, self-discipline, quality circles, and suggestions. Management (especially Western management) must regain the power of common sense and start applying it in *gemba*. These low-cost practices will provide management with the opportunity for a future phase of rapid growth via innovation—something Western management excels at. When Western management combines *kaizen* with its innovative ingenuity, it will greatly improve its competitive strength.

Masaaki Imai

ACKNOWLEDGMENTS

G*emba Kaizen* was born out of 10 years' *kaizen* consulting following the publication of my book *Kaizen: The Key to Japan's Competitive Success* in 1986.

This book is a product of joint collaborations with my fellow consultants at the Kaizen Institute; with many workers, engineers, and managers who were engaged in *gemba kaizen* at our clients' sites; and with many experts who supported our work, and I am deeply indebted to all of them.

Besides those whose names appear in the book, I am particularly indebted to Professor Zenjiro Sawada at Kurume University, who gave me the inspiration for the House of *Gemba* Management through his book *Visual Control of Factory Management* (published in English in 1991 from Nikkan Kogyo Shinbun); Ichiro Majima, Dean of Faculty of Business Administration of Miyazaki Sangyo-Keiei University, who provided much valuable information in writing this book; Kaizen consultants Kenji Takahashi, Yukio Kakiuchi, and Hitoshi Takeda, and many others who worked together with us in giving many *gemba kaizen* sessions at the clients' sites around the world.

My thanks also go to: Stu Chalmers, Kim Kaddatz, Tom Lane, Peter Teufel, Serge Le Berre, Jaap Postma, Hiromi Omoto, Kimie Anshita, Yumi Yuzawa, and others from Kaizen Institute; Carlos D. Tramutola, Renzo Terzano, Jorge Zino Gutierrez, Jorge Tesler, and Mario Muriago from STRAT of Argentina; Angel Perversi, former CEO of Bunge y Born; Joop Bokern and Dr. Siegfried Hoyler, who made tremendous contributions in advancing the cause of *kaizen* but unfortunately have since passed away. I should also add Peter Willats who contributed in developing the first few years of Kaizen Institute activities in Europe.

I also would like to thank those people who assisted in writing the cases in the book. They include Natacha Muro and Fernando Coletti of La Buenos Aires, Nestor Herrerra of Molinos Rio de la Plata, Axel Pause of Lucas Automotive, Gary Buchanan and Valerie Oberle of Disney University, Darla Hastings of Quality Inc., Bill Nigreen and Sandra Sucher of Fidelity, Shoji Shiratori of Aisin Seiki, Vittorio Neri of Infotec, and Yutaka Mori of Toyoda Automatic Loom Works as well as Yoshikazu Sano and Katsuo Inoue of Toyoda Machine Works.

Last but not least, I wish to thank my Executive Assistant Ruth Eiyama who worked on this book for months and months, putting in many hours of work going into late hours with no end, and my wife Noriko who had to accept my lifestyle, traveling around the world most of the time, though she had the pleasure of accompanying me more often than not; also to those who assisted in the making of this book, in particular, Bob Zenowich who reviewed my manuscripts and Jane Palmieri, Pamela Pelton, and Philip Ruppel of McGraw-Hill, who had the vital role of making this book a reality.

Masaaki Imai
JANUARY 1997

GLOSSARY

AQL: Acceptable Quality Level is a practice between customers and suppliers that allows suppliers to deliver a certain percentage of rejects by paying penalties.

Ask why five times: A commonsense principle of determining the root cause of a problem.

Check *gembutsu*: Examining tangible objects in *gemba* when attempting to determine the root cause of problems.

Conformance: An affirmative indication or judgment that a product or service has met the requirements of a relevant specification, contract, or regulation.

Control chart: A chart with upper and lower control limits on which values of some statistical measures for a series of samples or subgroups are plotted. The chart frequently shows a central line to help detect a trend of plotted values toward either control limit.

Cost: When used in the context of QCD, the word cost usually refers to cost management, and *not* cost cutting. Cost management refers to managing various resources properly, and eliminating all sorts of *muda* in such a way that the overall cost goes down.

Cross-functional management: An interdepartmental management activity to realize QCD.

Cycle time: The actual time taken by an operator to process a piece of product. (See *takt* time.)

Delivery: When used in the context of QCD, the word delivery refers to meeting both the delivery as well as the volume requirements of the customer.

Don't get it, don't make it, don't send it: A commonsense slogan to be implemented in *gemba* that puts into practice the belief that quality is the first priority in any program of QCD, for example, don't accept inferior quality from the previous process, don't make rejects in one's product, and if a reject has been produced, don't knowingly send it to the next process.

Failure Tree Analysis: Failure Tree Analysis is used to analyze and avoid in advance any safety and reliability problems by identifying cause-and-effect relationships and probability of problems by using the tree diagram.

Five golden rules of *gemba* management: A set of the most practical reminders in implementing *kaizen* in *gemba:* (1) Go to *gemba* when problems arise; (2) check *gembutsu*; (3) take temporary measures on the spot; (4) find and eliminate the root cause; and (5) standardize to prevent recurrence.

Five M's (5M): A method for managing resources in *gemba*—specifically those known as "5M"—manpower, machine, material, method, and measurement.

Five S's (5S): A checklist for good housekeeping to achieve greater order, efficiency, and discipline in the workplace. It is derived from the Japanese words *seiri, seiton, seiso, seiketsu,* and *shituke* and adopted to the English equivalents of *sort, straighten, scrub, systematize,* and *standardize.* In some companies it is adopted as the 5C's campaign: *clear out, configure, clean & check, conform,* and *custom & practice.*

Flow production: One of the basic pillars of just-in-time production system. In the flow production, machines are arranged in the order of processing so that the work piece flows between processes without interruptions and stagnation.

FMEA: Failure Mode and Effect Analysis is an analytical tool used to predict and eliminate in advance any potential design defect in a new product by analyzing the effects of failure modes of component parts on the final product performance. FMEA is also used for design review activities of a new production facility (called process FMEA).

FTA: See *Failure Tree Analysis.*

Gemba: A Japanese word meaning "real place"—now adapted in management terminology to mean the "workplace"—or that place where value is added. In manufacturing, it usually refers to the shop floor.

Gembutsu: The tangible objects found at *gemba* such as work pieces, rejects, jigs and tools, and machines.

Go to *gemba*: The first principle of *gemba kaizen.* This is a reminder that whenever abnormality occurs, or whenever a manager wishes to know the current state of operations, he or she should go to *gemba* right away, since *gemba* is a source of all information.

Heinrich's Law: A principle related to occurrence ratio of accidents with injuries. Heinrich expressed the ratio as follows:

$$\text{Serious injury:minor injury:no injury} = 1:29:300.$$

This equation expresses that when you see 1 person who was seriously injured by an accident, the same accident might have hurt 29 persons slightly. At the same time, there might have been 300 people who were luckily not injured but experienced the same accident.

Hiyari KYT (*kiken-yochi* training): *Hiyari* KYT refers to the practice of anticipating danger in advance and taking steps to avoid it.

Hiyari report (scare report): *Hiyari* Report (the scare report) is a written form from a worker to a supervisor that reports a condition that is unsafe and could lead to quality problems and/or accident.

Ishikawa (fishbone) diagram: A diagram originally developed by Professor Kaoru Ishikawa to show causes (process) and the effect (result). The diagram is used to determine the real cause(s) and is one of the seven basic tools of problem solving.

ISO 9000 Series Standards: A set of international standards on quality management and quality assurance developed to help companies document the quality system elements to be implemented to ensure the conformance of a product to specifications.

Jidhoka (auto<u>nom</u>ation): A device that stops a machine whenever a defective product is produced. This device is essential in introducing JIT.

Jishuken gemba kaizen: In the early 1960s, *jishuken* (autonomous JIT study team) was started to implement JIT activities in *gemba* among the Toyota Group of companies.

JIT (just-in-time): A system designed to achieve the best possible quality, cost, and delivery of products and services by eliminating all kinds of *muda* in a company's internal processes and deliver products just-in-time to meet customers' requirements. Originally developed by Toyota Motor Company, it is also called by such names as Toyota Production System, lean production system, and *kanban* system.

JK (*jishu kanri*): *Jishu kanri* means autonomous management in Japanese and refers to workers' participation in *kaizen* activities as a part of their daily activities under the guidance of the line manager; it is different from quality circle activities which are voluntary and are carried out by the workers' own volition.

Kaizen concepts: Major concepts that must be understood and practiced in implementing kaizen.

- *Kaizen* and management
- Process versus result
- Following the PDCA/SDCA
- Putting quality first
- Speaking with data
- Treating the next process as the customer

Kaizen story: A standardized problem-solving procedure to be used at each level of organization. *Kaizen* story has eight steps: (1) select a project, (2) understand current situations and set objectives, (3) analyze data to identify root causes, (4) establish countermeasures, (5) implement countermeasures, (6) confirm the effect, (7) standardize, and (8) review the above process and work on the next steps.

Kaizen **systems:** Major systems that must be established to attain a world-class status.

- Total Quality Control (Total Quality Management)
- Just-in-time production system
- Total productive maintenance
- Policy deployment
- Suggestion system
- Small-group activities

Kanban: A communication tool in the just-in-time system whenever a batch production is involved. A *kanban*, which means a sign board in Japanese, is attached to a given number of parts or products in the production line, instructing the delivery of a given quantity. When the parts have all been used, the *kanban* is returned to its origin where it becomes an order to produce more.

Kosu: Manufacturing operations can be divided between machining hours and man hours. *Kosu* refers to the specific man hours it takes to process one unit of a product in a given process and is calculated by multiplying the number of workers involved in a process by the actual time it takes to complete the process, and dividing that by the units produced. It is used as a measure of operators' productivity. *Kosu* reduction is one of the key measures of productivity improvement in *gemba*.

Morning market: A daily routine at *gemba* that involves examining rejects (*gembutsu*) made the previous day before the work begins so that countermeasures can be adopted as soon as possible, based on *gemba-gembutsu* principles. This meeting involving the *gemba* people (and not staff) is held first thing in the morning.

Muda: The Japanese word meaning "waste" which, when applied to management of the workplace, refers to a wide range of non-value-adding activities. In *gemba,* there are only two types of activities: value adding and non-value adding. In *gemba kaizen,* efforts are directed first to eliminate all types of non-value-adding activities. Elimination of *muda* in the following areas can contribute to significant improvements in QCD: overproduction, inventory, rejects, motion, processing, waiting, transport, and time. *Muda* elimination epitomizes the low-cost, commonsense approach to improvement.

Mura: Japanese word meaning irregularity or variability.

Muri: Japanese word meaning strain and difficulty.

One-piece flow: Only one work piece is allowed to flow from process to process to minimize *muda* in a just-in-time production system.

Pareto chart: A graphical tool for ranking causes from the most significant to the least significant. It is based on the Pareto principle, first defined by J. M. Juran. This 80:20 principle suggests that 80 percent of effects come from 20 percent of the possible causes. The Pareto chart is one of the seven basic tools of problem solving.

PDCA: Plan-Do-Check-Act—the basic steps to be followed in making continual improvement (*kaizen*).

Pull production: One of the basic requirements of a just-in-time production system. The previous process produces only as many products as are consumed by the following process.

Push production: The opposite of pull production. The previous process produces as much as it can without regard to the actual requirements of the next process and sends them to the next process whether there is a need or not.

QA Best-Line Certification: An in-house certification system to certify a world-class level of quality assurance performance of a particular process.

QC Circles: See *Quality Circles.*

QCD (Quality, Cost, Delivery): Quality, cost, and delivery is regarded as an ultimate goal of management. When management is successful in achieving QCD, both customer satisfaction and corporate success follow.

QCDMS: In *gemba*, often M(morale) and S(safety) are added to QCD as a target to be achieved.

QFD (Quality Function Deployment): A management approach to identify customer requirements first, and then work back through the stages of design, engineering, production, sales, and after-service of products.

QS 9000: A U.S. version of ISO 9000 series imposed by the Big Three automotive companies to the suppliers as compared with the general description of requirements by ISO 9000. QS 9000 specifies additional requirements, in particular, the need for continuous improvement of the standard and corrective actions.

Quality: In the context of QCD, quality refers to the quality of products or services delivered to the customer. In this instance, quality refers to conformance to specifications and customer requirements. In a broader sense, quality refers to the quality of work in designing, producing, delivering, and after-servicing the products or services.

Quality circles: Quality improvement or self-improvement study groups composed of a small number of employees (ten or fewer). Quality circles were originated in Japan and are called quality control (QC) circles. The QC circle voluntarily performs improvement activities within the workplace, carrying out its work continuously as a part of a companywide program of mutual education, quality control, self-development, and productivity improvement.

Scare report: See *Hiyari* report.

SDCA: Standardize-Do-Check-Act—the basic steps to be followed to maintain the current status.

Simultaneous realization of QCD: The top management must make certain that all levels of the company work to achieve Quality, Cost, and Delivery. The ultimate goal is to realize QCD simultaneously, but first of all, priority must be established among the three, quality always being the first.

Small-group activity: Shop-floor group activity to solve problems which appear at their own workplace. Groups are usually formed by five to ten shop-floor operators. Their activities are mostly similar to quality circle's. However, small-group activities are implemented not only for such activities as quality improvement, cost reduction, TPM, and productivity improvement, but also recreational and other social activities.

Standardization: Standardization is one of the three foundations of *gemba kaizen* activities and means the documentation of the best way to do the job.

Standardized work: An optimum combination of man, machine, and material. The three elements of standardized work are *takt* time, work sequence, and standard work-in-process.

Standards: A best way to do the job, namely, a set of policies, rules, directives, and procedures established by management for all major operations, which serve as guidelines that enable all employees to perform their jobs to assure good results.

Statistical process control (SPC): The application of statistical techniques to control a process. Often the term "statistical quality control" is used interchangeably.

Statistical quality control (SQC): The application of statistical techniques to control quality. Often used interchangeably with statistical process control, but includes acceptance sampling as well as statistical process control.

Store room: The place where work-in-processes and supplies are stored in *gemba*. A store room is different from the normal warehouse since only *standardized* inventory is kept in the store room.

Suggestion system: In Japan, the suggestion system is a highly integrated part of individual-oriented *kaizen*. The Japanese-style suggestion system emphasizes morale-boosting benefits and positive employee participation over the economic and financial incentives that are stressed in a Western-style system.

***Takt* time:** The theoretical time it takes to produce a piece of product ordered by the customer—as determined by dividing the total production time by the number of units to be produced.

Three K's (3K): The Japanese words referring to conventional perception of *gemba—kiken* (dangerous), *kitanai* (dirty), and *kitsui* (stressful)—in direct contrast to the idea of *gemba* being the place where real value is added and the source of ideas for achieving QCD.

Three M's (3M): *Muda* (waste), *mura* (irregularity), and *muri* (strain). These three words are used as *kaizen* checkpoints to help workers and management to identify the areas for improvement.

Three M's (3M) in *gemba*: The three major resources to be managed in *gemba*—manpower, material, and machine. (Sometimes referred to as 5M with the addition of "methods" and "measurement.")

Total productive maintenance (TPM): Total productive maintenance aims at maximizing equipment effectiveness throughout the entire life of the equipment. TPM involves everyone in all departments and at all levels; it motivates people for plant maintenance through small-group and autonomous activities, and involves such basic elements as developing a maintenance system, education in basic housekeeping, problem-solving skills, and activities to achieve zero breakdowns and accident-free *gemba*. Autonomous maintenance by workers is one of the important elements of TPM. 5S is an entry step of TPM.

Total quality control (TQC): Organized *kaizen* activities on quality involving everyone in a company—managers and workers—in a totally integrated effort toward *kaizen* at every level. It is assumed that these activities ultimately lead to increased customer satisfaction and the success of the business. In Japan, the term "total quality management" (TQM) is getting increasingly popular in usage and now is taking the place of TQC.

Total quality management (TQM): See *Total quality control (TQC)*.

TQC: See *Total quality control*.

Two-day *gemba kaizen*: *Gemba kaizen* practices at Nissan Motor Company and its suppliers. A particular process is selected and a group of internal *kaizen* consultants, engineers, and line managers spend two days in *gemba* using just-in-time and other related checklists to attain the target.

Value analysis (VA): A method for cost reduction introduced by L. D. Miles at GE in 1947. It aims at reducing material and component costs at the upstream stages of designing and design reviews and involves cross-functional collaborations of product design, production engineering, quality assurance, and manufacturing, etc. VA is also employed for competitive benchmarking.

Value engineering (**VE**): A method and practice for cost reduction developed by the U.S. Department of Defense in 1954. In Japan, both VA and VE are used almost for the same purposes (see *value analysis*).

Visual management: An effective management method to provide information and *gembutsu* in a clearly visible manner to both workers and managers so that the current state of operations and the target for *kaizen* are understood by everybody. It also helps people to identify abnormality promptly.

AN INTRODUCTION TO *KAIZEN*

Since 1986, when the book *Kaizen: The Key to Japan's Competitive Success* was published, the term *kaizen* has come to be accepted as one of the key concepts of management.

The 1993 edition of the *New Shorter Oxford English Dictionary* contained the word *kaizen.** (The *New Shorter Oxford English Dictionary* defines *kaizen* as continuous improvement of working practices, personal efficiency, etc., as a business philosophy.) Thus *kaizen* has finally gained recognition in the English vocabulary. Readers who are unfamiliar with *kaizen* may find it helpful to begin with a brief summary of the concepts of *kaizen*. For those who are already familiar with *kaizen*, this chapter may serve as a review.

In Japanese, *kaizen* means continuous improvement. The word implies improvement that involves everyone—both managers and workers—and entails relatively little expense. The *kaizen* philosophy assumes that our way of life—be it our working life, our social life, or our home life—should focus on constant-improvement efforts. This concept is so natural and obvious to many Japanese that they don't even realize they possess it! In my opinion, *kaizen* has contributed greatly to Japan's competitive success.

Although improvements under *kaizen* are small and incremental, the *kaizen* process brings about dramatic results over

---

*It should be noted that the Kaizen Institute AG and its subsidiaries and licensees have exclusive right to the use of *kaizen*,® as well as *gemba kaizen*,® as trademarks registered in major countries in the world.

time. The *kaizen* concept explains why companies cannot remain static for long in Japan. Western management, meanwhile, worships innovation: major changes in the wake of technological breakthroughs; the latest management concepts or production techniques. Innovation is dramatic, a real attention getter. *Kaizen,* on the other hand, is often undramatic and subtle. But innovation is one-shot, and its results are often problematic, while the *kaizen* process, based on common sense and low-cost approaches, assures incremental progress that pays off in the long run. *Kaizen* is also a low-risk approach. Managers can always go back to the old way without incurring large costs.

Most "uniquely Japanese" management practices, such as total quality control or companywide quality control, quality circles, and our style of labor relations, can be reduced to one word: *kaizen.* Using the term *kaizen* in place of such buzzwords as productivity, total quality control (TQC), zero defects (ZD), just-in-time (JIT), and the suggestion system paints a clearer picture of what has been going on in Japanese industry. *Kaizen* is an umbrella concept for all these practices. However, I hasten to add that these practices are not necessarily confined to Japanese management, but should rather be regarded as sound principles to be applied by managers everywhere. By following the right steps and applying the processes properly, any company, no matter what its nationality, should be able to benefit from *kaizen.*

MAJOR *KAIZEN* CONCEPTS

Management must learn to implement certain basic concepts and systems in order to realize *kaizen* strategy:

- *Kaizen* and management
- Process versus result
- Following the PDCA/SDCA cycles
- Putting quality first
- Speak with data
- The next process is the customer

By way of introduction, top management must put forth a very careful and very clear policy statement. It must then establish an implementation schedule and demonstrate leadership by practicing a *kaizen* procedure within its own ranks.

KAIZEN AND MANAGEMENT

In the context of *kaizen,* management has two major functions: maintenance and improvement. (See Figure 1-1.) Maintenance refers to activities directed toward maintaining current technological, managerial, and operating standards and upholding such standards through training and discipline. Under its maintenance function, management performs its assigned tasks so that everybody can follow standard operating procedure (SOP). Improvement, meanwhile, refers to activities directed toward elevating current standards. The Japanese view of management thus boils down to one precept: Maintain and improve standards.

As Figure 1-2 shows, improvement can be classified as either *kaizen* or innovation. *Kaizen* signifies small improvements as a result of ongoing efforts. Innovation involves a dras-

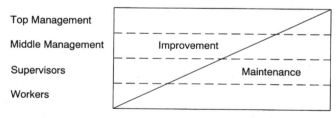

FIGURE 1-1.   Japanese perceptions of job functions.

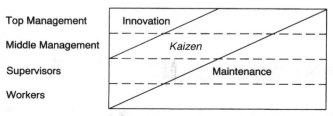

FIGURE 1-2.   Improvement broken down into innovation and *Kaizen.*

tic improvement as a result of a large investment of resources in new technology or equipment. (Whenever money is a key factor, innovation is expensive.) Because of their fascination with innovation, Western managers tend to be impatient and overlook the long-term benefits *kaizen* can bring to a company. *Kaizen,* on the other hand, emphasizes human efforts, morale, communication, training, teamwork, involvement, and self-discipline—a commonsense, low-cost approach to improvement.

PROCESS VERSUS RESULT

Kaizen fosters process-oriented thinking, since processes must be improved for results to improve. Failure to achieve planned results indicates a failure in the process. Management must identify and correct such process-based errors. *Kaizen* focuses on human efforts—an orientation that contrasts sharply with the result-based thinking in the West.

A process-oriented approach should also be applied in the introduction of the various *kaizen* strategies: the plan-do-check-act (PDCA) cycle; the standardize-do-check-act (SDCA) cycle; quality, cost, and delivery (QCD); total quality management (TQM); just-in-time; and total productive maintenance (TPM). *Kaizen* strategies have failed many companies simply because they ignored process. The most crucial element in the *kaizen* process is the commitment and involvement of top management. It must be demonstrated immediately and consistently to assure success in the *kaizen* process.

FOLLOWING THE PDCA/SDCA CYCLES

The first step in the *kaizen* process establishes the plan-do-check-act (PDCA) cycle as a vehicle that assures the continuity of *kaizen* in pursuing a policy of maintaining and improving standards. It is one of the most important concepts of the process. (See Figure 1-3.)

Plan refers to establishing a target for improvement (since *kaizen* is a way of life, there should always be a target for improvement in any area) and devising action plans to achieve the target. *Do* refers to implementing the plan. *Check* refers to determining whether the implementation remains on track

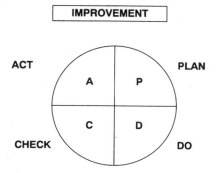

FIGURE 1-3. The plan-do-check-act (PDCA) cycle.

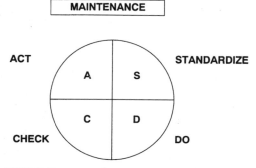

FIGURE 1-4. The standardize-do-check-act (SDCA) cycle.

and has brought about the planned improvement. *Act* refers to performing and standardizing the new procedures to prevent recurrence of the original problem or to set goals for the new improvements. The PDCA cycle revolves continuously; no sooner is an improvement made than the resulting status quo becomes the target for further improvement. PDCA means never being satisfied with the status quo. Because employees prefer the status quo and frequently do not have initiative to improve conditions, management must initiate PDCA by establishing continuously challenging goals.

In the beginning, any new work process is unstable. Before one starts working on PDCA, any current process must be stabilized in a process often referred to as the standardize-do-check-act (SDCA) cycle. (See Figure 1-4.)

Every time an abnormality occurs in the current process, the following questions must be asked: Did it happen because we did not have a standard? Did it happen because the standard was not followed? Or did it happen because the standard was not adequate? Only after a standard has been established and followed, stabilizing the current process, should one move on to PDCA.

Thus, SDCA standardizes and stabilizes the current processes, while PDCA improves them. SDCA refers to maintenance and PDCA refers to improvement; these become the two major responsibilities of management.

PUTTING QUALITY FIRST

Of the primary goals of quality, cost, and delivery, quality should always have the highest priority. No matter how attractive the price and delivery terms offered to the customer, the company will not be able to compete if the product or service lacks quality. Practicing a quality-first credo requires management commitment because managers often face the temptation to make compromises in meeting delivery requirements or cutting costs. In doing so, they risk sacrificing not only quality but the life of the business as well.

SPEAK WITH DATA

Kaizen is a problem-solving process. In order for a problem to be correctly understood and solved, the problem must be recognized and the relevant data gathered and analyzed. Trying to solve a problem without hard data is akin to resorting to hunches and feelings—not a very scientific or objective approach. Collecting data on the current status helps you understand where you are now focusing; this serves as a starting point for improvement. Collecting, verifying, and analyzing data for improvement is a theme that recurs throughout this book, as you will see later.

The Next Process Is the Customer

All work is a series of processes, and each process has its supplier as well as its customer. A material or a piece of information provided by process A (supplier) is worked on and improved in process B and then sent on to process C. The next process should always be regarded as a customer. This axiom—the next process is the customer—refers to two types of customers: internal (within the company) and external (out in the market).

Most people working in an organization deal with internal customers. This realization should lead to a commitment never to pass on defective parts or inaccurate pieces of information to those in the next process. When everybody in the organization practices this axiom, the external customer in the market receives a high-quality product or service as a result. A real quality-assurance system means that everybody in the organization subscribes to and practices this axiom.

MAJOR *KAIZEN* SYSTEMS

The following are major systems that should be in place in order to successfully achieve a *kaizen* strategy:

- Total quality control/total quality management
- A just-in-time production system (Toyota Production System)
- Total productive maintenance
- Policy deployment
- A suggestion system
- Small-group activities

Total Quality Control/Total Quality Management

One of the principles of Japanese management has been total quality control (TQC), which, in its early development, emphasized control of the quality process. This has evolved into a system encompassing all aspects of management, and is now referred to as total quality management (TQM), a term used internationally.

Regarding the TQC/TQM movement as a part of *kaizen* strategy gives us a clearer understanding of the Japanese approach. Japanese TQC/TQM should not be regarded strictly as a quality control activity; TQC/TQM has been developed as a *strategy* to aid management in becoming more competitive and profitable by helping it to improve in all aspects of business. In TQC/TQM, Q, meaning *quality,* has priority, but there are other goals, too—namely, cost and delivery.

The T in TQC/TQM signifies *total,* meaning that it involves everybody in the organization, from top management through middle managers, supervisors, and shop floor workers. It further extends to suppliers, dealers, and wholesalers. The T also refers to top management's leadership and performance—so essential for successful implementation of TQC/TQM.

The C refers to *control* or *process control.* In TQC/TQM, key processes must be identified, controlled, and improved on continuously in order to improve results. Management's role in TQC/TQM is to set up a plan to check the process against the result in order to improve the process, not to criticize the process on the basis of the result.

TQC/TQM in Japan encompasses such activities as policy deployment, building quality assurance systems, standardization, training and education, cost management, and quality circles.

THE JUST-IN-TIME PRODUCTION SYSTEM

Originating at Toyota Motor Company under the leadership of Taiichi Ohno, the just-in-time (JIT) production system aims at eliminating non-value-adding activities of all kinds and achieving a lean production system flexible enough to accommodate fluctuations in customer orders. This production system is supported by such concepts as *takt* time (the time it takes to produce one unit) versus cycle time, one-piece flow, pull production, *jidohka* (auto*no*mation), U-shaped cells, and setup reduction.

To realize the ideal just-in-time production system, a series of *kaizen* activities must be carried out continuously to eliminate non-value-adding work in *gemba*. JIT dramatically reduces cost, delivers the product in time, and greatly enhances company profits.

Total Productive Maintenance (TPM)

An increasing number of manufacturing companies now practice total productive maintenance (TPM) within as well as outside of Japan. Whereas TQM emphasizes improving overall management performance and quality, TPM focuses on improving equipment quality. TPM seeks to maximize equipment efficiency through a total system of preventive maintenance spanning the lifetime of the equipment.

Just as TQM involves everybody in the company, TPM involves everybody at the plant. The five S's of housekeeping (discussed in Chapter 5), another pivotal activity in *gemba*, may be regarded as a prelude to TPM. However, five-S activities have registered remarkable achievements in many cases even when carried out separately from TPM.

Policy Deployment

Although *kaizen* strategy aims at making improvements, its impact may be limited if everybody is engaged in *kaizen* for *kaizen*'s sake without any aim. Management should establish clear targets to guide everyone and make certain to provide leadership for all *kaizen* activities directed toward achieving the targets. Real *kaizen* strategy at work requires closely supervised implementation.

First, top management must devise a long-term strategy, broken down into medium-term and annual strategies. Top management must have a plan to deploy strategy, passing it down through subsequent levels of management until it reaches the shop floor. As the strategy cascades down to the lower echelons, the plan should include increasingly specific action plans and activities. For instance, a policy statement along the lines of "We must reduce our cost by 10 percent to stay competitive" may be translated on the shop floor to such activities as increasing productivity, reducing inventory and rejects, and improving line configurations.

Kaizen without a target would resemble a trip without a destination. *Kaizen* is most effective when everybody works to achieve a target, and management should set that target.

THE SUGGESTION SYSTEM

The suggestion system functions as an integral part of individual-oriented *kaizen,* and emphasizes the morale-boosting benefits of positive employee participation. Japanese managers see its primary role as that of sparking employee interest in *kaizen* by encouraging them to provide many suggestions, no matter how small. Japanese employees are often encouraged to discuss their suggestions verbally with supervisors and put them into action right away, even before submitting suggestion forms. They do not expect to reap great economic benefits from each suggestion. Developing *kaizen*-minded and self-disciplined employees is the primary goal. This outlook contrasts sharply with that of Western management's emphasis on the economic benefits and financial incentives of suggestion systems.

SMALL-GROUP ACTIVITIES

A *kaizen* strategy includes small-group activities—informal, voluntary, intracompany groups organized to carry out specific tasks in a workshop environment. The most popular type of small-group activity is quality circles. Designed to address not only quality issues but also such issues as cost, safety, and productivity, quality circles may be regarded as group-oriented *kaizen* activities. Quality circles have played an important part in improving product quality and productivity in Japan. However, their role has often been blown out of proportion by overseas observers, who believe that these groups are the mainstay of quality activities in Japan. Management plays a leading role in realizing quality—in ways that include building quality assurance systems, providing employee training, establishing and deploying policies, and building cross-functional systems for quality, cost, and delivery. Successful quality circle activities indicate that management plays an invisible but vital role in supporting such activities.

THE ULTIMATE GOAL OF *KAIZEN* STRATEGY

Since *kaizen* deals with improvement, we must know which aspects of business activities need to be improved most. And the answer to this question is quality, cost, and delivery (QCD). My previous book, *Kaizen: The Key to Japan's Competitive Success*, used the term quality, cost, and scheduling (QCS). Since that time QCD has replaced QCS as the commonly accepted terminology.

Quality refers not only to the quality of finished products or services, but also to the quality of the processes that go into those products or services. *Cost* refers to the overall cost of designing, producing, selling, and servicing the product or service. *Delivery* means delivering the requested volume in time. When the three conditions defined by the term QCD are met, customers are satisfied.

QCD activities bridge such functional and departmental lines as research and development, engineering, production, sales, and after-sales service. Therefore, cross-functional collaborations are necessary, as are collaborations with suppliers and dealers. It is top management's responsibility to review the current position of the company's QCD in the marketplace and to establish priorities for its QCD improvement policy.

Following the chapters of this book we have assembled a number of cases that illustrate how various companies from both manufacturing and service sectors have implemented the concepts and systems of *gemba kaizen*.

CHAPTER TWO

GEMBA KAIZEN

In Japanese *gemba* means *real place*—the place where real action occurs. Japanese use the word *gemba* in their daily speech. When the earthquakes shook Kobe in January 1995, TV reporters at the scene referred to themselves as "reporting from *gemba*"; in the background, one could see houses in flames or collapsed elevated highways. In business, the value-adding activities that satisfy the customer happen in *gemba.*

Within Japanese industry, the word *gemba* is almost as popular as *kaizen.* Joop Bokern, one of the first *kaizen* consultants in Europe, had worked at Philips Electronics N.V. in Europe as production manager, as plant director, and finally as corporate quality manager. Bokern said that whenever he visited a Japanese company, he had a rule of thumb to determine whether the company was a good one or not. If, in his conversation with the Japanese manager, he heard the word *kaizen* within the first five minutes and the word *gemba* within the first ten minutes, he concluded that it must be a good company. Bokern's example shows that *kaizen* and *gemba* are subjects close to managers' hearts and that they often make decisions based on their understanding of *gemba.*

All businesses practice three major activities directly related to earning profit: developing, producing, and selling. Without these activities, a company cannot exist. Therefore, in a broad sense, *gemba* means the sites of these three major activities.

In a narrower context, however, *gemba* means the place where the products or services are formed. This book will use the word in this narrower context, since these sites have been one of the business arenas most neglected by management. Managers seem to overlook the workplace as a means to generate revenue, and they usually place far more emphasis on such sectors as financial management, marketing and sales, and product development. When management focuses on *gemba* or worksites, they discover opportunities for making the company far more successful and profitable.

In many service sectors, *gemba* is where the customers come into contact with the services offered. In the hotel business, for instance, *gemba* is everywhere: in the lobby, the dining room, guest rooms, the reception desk, the check-in counters, and the concierge station. At banks, the tellers are working in *gemba,* as are the loan officers receiving applicants. The same goes for employees working at desks in offices and for telephone operators sitting in front of switchboards. Thus *gemba* spans a multitude of office and administrative functions. Most departments in these service companies have internal customers with whom they have inter-departmental activity, which also represents *gemba.* A telephone call to a general manager, production manager, or quality manager at a Japanese plant is likely to get a response from the manager's assistant to the effect that "He is out at *gemba.*"

GEMBA AND MANAGEMENT

In or at *gemba,* customer-satisfying value is added to the product or service that enables the company to survive and prosper. Figure 2-1 places *gemba* at the top of the organization, showing its importance to the company. The regular management layers—top management, middle management, engineering staff, and supervisors—exist to provide the necessary support to the worksite. For that matter, *gemba* should be the site of all improvements and the source of all information. Therefore, management must maintain close contact with the realities of *gemba* in order to solve whatever problems arise there. To put it differently, whatever assistance management provides should start from the specific needs of the worksite. When management does not respect and appreciate *gemba,* it tends to "dump" its instructions, designs, and other supporting services—often in complete disregard of actual requirements.

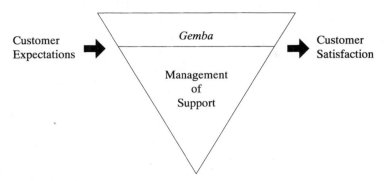

FIGURE 2-1.   In this view of *gemba*-management relations, management's role is to provide support to *gemba,* which is seen as being at the top of management structure.

Management exists to help *gemba* do a better job by reducing constraints as much as possible. In reality, however, I wonder how many managers correctly understand their role. More often than not, managers regard *gemba* as a failure source where things always go wrong, and they neglect their responsibility for those problems.

In some Western companies where the influence of strong unions practically controls *gemba,* management avoids involvement in *gemba* affairs. Sometimes management even appears afraid of the plant, and seems almost lost or helpless. Even in places where the union does not exercise a firm grip, *gemba* work is left to veteran supervisors who are allowed by management to run the show as they please. In such cases, management has lost control of the workplace.

Subsequent chapters will discuss in depth what management of *gemba* really means. Supervisors should play a key role in *gemba* management, and yet they often lack the basic training to manage or to do their most important job: maintaining and improving the standards and achieving quality, cost, and delivery.

Eric Machiels, who came to Japan from Europe as a young student to learn about Japanese management practices, was placed in a Japanese automotive assembly plant as an operator: Comparing his experience there with his previous experience in European *gemba,* Machiels observed much more intense communication between management and operators in Japan, resulting in a much more effective two-way information flow between them. Workers had a much clearer understanding of management expectations and of their own responsibilities in the whole *kaizen* process. The resulting constructive tension on the work floor made the work much more challenging in terms of meeting management expectations and giving workers a higher sense of pride in their work.

Maintaining *gemba* at the top of the management structure requires committed employees. Workers must be inspired to fulfill their roles, to feel proud of their jobs, and to appreciate the contribution they make to their company and society. Instilling a sense of mission and pride is an integral part of management's responsibility for *gemba*.

This approach contrasts sharply with perceptions of *gemba* (Figure 2-2) that regard it as a place where things always go wrong, a source of failure and customer complaints. In Japan, production-related work is sometimes referred to as three-K, signifying the Japanese words for dangerous (*kiken*), dirty (*kitanai*), and stressful (*kitsui*). Once upon a time, *gemba* was a place good managers avoided, and being assigned a position there amounted to a career dead end. Today, in contrast, the presidents of some better-known Japanese companies have rich backgrounds in *gemba* areas. They possess a good understanding of what goes on in *gemba* and provide support accordingly.

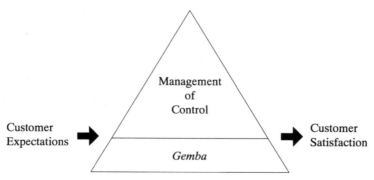

FIGURE 2-2. In this view of *gemba*-management relations, management's role is to manage *gemba* by providing policies and resources.

The two opposite views of *gemba*—as sitting on top of the management structure (inverted triangle) and as sitting on the bottom of management structure (normal triangle)—are equally valid in terms of *gemba*-management relations. *Gemba* and management share an equally important place—*gemba* by providing the product or service that satisfies the customer and management by setting strategy and deploying policy to achieve that goal in *gemba*. Thus the thrust for improvement should be both bottom-up and top-down. In Figure 2-2, management stays on top of the organization. It takes the initiative in establishing policies, targets, and priorities and in allocating resources such as manpower and money. In this model, management must exercise leadership and determine the kind of *kaizen* most urgently needed. This process of achieving corporate objectives is called policy deployment. Because of their attachment to the *gemba*-management relationship as shown in the regular triangle (Figure 2-2), many managers tend to believe that their job is always to tell *gemba* what to do. However, by looking at the inverted triangle (Figure 2-1) showing *gemba* at the top, managers can see that they should listen to and learn from employees in *gemba* in order to provide appropriate help. *Gemba* becomes the source for achieving commonsense, low-cost improvements.

The respective roles of management and *gemba* in these two models should never be confused.

Assistant Professor Takeshi Kawase of Keio University writes, in *Solving Industrial Engineering Problems* (published by Nikkan Kogyo Shinbun in Japanese, 1995):

> People within a company can be divided into two groups: those who earn money and those who don't. Only those frontline people who develop, produce, and sell products are earning money for the company. The ideal company would have only one person who does not earn money—the president—leaving the rest of the employees directly involved in revenue-generating activity.

The people who do not earn money are those who sit on top of the money earners—all employees with titles such as chief, head, or manager, including the president and all staff, and spanning areas that include personnel, finance, advertising, quality, and industrial engineering. No matter how hard these people may work, they do not directly earn money for the company. For this reason, they might be better referred to as "dependents." If money earners stop work for one second, the company's chances of making money will be lost by one second.

The trouble is that non–money earners often think that they know better and are better qualified than money earners because they are better educated. They often make the job of the latter more difficult. Non–money earners may think, "Without us, they cannot survive," when they should be thinking, "What can we do to help them do their job better without us?"

If we call the customer king, we should call the *gemba* people Buddha.

Historically, the corporate staff played a leading role in regard to *gemba*; the staff were accountable for achieving greater efficiency by providing guidance for *gemba* people to follow. The shortcoming of this system is the separation between those who pass down directives and those who carry them out. The new approach should be what we might call a *gemba*-centered approach, where *gemba* is accountable not only for production but also for quality and cost, while staff assist from the sidelines. The following are the conditions for successful implementation of a *gemba*-centered approach.

- *Gemba* management must accept accountability for achieving QCD.
- *Gemba* must be allowed enough elbow room for *kaizen*.
- Management should provide the target for *gemba* to achieve but should be accountable for the outcome. (Also, management should assist *gemba* in achieving the target.)

The benefits of the *gemba*-centered approach are many:

- *Gemba*'s needs are more easily identified by the people working there.
- Somebody on the line is always thinking about all kinds of problems and solutions.
- Resistance to change is minimized.
- Continual adjustment becomes possible.
- Solutions grounded in reality can be obtained.
- Solutions emphasize commonsense and low-cost approaches rather than expensive and method-oriented approaches.
- People begin to enjoy *kaizen* and are readily inspired.
- *Kaizen* awareness and work efficiency can be enhanced simultaneously.
- Workers can think about *kaizen* while working.
- It is not always necessary to gain upper management's approval in order to make changes.

THE HOUSE OF *GEMBA*

Two major activities take place in *gemba* on a daily basis as regards resource management—namely, maintenance and *kaizen*. The former relates to following existing standards and maintaining the status quo, and the latter relates to improving such standards. *Gemba* managers engage in one or the other of these two functions, and quality, cost, and delivery (QCD) is the outcome.

Figure 2-3, the House of *Gemba*, shows a bird's-eye view of activities taking place in *gemba* that achieve QCD. A company that produces quality products or services at a reasonable price and delivers them on time satisfies its customers, and they in turn remain loyal. (For a more detailed explanation of quality, cost, and delivery, see Chapter 3.)

STANDARDIZATION

In order to realize QCD, the company must manage various resources properly on a daily basis. These resources include manpower, information, equipment, and materials. Efficient

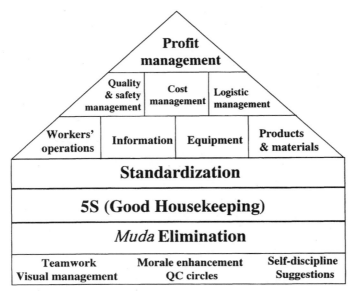

FIGURE 2-3.   House of *Gemba* management.

daily management of resources requires standards. Every time problems or irregularities arise, the manager must investigate, identify the root cause, and revise the existing standards or implement new ones to prevent recurrence. Standards become an integral part of *gemba kaizen* and provide the basis for daily improvement.

Properly applied, *kaizen* can improve quality, reduce cost considerably and meet customers' delivery requirements without any significant investment or introduction of new technology. Three major *kaizen* activities—standardization, the five S's, which cover various housekeeping tasks, and the elimination of *muda* (waste) contribute to successful QCD. These three activities are indispensable in building lean, efficient, and successful QCD. Standardization, *muda* elimination, and the five S's are easy to understand and implement and do not require sophisticated knowledge or technology. Anybody—any manager, any supervisor, or any employee—can readily introduce these commonsense, low-cost activities. The difficult part is building the self-discipline necessary to maintain them.

Standardization in *gemba* often means the translation of

technological and engineering requirements specified by engineers into workers' day-to-day operational standards. Such a translating process does not require technology or sophistication. It does require a clear plan from management deployed in logical phases. (For details of standards, refer to Chapter 4.)

THE FIVE S's OF GOOD HOUSEKEEPING

The five S's stand for five Japanese words that constitute housekeeping. Today, practicing the five S's has become almost a must for any company engaged in manufacturing. An observant *gemba* management expert can determine the caliber of a company in five minutes by visiting the plant and taking a good look at what goes on there, especially in regard to *muda* elimination and the five S's. A lack of the five S's in *gemba* indicates inefficiency, *muda*, insufficient self-discipline, low morale, poor quality, high costs, and an inability to meet delivery terms. Suppliers not practicing the five S's will not be taken seriously by prospective customers. These five points of housekeeping represent a starting point for any company that seeks to be recognized as a responsible manufacturer eligible for world-class status. (The implications of the five S's will be explained in detail in Chapter 5.)

Recently, before starting assembly operations in Europe, a Japanese automobile manufacturer sent purchasing managers to visit several prospective European suppliers. Eagerly anticipating new business, one of the suppliers prepared a detailed schedule for receiving the potential customers, starting with an hour-long presentation, complete with graphs and charts, on their efforts to improve quality. Next, the visitors would receive a tour of *gemba*. On arrival, the purchasing managers were shown into the conference room. However, they insisted on being taken to *gemba* right away, skipping the conference agenda. Once at the plant, they stayed only a few minutes before preparing to leave.

Bewildered, the general manager of the plant implored, "Please tell us about your findings!" The purchasing group replied, "We saw a very low level of housekeeping and found the plant very disorderly. Even worse, we saw some workers smoking while working on the line. If management allows these things to happen in *gemba*, it cannot be serious enough about making components vital for automotive safety, and we do not want to deal with management that is not serious enough."

MUDA ELIMINATION

Muda means *waste* in Japanese; however, the implications of the word include anything or any activity that does not add value. In *gemba*, only two types of activities go on: value adding or non–value adding. A worker looking at an automatic machine while the machine processes a piece does not add any value. The machine does the only value-adding work, no matter how attentively and affectionately the worker may look at it. When a maintenance engineer walks a long distance with a tool in his hand, he is not adding any value. The value is added by using the tool to fix, maintain, or set up the machine.

Customers do not pay for non-value-adding activities. Why, then, do so many people in *gemba* engage in non-value-adding activities?

A manager of one factory once checked how far a worker walked in *gemba* in the course of a year and found that the worker walked a distance of 400 kilometers. Jogging for health should be done in the gym, not in *gemba*! Ironically, some factories are equipped with gyms that have running tracks, but the workers spend more time jogging in *gemba* during working hours than in the gym during off hours.

Once, when I was at Dallas–Fort Worth Airport in Texas, I needed to have my ticket endorsed in order to switch to another airline company. After I had stood in line at the ticket counter for several minutes, my turn came, whereupon I was told that I had to go to another desk in another terminal to get the endorsement. I had to take a tram to the other terminal because the terminals at Dallas–Forth Worth are so far apart (a big *muda* in *kaizen* terms!). At the counter there, I waited in line again for several minutes. When my turn came, the airline employee stamped my ticket with a bang! and said, "Here you are, sir!" I asked myself, "Did I deserve to wait almost half an hour for this?" At what moment did I get my value? Bang! That was the moment of truth, as far as I was concerned. When a company in the service industry conducts its business inefficiently, the company is not only wasting its own resources but also stealing the valued customer's time.

Any work that takes place in *gemba* is actually a series of processes. Assuming 100 processes from receipt of raw materials and components until final assembly and shipment, the value-adding time at each process is just like that bang! Just think about how little time it takes to press a sheet of metal, shape a piece of work on a lathe, process a sheet of paper, or give a signature for approval. These value-adding activities take only seconds. Even supposing that each process takes one minute, value-adding activity for 100 processes should take no more than a total of 100 minutes. Why is it, then, that in most companies days or weeks pass from the time raw materials and parts are brought in and finished products emerge, or for a document to go through the production process? There is far too much *muda* between the value-adding moments. We should seek to realize a series of processes in which we can concentrate on each value-adding process—Bang! Bang! Bang!—and eliminate intervening downtime. (Chapter 6 offers a more detailed explanation of *muda*.)

Muda elimination and good housekeeping often go hand in hand. Facilities where *muda* has been eliminated are orderly and show a high level of the five S's.

Good housekeeping indicates good employee morale and self-discipline. Any company can achieve a high level of self-discipline among employees temporarily. Sustaining that level, however, is a very challenging job. And the moment it disappears, its absence shows up in the form of a disorderly *gemba*. Increased morale and self-discipline within *gemba* require involvement, participation, and information sharing with employees. Certain activities expedite the process of *kaizen* and maintain its momentum, eventually bringing change to the culture. These include teamwork, such as quality-circle and other small-group activities, and employee suggestion schemes, in which workers remain continuously on the lookout for potential *kaizen* targets. When *gemba* employees participate in *kaizen* activities and notice the dramatic changes that have taken place as a result, they grow much more enthusiastic and self-disciplined.

More positive communication on policy deployment at the plant as well as in a company's offices, worker participating in setting up goals for *kaizen,* and the use of various kinds of visual management also play a vital role in sustaining the momentum of *kaizen* in *gemba.* (Chapter 7 addresses employee empowerment, involvement, and participation.)

THE GOLDEN RULES OF *GEMBA* MANAGEMENT

Most managers prefer their desk as their workplace and wish to distance themselves from the events taking place in *gemba*. Most managers come into contact with reality only through their daily, weekly, or even monthly reports and meetings.

Staying in close contact with and understanding *gemba* is the first step in managing a production site effectively. Hence the five golden rules of *gemba* management:

1. When a problem (abnormality) arises, go to *gemba* first.
2. Check the *gembutsu* (relevant objects).
3. Take temporary countermeasures on the spot.
4. Find the root cause.
5. Standardize to prevent recurrence.

GO TO GEMBA FIRST

Management responsibilities include hiring and training workers, setting the standards for their work, and designing the product and processes. Management sets the conditions in *gemba,* and whatever happens there reflects upon management. Managers must know firsthand the conditions in *gemba;* thus the axiom "Go to *gemba* first." As a matter of routine, managers and supervisors should immediately go to the site and stand in one spot attentively observing what goes on. After developing the habit of going to *gemba,* the manager will develop the confidence to use the habit to solve specific problems.

Kristianto Jahja, a *kaizen* consultant who worked for the joint venture in Indonesia between the Astra group and Toyota Motor company, recalls the first time he was sent to Toyota's plant in Japan for training. On the first day, a supervisor who was assigned as his mentor took him to a corner of the plant, drew a small circle on the floor with chalk, and told him to stay within the circle all morning and keep his eyes on what was happening.

So Kristianto watched and watched. Half an hour and then an hour went by. As time passed, he became bored because he was simply watching routine and repetitive work. Eventually, he became angry and said to himself, "What is my supervisor trying to do? I'm supposed to learn something here, but he doesn't teach me anything. Does he want to show his power? What kind of training is this?" Before he became too frustrated, though, the supervisor came back and took him to the meeting room.

There, Kristianto was asked to describe what he had observed. He was asked specific questions like "What did you see there?" and "What did you think about that process?" Kristianto could not answer most of the questions. He realized that he had missed many vital points in his observations.

The supervisor patiently explained to Kristianto the points he had failed to answer, using drawings and sketches on a sheet of paper so that he could describe the processes more clearly and accurately. At this point Kristianto understood his mentor's deep understanding of the process and realized his ignorance.

Slowly but steadily, it became clear to Kristianto: *Gemba* is a source of all information. Then his mentor said that to qualify as a Toyota man, one must love *gemba,* and that every Toyota employee believes *gemba* is the most important place in the company.

Says Kristianto, "Definitely, this was the best training I ever had, as it helped me to truly become a *gemba* man, and this *gemba* thinking has influenced me throughout my career. Even now, every time I see a problem, my mind immediately shouts out loud and clear: Go to *gemba* first and have a look!"

This is a common training method in Japanese *gemba.* Taiichi Ohno is credited with having developed the Toyota production system. When Ohno noticed a supervisor out of touch with the realities of *gemba,* he would take the supervisor to the plant, draw a circle, and have the supervisor stand in it until he gained awareness. Ohno urged managers, too, to visit *gemba.* He would say, "Go to *gemba* every day. And when you go, don't wear out the soles of your shoes in vain. You should come back with at least one idea for *kaizen.*"

When he first began introducing just-in-time concepts at Toyota, Ohno encountered resistance from all quarters. One source of strong opposition was the company's financial people, who only believed written financial reports and often did not support allocating resources to *gemba*-related *kaizen* because doing so did not always yield immediate bottom-line results. To soften this opposition, Ohno urged accountants to go to the plant. He told them to wear out two pairs of shoes per year just walking around the site observing how inventory, efficiency, quality, etc., were improved and how the improvements contributed to cost reductions that ultimately produced higher profits.

In his later years Ohno made public speeches sharing his experiences. He is reported to have opened one such speech by asking, "Are there any financial people in the audience?" When several people raised their hands, he told them, "You are not going to understand what I am going to say. Even if you understand, you are not going to be able to implement it, since you live far away from *gemba*. Knowing how busy you are, I believe your time will be better spent if you go back to your desk to work." He said this facetiously, knowing that the support of financial managers is crucial for *gemba kaizen*.

Fuji Xerox President Akira Miyahara started his career at the Fuji Photo Film Company as a cost accountant. Knowing that *gemba* was the source of the real data, he would go to *gemba* to ascertain the information he obtained. When he received the data about rejects for his financial report, he felt compelled to go to *gemba* and observe the reason for the rejects, as he believed that an accountant's job was not simply to deal with numbers, but to understand the process behind the numbers. As Miyahara was seen in *gemba* so often, the supervisor finally had to prepare a special desk for his use near the production line.

Miyahara's attachment to *gemba* remained with him even after he was transferred to Fuji Xerox Company and was promoted to other management positions. When he was general manager of the sales division, for instance, *gemba* meant where his sales and service people were—that is, at the customers' sites. He accompanied service reps and visited customers which gave him a far better understanding of the customers' needs than did reading the reports.

I once traveled to Central America and visited a branch of Yaohan, a Japanese supermarket chain headquartered in Hong Kong, whose stores span the globe. I asked the general manager, who had his office in the corner of a warehouse, how often he went to *gemba* (at a supermarket, *gemba* is used to refer to the sales floor, warehouse, and checkout counter). The manager answered very apologetically, "You know, I have an assistant who is in charge of *gemba,* so I don't go there as often as I should." When I pressed him to tell me exactly how often, he said, "Well, I must go there about thirty times a day." This manager felt apologetic about "only" going to *gemba* thirty times a day!

"As I walk through *gemba*," he told me, "I not only look around me to see how many customers we have, whether merchandise is properly displayed, which items are popular, and so on, but also look up the ceiling and down the floor to see if there is any abnormality. Going through *gemba* and looking straight ahead is something any manager can do, you know?"

One place that is definitely not *gemba* is the manager's desk. When a manager makes a decision at his or her desk based on data, the manager is not in *gemba*, and the source of the original information must be questioned carefully.

An example will illustrate. Because of its volcanic terrain, Japan has many hot-spring resorts. A key attraction of the spas is the open-air bath (*rotemburo*), where guests can soak while enjoying a view of river or mountains. I recently spent several days at a large hot-spring hotel that had both an indoor and an outdoor bath. Most guests would bathe in the indoor bath first, then walk down the stairs to the *rotemburo*. I normally found about half of the guests in each bath. One evening I found the indoor bath almost empty. When I went in, I found out why: the water was too hot. Consequently, there was a crowd in the *rotemburo*, where the temperature was fine.

Clearly something was wrong with the indoor bath. A housekeeper who was bringing in additional towels and cleaning the bath had apparently not noticed anything amiss. When I brought the problem to her attention, she quickly made a telephone call and the temperature was restored to normal.

Later, I discussed this incident with the hotel's general manager, a good friend of mine. He told me that the temperature of the indoor bath was set at 42.5 degrees Celsius and that of the outdoor bath at 43 degrees Celsius. The manager went on to explain, "We have a monitoring room whereby our engineer keeps close watch over the temperatures of the baths, along with room temperatures, fire alarms, and such. Whenever he sees an abnormality on the meters, he's supposed to take a corrective action."

To this, I responded, "Wrong! The guy who watches the meters is only relying on secondary information. The information on the baths is first collected by the thermometer submerged in the tub, then transferred to the monitoring room by the electromechanical device, which moves the dial on the chart. Anything could go wrong in this process. The reality in *gemba* is that, at that time on that day, there were very few people in the indoor bath, and if the housekeeper had been trained to be more attentive, she could have noticed the situation, stuck her hand into the water, and found that it was too hot.

"The information you get directly from *gemba*," I told my friend, "is the most reliable. The feeling of the hot water you experience with your hand is the reality. Often, you don't even need substantiating data when you are in *gemba*, since what you feel and see *is* the original data! People in *gemba* should be responsible for quality because they are in touch with reality all the time. They are better equipped at maintaining quality than the guy in the monitoring room!"

Dr. Kaoru Ishikawa, one of the gurus of quality management in Japan, used to say, "When you see data, doubt it! When you see measurements, doubt them!" He knew that many data are collected in the company to please the boss and that measurements are often made or recorded incorrectly by devices. At best, measurements are only secondary information that does not always reflect the actual conditions.

Many Western managers tend to choose not to visit *gemba*. They may take pride in not going to the site and not knowing much about it. Recently, on learning from the president of one company that he never visited the plant, I suggested he do so once in a while. He replied, "I am an engineer by background and I know how to read and interpret data. So, I can make a good decision based on the data. Why should I go to the plant?"

At another plant I visited, I was told that whenever the big shots came from corporate headquarters to visit, the plant managers had to spend hours on end in the conference room answering foolish questions by managers who did not understand what was going on in *gemba* and who often left inappropriate and disturbing instructions. "We would be much better off without these meetings," the plant managers told me.

The plant managers' opinion of the meetings illustrate the tremendous gap between top management and the workplace, a condition that can make a company vulnerable to challenge from internal waste and external competition. This attitude at the management level usually sponsors a similar disrespect from workers.

CHECK THE *GEMBUTSU*

Gembutsu in Japanese means something physical or tangible. In the context of *gemba,* the word can refer to a broken-down machine, a reject, a tool that has been destroyed, returned goods, or even a complaining customer. In the event of a problem or abnormality, managers should go to *gemba* and check the *gembutsu.* By looking closely at the *gembutsu* in *gemba,* repeatedly asking, "Why?" and using a commonsense, low-cost approach, managers should be able to identify the root cause of a problem without applying sophisticated technology. If a reject is produced, for example, simply holding it in your hands, touching it, feeling it, closely examining it, and looking at the production method will probably reveal the cause.

Some executives believe that when one of the company's machines breaks down, the *gemba* for the managers is not where the machine is, but the conference room. There, the managers get together and discuss the problem without ever looking at the *gembutsu* (in this case the machine), and then everybody disavows his or her culpability.

Kaizen starts with recognizing the problem. Once aware, we are already halfway to success. One of the supervisor's jobs should be to keep constant watch at the site of the action and identify problems based on the *gemba* and *gembutsu* principles.

One supervisor recently remarked, "I walk through *gemba* every day and try to look at *gembutsu* to find something unusual so that I can take it back to my desk and start working on it. When I do not find any item for *kaizen,* I feel frustrated."

Soichiro Honda, the founder of Honda Motor Co., did not have a president's office; he was always found somewhere in *gemba.* Being a mechanic by background and having worked close to *gemba* all his life tuning and adjusting engines with screwdrivers and wrenches, he had many scars on his hands. Later in his life, when Honda visited nearby grade schools to talk with the children, he would proudly show them his hands and let them touch the scars there.

TAKE TEMPORARY COUNTERMEASURES ON THE SPOT

Once I visited a plant where I found a small broom attached to a machine engaged in cutting operations. I noticed that the machine kept stopping because metal chips were falling on the belt that was driving the machine, thus clogging the belt's movement. At this point the operator would pick up the broom and sweep the chips off the belt to start the machine again. After a while, the machine would stop, and the operator would repeat the same process to get it started again.

If a machine goes down, it must be started promptly. The show must go on. Sometimes kicking the machine will do the job! However, temporary measures address only the symptoms, not the root cause, of machine stoppages. This is why you need to check *gembutsu* and keep asking "Why?" until you identify the root causes of the problem.

Determination and self-discipline never stop the *kaizen* effort at the third stage (temporary countermeasures). They continue to the next stage, identifying the real cause of the problem and taking action.

FIND THE ROOT CAUSE

Many problems can be solved quite readily using the *gemba-gembutsu* principles and common sense. With a good look at *gembutsu* at the site of the problem, and the determination to identify root causes, many *gemba*-related problems can be solved on the spot and in real time. Other problems require substantial preparation and planning to solve; examples include some engineering difficulties or the introduction of new technologies or systems. In these cases, managers need to collect data from all angles, and may also need to apply some sophisticated problem-solving tools.

For instance, if the chips falling on a conveyor belt are causing stoppages, a temporary guide or cover can be fashioned from cardboard on the spot. Once the effectiveness of the new method has been confirmed, a permanent metal device can be installed. Such a change can be made within hours, and certainly within a day or two. The opportunities for making such a change abound in *gemba,* and one of the most popular axioms of *gemba kaizen* is "Do it now. Do it right away!"

Unfortunately, many managers believe that one must make a detailed study of every situation before implementing any *kaizen.* In reality, about 90 percent of all problems in *gemba* can be solved right away if managers see the problem and insist that it be addressed on the spot. Supervisors need training on how to employ *kaizen* and what role they should play.

One of the most useful tools for finding the root cause in *gemba* is to keep asking "Why?" until the root cause is reached. This process is sometimes referred to as the five why's, since chances are that asking "Why?" five times will uncover the root cause.

Suppose, for example, you find a worker throwing sawdust on the floor in the corridor between machines.

YOUR QUESTION: "Why are you throwing sawdust on the floor?"
HIS ANSWER: "Because the floor is slippery and unsafe."
YOUR QUESTION: "Why is it slippery and unsafe?"
HIS ANSWER: "Because there's oil on it."
YOUR QUESTION: "Why is there oil on it?"
HIS ANSWER: "Because the machine is dripping."
YOUR QUESTION: "Why is it dripping?"
HIS ANSWER: "Because oil is leaking from the oil coupling."
YOUR QUESTION: "Why is it leaking?"
HIS ANSWER: "Because the rubber lining inside the coupling is worn out."

Very often—as in this case—by asking "Why?" five times we can identify the root cause and take a countermeasure, such as replacing the rubber lining with a metal lining to stop the oil leakage once and for all. Of course, depending on the complexity of the problem, the question "Why?" may need to be asked more or fewer times. However, I have noticed that people tend to look at a problem (in this case, oil on the floor) and jump to the conclusion that throwing sawdust on it will solve everything.

STANDARDIZE TO PREVENT RECURRENCE

A manager's task in *gemba* is to realize QCD. However, all manner of problems and abnormalities occur at plants every day; there are rejects, machines break down, production targets are missed, and people arrive late for work. Whenever a given problem arises, management must solve it and make sure it will not recur for the same reason. Once a problem has been solved, therefore, the new procedure needs to be standardized and the standard-do-check-act cycle invoked. Otherwise, people are always busy firefighting. Thus the fifth and last golden rule of *gemba* management is standardization. When a problem occurs in *gemba,* whether a machine breaks down from metal chips clogging the conveyors or hotel guests complain about the way fax messages are handled, the problem must first be carefully observed in light of *gemba-gembutsu* principles. Next, the root causes must be sought out, and finally, after the effectiveness of the procedure devised to solve the problem has been confirmed, the new procedure must be standardized.

In this manner, every abnormality gives rise to a *kaizen* project, which should eventually lead, either to introducing a new standard or to upgrading the current standard. Standardization assures the continuity of the effects of *kaizen.*

One definition of a *standard* is *the best way to do the job.* If *gemba* employees follow such a standard, they assure that the customer is satisfied. If a standard means the best way, it follows that the employee should adhere to the same standard in the same way every time. If employees do not follow standards in repetitive work—which is often the case in manufacturing *gemba*—the outcome will vary, leading to fluctuations in quality. Management must clearly designate standards for employees as the only way to assure customer-satisfying QCD. Managers who do not take the initiative to standardize the work procedure forfeit their job of managing *gemba.*

At Giorgi Foods, Inc., in Temple, Pennsylvania, the administrative rooms were once located upstairs while *gemba* was downstairs. Upstairs, walls separated the rooms for each function: sales, marketing, engineering, research and development, and personnel.

But the company's chairman, Fred Giorgi, decided that everyone whose job was to support *gemba* should move their desks to *gemba*. He declared: "We are all going to move to *gemba*, and we are going to work together in a big room without walls!" An uproar of protests followed: "It will be too noisy!" "We won't be able to concentrate on our work!" "Some subordinates will quit!" "We won't be able to keep the company's secrets!" Giorgi was undaunted. He said, "If a secret leaks out this way, then it can't be kept a secret anyway. If people don't like it, let them go!"

But, in the end, everybody moved, if not wholeheartedly.

Today, a visitor to the company can see at a glance everyone working in one big room. If the visitor is attentive, he will find Fred Giorgi among them, inconspicuously sitting at a small desk flanked by two other desks, each occupied by an executive of the company. "Before," says Giorgi," "whenever I wanted to have a meeting with managers, I had to check who was in and who was out before calling such a meeting. Now, I look around and see who is present. Then, I yell out and say, "Hey, let's go to the meeting room and discuss this matter! No *muda!*"

This arrangement of the company's staff offers other advantages as well. At the entrance to the administrative floor are two small rooms: a telephone operator's room and the personnel department. In the wall of the former is a window allowing the operator to see at a glance who is in and who is out. And because employees must pass the personnel office whenever they have business on the administrative floor, it has become easier for them to approach personnel people to discuss matters of concern.

Says Tony Puglio, former department manager of the labeling department at Giorgio Foods, "Five years ago, I spent a lot of time in my office doing paperwork. I thought I had all the answers and I could do everything myself. Now I find that we can make a difference through our *kaizen* activities like the quality circle meetings and listening to workers' suggestions, going out to the workplace, spending more time there, looking at each and every problem and correcting them. I found out that my employees have great ability—artistic talent and practical skills—that I didn't realize they had. They were able to do all the *kaizen* work themselves and make a difference on the lines.

"I spend around 90 percent of my time on the shop floor, which enables me to see workers' problems," says Puglio. "Before, when they would come into the office and tell me their problems, I would listen to them but not do much about it. I didn't realize that we'd been running like this for years and years, and I assumed everything was OK. But it wasn't. By going on the floor I could really see what the workers were talking about.

"Now I notice that everybody is putting a little more effort in; they're excited, they're proud of their department. They're keeping everything in order and in place; they are keeping everything much cleaner. The workplace looks good, and when people come in, they want to be at work. They feel good about themselves. They look good, they feel good. They see these changes are working and it's making a difference, making their jobs a little bit easier."

APPLICATION OF THE GOLDEN RULES

Let me explain how these golden rules have been applied in my own experience.

The fax is becoming an indispensable business tool. As a *kaizen* consultant who spends more than half of his time traveling around the world, I do not know how I would accomplish my business without faxes. During a recent hotel stay lasting a few days, I had a series of problems with the way the hotel handled incoming faxes. I was supposed to have received an urgent fax from Tokyo. When I called my executive assistant there, I was assured that the transmission had gone through a few hours before. As the document had not been delivered to me, I had to inquire at the front desk. The person at the desk was sure that no fax had arrived for me. Earlier, at this same hotel, I had received several faxes addressed to me, together with several meant for somebody else. I was so annoyed that I finally asked myself what I would do if I were the general manager of this hotel and received many complaints from customers on the way employees handled faxes. My conclusion: Apply the golden rules, by all means!

So I put myself in the shoes of a hotel manager interested in applying *gemba kaizen*. The first step was to go to *gemba*, in this case the lobby. I stood on an elevated platform in a corner of the lobby (but did not draw a chalk circle), and stayed there a few minutes watching attentively how people at the front office handled faxes. It did not take five minutes to find out that there were no special procedures! For instance, there was no fixed place to store the incoming documents (no standard). Some employees put them in the key boxes. Others left them on the desk. Still others put them wherever they found a space. Also, when the fax papers (*gembutsu*) came out of the fax machine (another *gembutsu*) in the reverse order of pages, employees didn't even take time to put them in the right order. This appeared to be the reason somebody else's faxes were delivered to me along with my own.

If I had actually been the hotel's general manager, I would, after observing this situation, have called a meeting with the *gemba* people and asked them to work out procedures for handling faxes. We might have agreed that the documents' pages should be arranged in the right sequence and that all incoming faxes should be placed in the key boxes, for example. We might also have arranged to record the times that faxes were delivered to guests (standardization) to avoid any arguments over whether or not a guest received a fax. Discussing and agreeing on the new procedures would probably have taken no more than half an hour. (This is the essence of "Go to *gemba* and do it right away.") The agreed-upon procedure would then be consistently followed. In response to problems or customer complaints, the procedure could be refined, so that the hotel's fax-handling system could be continuously improved over time.

HOW TO MANAGE QUALITY, COST, AND DELIVERY IN *GEMBA*

Quality, cost, and delivery are not distinctly separate sub-jects, but rather are closely interrelated. It is pointless to buy products or services lacking in quality, no matter how attractive their price. Conversely, it is meaningless to offer products or services of good quality and attractive price if those products cannot be delivered in time to meet the customer's need and in the quantity that the customer wants.

QUALITY: MORE THAN JUST A RESULT

Quality in this context means the quality of products or services. In a broad sense, however, it also means the quality of the processes and of the work that yields these products or services. We may call the former *result quality* and the latter *process quality*. By this definition, quality runs through all phases of company activity—namely, throughout the processes of developing, designing, producing, selling, and servicing the products or services.

Figure 3-1, a quality assurance system diagram of Toyoda Machine Works, shows how quality-assuring activities take place on an ongoing basis at a tool manufacturing company. One might say that this diagram shows all the key steps of process quality. Reading from top to bottom, Figure 3-1 shows the flow of activities from the identification of customer requirements through such stages as Product Planning 1 (the customer's standpoint),

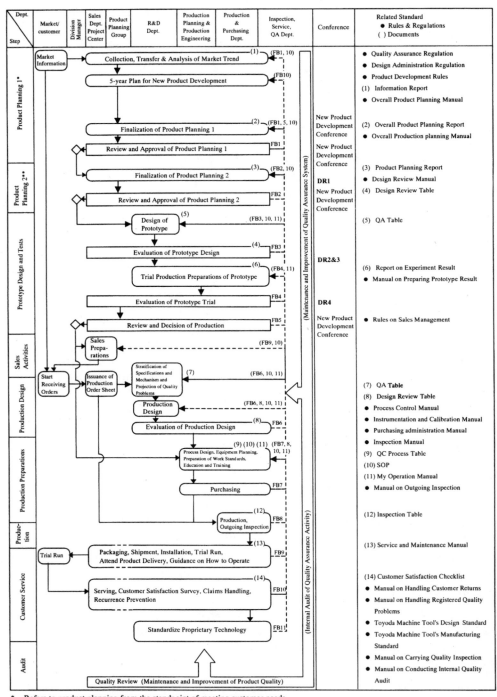

* Refers to product planning from the standpoint of meeting customer needs.
** Refers to product planning from the standpoint of making the product.

FIGURE 3-1. QA system diagram.

38

Product Planning 2 (the manufacturer's standpoint), Prototype Design and Test, Sales Activities, Production Design, Production Preparations, Production, Customer Service, and Audit.

Reading the diagram from left to right shows the involvement of people from various departments. The main body of the diagram shows activities that assure quality at every process. The flow of quality-related information also appears here. For instance, below the Division Manager column appear four stages of design review (DR), meaning that the division manager is involved in all design review stages.

The Conference column in Figure 3-1 shows cross-functional meetings and conferences in which the departments concerned must participate at each key stage before moving on to the next stage.

The last column on the right shows the related standards, regulations, or documents corresponding to each stage of quality assurance. This diagram shows that before *gemba* starts making the products, a long list of quality-assuring actions take place. For instance, items 8 through 12 of Standards and Regulations (including the process control manual, the instrumentation and calibration manual, the inspection manual, the QC process table, the standard operating procedures manual, my operation manual, and the manual on outgoing inspection) list typical procedures that assure quality at *gemba*. But the diagram also shows that items 1 through 7 have been completed by the time *gemba* work begins.

Activities that precede *gemba* (standards 1 through 8) are called *upstream management*. Traditionally, when quality was perceived primarily as a matter of workmanship, quality-related efforts focused mainly on *gemba*. While workmanship remains one of the most important pillars of quality, people increasingly recognize that quality in the area of design, product concepts, and understanding of customer requirements must precede *gemba* work.

Most activities in *gemba* relate to workmanship and seldom reach upstream management, although *gemba*-based *kaizen* activities arise from management's policy deployment, which in turn identifies the need for *kaizen* upstream as well. Top management must establish standards for quality of planning.

Planning correctly the first time around—accurately understanding customer needs, translating this understanding into the engineering and designing requirements, and making advance preparations for a smooth start-up—makes it possible to avoid many problems in *gemba* during process stages as well as in after-sales service.

The job of developing a new product or designing a new process starts with paperwork. Bugs or malfunctions can be rectified with the stroke of a pen at no cost. Malfunctions identified later, in the production stage or—even worse—after the product has been delivered to the customer, necessitate very expensive corrections.

Quality function deployment (QFD) is a powerful tool that enables management to identify the customer's needs, convert those needs into engineering and designing requirements, and eventually deploy this information to develop components and processes, establish standards, and train workers.

The system diagram in Figure 3-1 shows that the company is using the tools of QFD in the daily quality assurance activities listed in the right-hand column. These tools include QA tables, which are matrixes correlating between such items as customers' requirements and corresponding engineering parameters.

Upstream management plays an indispensable role in assuring quality. On the other hand, if *gemba* is not sufficiently robust, the company will not be able to enjoy the full benefits of even the most effective upstream management. Such a situation is analogous to making a sophisticated plan to climb Mount Everest only to find that one's legs are too weak to make the climb.

QUALITY MANAGEMENT IN *GEMBA*

Gemba confronts quality issues from a different angle than upstream management. While upstream management requires sophisticated tools, such as design reviews, design of experiments, value analysis, value engineering, and the various tools of QFD, many problems in *gemba* relate to simple matters, such as workmanship and handling the difficulties and variabilities that come up every day, like inadequate working standards and operators' careless mistakes.

In order to reduce variability, management must establish standards, build self-discipline among employees to maintain standards, and make certain that no defects are passed on to the next customer. Most quality problems can be solved using *gemba-gembutsu* principles, the low-cost, commonsense approach explained in Chapter 2.

Management must introduce teamwork among operators, because the operators' involvement is a key issue. Statistical quality control (SQC) is often effectively employed in *gemba,* but SQC is a tool to confine the variability of the processes and will work well only if everybody—particularly management—understands the concept of variability control and makes an effort to practice it.

I once visited a plant whose manager was proud of his achievement of SQC. I saw many control charts posted on the walls in his room. But once I stepped into *gemba,* I realized that nobody understood variability. The operators had no standards, and they did their job differently with each piece they assembled. Sometimes they didn't even have a designated place for assembly work. During my visit, machines broke down repeatedly and many rejects were produced. Yet this manager was proud of his SQC!

Professor Hitoshi Kume of Tokyo University has said: "I think that while quality control in the West aims at 'controlling' the quality and conformance to standards and specifications, the feature of the Japanese approach centers around improving (*kaizen*) quality. In other words, the Japanese approach is to do such *kaizen* systematically and continually."

The landmark case of line assembly quality improvement of the dip soldering process at Yokogawa Hewlett Packard (YHP), in which the company succeeded in reducing the failure rate from 4000 ppm to 3 ppm between 1978 and 1982, may well illustrate his point. YHP's history of quality improvement is divided into two periods, 1978–1979 and 1980–1982.

Quality improvement activities differed considerably during the two periods.

During the first phase, for example, YHP took such actions as improving working standards, collecting and analyzing data on defects, introducing jigs for better control of the process, providing worker training, encouraging quality-circle activities, and reducing careless mistakes by operators. To do this, YHP assembled a project team of *gemba* supervisors and production engineers to collect data, train quality-circle members, and provide technical assistance in such areas as jig construction. These actions helped drive the failure rate down to 40 ppm from its previous level of 4000 ppm. (See Figure 3-2.)

Once the 40 ppm level had been reached, YHP needed to step up and refine these activities if it wanted to continue its momentum and make further gains. (See Figure 3-3.) At the same time, it had to apply new technologies: revised engineering standards, improved PC board designs, and production layout. It also needed to redesign its equipment as well as its layout, incorporating the just-in-time concepts. All the while, YHP's quality circles maintained their activities to gain a better understanding of the process. They also contributed great-

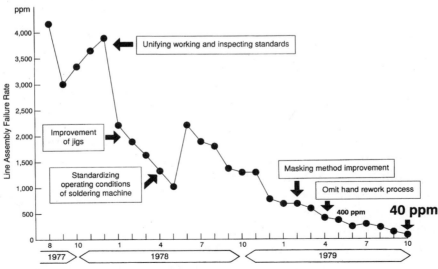

FIGURE 3-2.   Process quality improvement, phase 1.

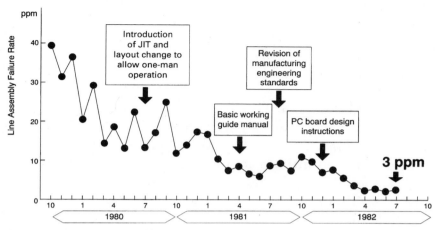

FIGURE 3-3.   Process quality improvement, phase 2.

ly to the continuous improvement of the process. As a result, YHP reached the level of 3 ppm in 1982.

Generally speaking, as long as the quality level remains in the percentile figures, companies can achieve dramatic improvement through such basic activities as reviewing the standards, housekeeping, collecting data on rejects, and conducting group activities for problem solving.

First review existing procedures, asking such questions as:

- Do we have standards?
- What about housekeeping (the five S's) in *gemba*?
- How much *muda* exists in *gemba*?

Then begin taking action. For example:

- Implement the five *gemba* principles.
- Train employees to be committed to never send rejects on to the next process.
- Encourage group activities and suggestions for problem solving.

- Start collecting data to gain a better understanding of the nature of the problems and solve them.
- Start making simple jigs and tools to make the job easier and its results more reliable.

These down-to-earth activities alone should reduce reject rates to a tenth of their original levels. When these fundamentals are lacking, the variables are so large that sophisticated technologies do little to improve the process. Only after the basic variabilities have been addressed are the more challenging applications of SQC and other sophisticated approaches cost-effective.

Quality begins when everybody in the organization commits to never sending rejects or imperfect information to the next process. Dr. Kaoru Ishikawa's axiom, "The next process is the customer," refers to the internal customer within the same company. One should never inconvenience the customers in the next process by sending rejects to them. In *gemba,* such a state of mind is often referred to as "Don't get it. Don't make it. Don't send it." When everybody subscribes to and lives by this philosophy, a good quality-assurance system exists.

COST REDUCTION IN *GEMBA*

In this context, the word *cost* does not mean cost cutting, but cost management. Cost management oversees the processes of developing, producing, and selling products or services of good quality while striving to lower costs or hold them to target levels. Cost reduction in *gemba* should come as a result of various activities carried out by management. Unfortunately, many managers try to reduce costs only by cutting corners; typical actions include firing employees, restructuring, and beating up suppliers. Such cost cutting invariably disrupts the process of quality and ends in quality deterioration. But today's customers are increasingly demanding; they want better quality at a lower price—complete with prompt delivery. When we respond to demand for lower prices simply by cost cutting, we soon find that quality and prompt delivery disappear. Cost management encompasses a wide spectrum of activities, including:

1. Cost planning to maximize the margin between costs and revenues
2. Overall cost reduction in *gemba*
3. Investment planning by top management

Opportunities for cost reduction on-site may be expressed in terms of *muda*. The best way to reduce costs in *gemba* is to eliminate excess use of resources. To reduce costs, the following seven activities should be carried out simultaneously, with quality improvement being the most important. The other six major cost-reduction activities may be regarded as part of the process quality in a broader sense:

1. Improve quality.
2. Improve productivity.
3. Reduce inventory.
4. Shorten the production line.
5. Reduce machine downtime.
6. Reduce space.
7. Reduce lead time.

These efforts to eliminate *muda* will reduce the overall cost of operations.

Improve Quality

Quality improvement actually initiates cost reduction. *Quality* here refers to the process quality of managers' and employees' work. Improving the work process quality results in fewer mistakes, fewer rejects and less rework, shorter lead time and reduced use of resources, therefore lowering the overall cost of operations. Quality improvement is synonymous with better yields as well.

Process quality includes the quality of work in developing, making, and selling products or services. In *gemba,* the term specifically refers to the way products or services are made and delivered. It refers mainly to managing resources in *gemba*; more specifically, it refers to managing <u>m</u>an (worker activity), <u>m</u>achine, <u>m</u>aterial, <u>m</u>ethod, and <u>m</u>easurement—known collectively as the five M's.

IMPROVING PRODUCTIVITY TO LOWER COSTS

Productivity improves when less input produces the same output, or when output increases with the same input. Input here refers to such items as human resources, utilities, and material. Output means such items as products, services, yield, and added value. Reduce the number of people on the line; the fewer line employees, the better. This not only reduces cost, but more important, reduces quality problems, since fewer hands present fewer opportunities to make mistakes. (I hasten to add that I do not advocate firing employees. There are many ways to use former line employees. Management should consider employees freed up by *kaizen* activities as resources for other value-adding activities.) When productivity goes up, cost goes down.

REDUCE INVENTORY

Inventory occupies space, prolongs production lead time, creates transport and storage needs, and eats up financial assets. Products and work-in-process sitting on the factory floor or in the warehouse do not yield any added value. On the contrary, they deteriorate in quality and may even become obsolete overnight when the market changes or competitors introduce a new product.

SHORTEN THE PRODUCTION LINE

In manufacturing, a longer production line requires more people, more work-in-process and a longer lead time. More people on the line also means more mistakes, which lead to quality problems. One company's line was fifteen times longer than its competitor's. The result—in terms of the number of people employed on the line, the quality level (more people producing more quality problems), the inventory (both work-in-process and finished products) and the much longer lead time—was an overall cost of operations much higher than it needed to be.

I once reviewed the layout of a production line that was to be introduced soon for manufacturing a new product. To my surprise, the new process was a carbon copy of the existing one, except that some of the existing machines were replaced with the latest models. The company had made no effort to shorten the line. Management had not included shortening the line as one of its targets, nor had the designers given it a thought.

In Japan, an engineer tasked with collecting catalogues from various machine makers and placing orders from among them to design a new layout is called a catalogue engineer—not a very prestigious title. Management should encourage such engineers to do a better production layout—to design ever-shorter assembly lines employing fewer and fewer people. Constantly challenging employees to do a better job than last time should be an integral part of any *kaizen*-driven manager's work. The situation is exactly the same in nonmanufacturing activities.

REDUCE MACHINE DOWNTIME

A machine that goes down interrupts production. Unreliable machinery necessitates batch production, extra work-in-process, extra inventory, and extra repair efforts. Quality also suffers. All these factors increase the cost of operations. Such problems are similar in the service sector. Downtime in the computer or communication system causes undue delay, greatly increasing the cost of machine operations. When a newly hired employee is assigned to a workstation without proper training to handle the equipment, the consequent delay in operation may be just as costly as if the equipment were down.

REDUCE SPACE

As a rule, manufacturing companies use four times as much space, twice as many people, and ten times as much lead time as they really need. Typically, *gemba kaizen* eliminates conveyor lines, shortens production lines, incorporates separate work stations into the main line of production, reduces inventory, and decreases transportation needs. All of these improvements reduce space requirements. Extra space freed up by *gemba kaizen* may be used to add new lines or may be reserved for future expansion. A similar improvement can be introduced in a nonmanufacturing environment.

REDUCE LEAD TIME (THROUGHPUT TIME)

Lead time begins when a company pays for raw materials and supplies and ends only when the company receives payment from its customer for products sold. Thus lead time represents the turnover of money. A shorter lead time means better use and turnover of resources, more flexibility in meeting customer needs, and a lower cost of operations. The lead time is the true measure of management's capability, and shortening this interval should be top management's paramount concern. *Muda* in the area of lead time presents a golden opportunity for *kaizen.*

Ways to cut lead time include improving and speeding feedback of customer orders and communicating better with suppliers; this reduces the inventory of raw materials and supplies. Streamlining and increasing the flexibility of *gemba* operations can also shorten production lead time. When everyone in an organization works toward this goal, there is a positive impact on cost effectiveness.

THE ROLE OF *GEMBA* IN OVERALL COST REDUCTION

If *gemba* cannot make its procedures very short, flexible, efficient, reject-free, and free of machine downtime, there is neither hope of reducing the inventory levels of supplies and parts nor of becoming flexible enough to meet today's stringent customer demands for high quality, low cost, and prompt delivery. *Gemba kaizen* can be the starting point for improvements in all three categories.

Gemba that are insufficiently reliable and robust cannot sustain improvements made in other functional areas, such as product development and process designs, purchasing, marketing, and sales.

Kaizen should start in *gemba*. To put it another way, by carrying out *gemba kaizen* and identifying the problems manifested at the worksite, we can identify the shortcomings of other supporting departments, such as research and development, design, quality control, industrial engineering, purchasing, sales, and marketing. In other words, *gemba kaizen* helps identify shortcomings in upstream management. *Gemba* becomes a mirror that reflects the quality of the company's management systems and a window through which we see the *real* capabilities of management.

DELIVERY

Delivery refers to the *timely* delivery of the *volume* of products or services. One of management's tasks is to deliver the required volume of products or services in time to meet the customer's needs. The challenge to management is how to live up to delivery commitment while meeting quality and cost targets. In line with the axiom "Quality first," quality is the foundation upon which cost and delivery are built.

A just-in-time (JIT) system addresses both cost and delivery issues, but it can be introduced only if a good quality-assurance system is in place. By eliminating all kinds of non-value-adding activities, JIT helps reduce costs. Indeed, it is a practical way to drastically cut costs for companies that have never tried it before.

Equally important, JIT addresses delivery. The conventional approach has been to deliver products out of inventory, with the customer paying for the added cost. In JIT, every effort is made to produce and deliver the product "just-in-time"— namely, to produce only *as many* as are needed, and only *when* needed, thereby eliminating the cost of excessive inventory. Through various *kaizen* activities, JIT makes it possible to build such a flexibility into the management system. (See Chapter 11, "JIT—The Ultimate Production System.")

It *is* possible to realize improved quality, cost, and delivery simultaneously by employing various management systems that have been developed over the years, and thus to make the company far more profitable than it has been in the past.

QUALITY IMPROVEMENT AND COST REDUCTION ARE COMPATIBLE

The recurring theme of this chapter has been that improving quality and reducing cost are compatible objectives. In fact, quality is the foundation upon which both cost and delivery can be built. Without creating a firm system to assure quality, there can be no hope of building effective cost management and delivery systems.

Not only is it *possible* to both improve quality and reduce cost, we *must* do both in order to meet today's customer requirements. Take, for example, international competition in the luxury automobile market. Suppose one company subscribes to the old philosophy that better quality costs more money. The company's major means of assuring quality has been to buy more expensive machines and testing equipment and hire more people to perform rework and inspections. The company has a reputation for world-class quality, but its prices are very high.

Suppose that a new company emerges as a competitor. This company believes that better quality and lower cost are compatible, and has succeeded in building a car of equal or better quality to the first company's, but at a lower price. How will the first company cope with its new rival? This is the real nature of the "clear and present danger" facing many of today's companies that continue to subscribe to the outdated notion that quality costs money.

Simultaneous realization of QCD: This is the task that the *kaizen*-minded manager should tackle in today's competitive environment. At a time when customers are demanding ever-better QCD, management must emphasize the proper priority to achieve all three: *quality first!* Resist the temptation to cut costs at the expense of quality! And do not sacrifice quality for delivery!

STANDARDS

Daily business activities function according to certain agreed-upon formulas. These formulas, when written down explicitly, become standards. Successful management on a day-to-day level boils down to one precept: Maintain and improve standards. This not only means adhering to current technological, managerial, and operating standards, but also improving current processes in order to elevate current standards to higher levels.

MAINTAIN AND IMPROVE STANDARDS

Whenever things go wrong in *gemba,* such as producing rejects or dissatisfying customers, management should seek out the root causes, take actions to remedy the situation, and change the work procedure to eliminate the problem. In *kaizen* terminology, managers should implement the standardize-do-check-act (SDCA) cycle.

With current standards in place and workers doing their jobs according to those standards with no abnormalities, the process is under control. The next step is to adjust the status quo and raise standards to a higher level. This entails the plan-do-check-act (PDCA) cycle.

In both cycles, the final stage of the cycle, *act* refers to standardizing and stabilizing the job. Thus standardization becomes an inseparable part of everybody's job. As will be explained later, standards are the best way to assure quality and the most cost-effective way to do the job.

Here, let's refer back to Chapter 2's anecdote about the way fax messages were improperly handled by the hotel's desk staff. In a case like this, each customer complaint gives rise to a need to review the existing standards. Depending on the level of sophistication involved, management might find that no standards at all existed to start with and that simply adding standards would make the system more robust. However, not every aspect of our work needs close scrutiny. For instance, if the hotel management had received no complaints from its guests, it might have concluded that its current way of handling fax messages was adequate. In such a case, one could look for *kaizen* in other areas rather than trying to improve fax-handling procedures. This would not mean, however, that one didn't need to look at the best benchmark practices of the industry and try to reach such a level even when no complaints had been received. An improved fax procedure might have saved time and work for the staff, thus freeing them for other work.

We should establish priorities in reviewing standards based on such factors as quality, cost, delivery, safety, the urgency and the gravity of the consequences, and the severity of customer complaints.

In daily routine work (called maintenance), workers either do the job the right way, causing no abnormalities, or encounter abnormalities, which should trigger a review of existing standards and perhaps lead to establishing new ones. The first requirement of management remains that of maintaining standards. The system is under control when standards exist that are followed by workers who produce no abnormalities. Once the system is under control, the next challenge is to improve the status quo.

Let's assume that a strong demand necessitates a production increase of 10 percent. In line with *kaizen* spirit, making better use of the existing resources would be the best way to cope with such a demand. To meet the goal, operators must change their way of doing their jobs. The existing standards must be upgraded through *kaizen* activities. At this stage, we have left the maintenance stage and moved on to the improvement stage.

Once such improvement has started, new and upgraded standards can be installed and efforts made to stabilize the new procedures, initiating a new maintenance stage. Figure 4-1

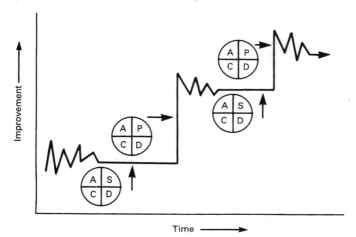

FIGURE 4-1. How improvements are registered from SDCA cycle to PDCA cycles.

shows how improvements are registered within a company between the standardize-do-check-act (SDCA) cycle and the plan-do-check-act (PDCA) cycle.

OPERATIONAL STANDARDS

Before we go any further, let's focus on the way we're using the word *standards.* In this context, there are two types of standards. One is *managerial standards,* which are necessary for managing employees for administrative purposes and which include administrative rules, personnel guidelines and policies, job descriptions, rules for preparing expense accounts, etc. The other is called *operational standards,* which have to do with the way people do a job to realize QCD. While managerial standards relate to the internal purpose of managing employees, operational standards relate to the external demand to achieve QCD to satisfy customers.

The standards referred to in this book are operational and point up a big disparity between Japanese and Western companies. Japan enthusiastically embraces the idea of establishing standards, while the West looks upon standards with a certain degree of cynicism. In the West, the word *standards* is often misinterpreted to mean the imposition of unfair conditions on workers—the introduction of a wage system based on piecework, for instance. However, the word *standards* as used in this book means using the process that's the safest and easiest for workers and the most cost-effective and productive way for the company to assure quality for the customer.

In extreme cases, standards in the West are seen as something that goes against human nature. There is a feeling that people should not be bound by standards and that human beings should be given maximum freedom to do their job the way they want to. But it's important to distinguish between the ideas of *controlling* and *managing*. When management talks about *control,* it means control over the process, not the person. Management manages employees so that employees can control the process. Following standards is like driving a car. The driver must follow certain regulations and yet, as a result, he or she gains the freedom to go where he/she wants to go. Likewise, when workers follow standards and do the job right, the customer is satisfied with the product or service, the company prospers, and the workers can look forward to job security.

KEY FEATURES OF STANDARDS

Standards have the following key features:

1. *Represent the best, easiest, and safest way to do a job.* Standards reflect many years of wisdom and know-how on the part of employees in doing their jobs. When management maintains and improves a certain way of doing something, making sure that all the workers on different shifts follow the same procedures, those standards become the most efficient, safe, and cost-effective way of doing the job.

2. *Offer the best way to preserve know-how and expertise.* If an employee knows the best way to do the job and leaves without sharing that knowledge, his or her know-how will also

leave. Only by standardizing and institutionalizing such know-how within the company does it stay in the company, regardless of the comings and goings of its individual workers.

3. *Provide a way to measure performance.* With established standards, managers can evaluate job performance. Without standards, there is no fair way to do this.

4. *Show the relationship between cause and effect.* Having no standards or not following standards invariably leads to abnormalities, variabilities, and waste. Let's apply this concept to the sport of sky diving, for example. When people first begin sky diving, they depend on their instructor to fold their parachute. As they become more experienced, they begin folding their parachute with the help of their instructor. Before they can become full-fledged sky divers, they must learn how to fold the parachute correctly by themselves.

    Suppose a sky diver has folded the parachute for the first time in his life and is going to jump tomorrow. He goes to bed but cannot sleep and starts wondering, "Did I fold it right?" He gets out of his bed, unfolds the parachute and starts all over again, goes back to bed, but still can't sleep. How many times does he need to fold it before he is convinced that everything is OK? The answer is that he should need to do it only once. The way to fold the parachute today is the best, easiest, and safest way, reflecting the experience of many thousands of parachutists—and the aftermath of various tragedies. Every time a parachute did not open up, it gave rise to wrenching questions: "Where in our way of folding the parachute did we go wrong? How can we change and improve the process to prevent a recurrence?" What are the consequences of not following the folding standards? By the time you find it out, it may be too late.

5. *Provide a basis for both maintenance and improvement.* By definition, following standards means *maintenance* and upgrading standards means *improvement.* Without standards, we have no way of knowing whether we have made improvements or not. Management's duty is, first and foremost, to maintain standards. When variability occurs due to a lack of standards, one must introduce new standards. If

variability occurs even with adherence to standards, management must first determine the cause, and then either revise and upgrade the existing standards, or train the operators to do the job as specified by the standards. Perhaps something about the existing standards is unclear, or the operators need more training to do the job properly.

Maintenance activities should constitute a majority of managers' tasks in their day-to-day activities in *gemba*.

Once maintenance stabilizes and controls the process, management can plan the next challenge: improvement, or upgrading the existing standards. Where there is no standard, there can be no improvement. For these reasons, standards are the basis for both maintenance and improvement.

6. *Provide objectives and indicate training goals.* Standards can be described as a set of visual signs that show how to do the job. As such, standards should communicate in a simple, understandable manner. Normally, standards come in the form of written documents, but at times, pictures, sketches, and photos may facilitate understanding.

7. *Provide a basis for training.* Once standards are established, the next step is to train operators to such an extent that it becomes second nature for them to do the job according to the standards.

8. *Create a basis for audit or diagnosis.* In *gemba,* work standards are often displayed, showing the vital steps and checkpoints of operators' work. These standards no doubt serve as reminders to operators. But even more important, they help managers check whether work is progressing normally. If maintaining and improving standards are the two major tasks of management, the primary job of *gemba* supervisors is to see whether standards are being maintained and, at the appropriate time, whether plans to upgrade current standards are being implemented.

9. *Provide a means for preventing recurrence of errors and minimizing variability.* As already stated, standardization is the last step of the five *gemba* principles. It is also the next-to-the-last step in the *kaizen* stories, explained later in this

chapter. Only when we standardize the effect of a *kaizen* project, can we expect that the same problem does not recur. Quality control means variability control. Management's task is to identify, define, and standardize key control points at each process and make certain that such control points will be followed at all times.

Often, company A turns out to be better than company B in quality—not because A is superior in *all* aspects of the processes, but because company A is making concerted efforts to ensure that *all* the processes are followed as specified in standards, while company B finds that one or two processes are not always followed.

Thus, standardization is an integral part of quality assurance, and without standards, there can be no way to build a viable quality system.

TOYODA MACHINE WORKS

Yoshio Shima, director of Toyoda Machine Works, says that the benefit of building systems and standards for quality assurance became apparent in the 1980s when the company introduced TQM with the aim of receiving the Deming Prize. Management's efforts to build a frame of reference for a quality assurance system culminated in the company's receiving the Deming Prize in 1985.

Shima admits that the various standards instituted during those early days reflected not only essential steps for quality assurance, but also the management's wishful thinking, their vision of ideal procedure. "You might say that we started out by putting in the form of standardization first, and later putting a soul into it," he says.

However, Shima found that after these standards were put into practice, they were not always usable. In order to remain practical, they had to be constantly reviewed and upgraded. Thus, the journey to quality improvement at the company meant a never-ending review of existing standards.

Says Shima, "The difficult part of standardization is that standards are not unchangeable. If you believe that standards are writ in stone, you will fail. When the environment changes, standards change as well. You have to believe that standards are there to be changed." He goes on to say that "Once standards are in place and being followed, if you find a deviation, you know there is a problem. Then you review the standards and either correct the deviation from the standard or change the standard. It is a never-ending process of PDCA! That is the reason why you see numerous feedback routes on our QA system diagram." (See Figure 3-1.)

Shima finds that the QA system diagram is very helpful, as it affords him a bird's-eye view of the total system of quality assurance within the company. When quality problems arise with the customer, the company uses the system diagram to explain how it will solve the problem. The customer understands and appreciates management's efforts.

THE *KAIZEN* STORY*

The *kaizen* story is a standardized format to record *kaizen* activities conducted by such small-group activities as quality circles. The same standardized format is also employed to report *kaizen* activities conducted by staff and managers.

The *kaizen* story follows the plan-do-check-act (PDCA) cycle. Steps 1 through 4 relate to P (plan), step 5 relates to D (do), step 6 relates to C (check), and steps 7 and 8 relate to A (act). The *kaizen* story format helps anybody to solve problems based on data analysis. One of its merits is to help managers visualize and communicate the problem-solving process. It is also an effective way to keep records of *kaizen* activities.

Various problem-solving tools are often shown in the *kaizen* story to help the reader understand the process.

---

*In Japan the term *QC* story is commonly used. In view of the fact that the term *kaizen* story is more often used in other countries these days, the term *kaizen* story is used throughout this book.

The *kaizen* story includes the following standardized steps:

1. *Selecting the theme.*   The story begins with the reason why the particular theme was selected. Often, the themes are determined in line with management policies or are dependent upon the priority, importance, urgency, or economics of current circumstances.

2. *Understanding the current status and setting objectives.* Before starting the project, current conditions must be understood and reviewed. One way to do this is to go to *gemba* and follow the five *gemba* principles. Another way is to collect data.

3. *Analyzing the data thus collected to identify root causes.*

4. *Establishing countermeasures based on the data analysis.*

5. *Implementing countermeasures.*

6. *Confirming* the effects of the countermeasures.

7. *Establishing or revising the standards to prevent recurrence.*

8. *Reviewing the above processes and working on the next steps.*

For an example of a *kaizen* story, see the case "Kaizen Experience at Alpargatas."

KAIZEN/ISO 9000/QS 9000

Today, it has become almost a must for any company to apply for national or international certification of standards, such as ISO 9000 and QS 9000, if they are to stay in business and gain the confidence of their major global customers. These certification programs place much emphasis on standardization of the key processes and continual improvement.

In *kaizen* terms, the standards are the best way to do the job, and *gemba kaizen* such as *muda* elimination and housekeeping (5S's in particular) should precede writing a standard. Writing down the working process in *gemba* as it is now is useless if the current process contains much *muda* and variability.

Once standards have been established, improvement of those standards must follow. Thus, it is imperative that *gemba kaizen* activities be carried out before applying for the certification as well as upgrading the standards after the certification has been awarded.

Sometimes an executive preparing for certification of ISO 9000 or QS 9000 would say, "We are too busy preparing for the certification and have no time to do *kaizen!*" Nothing can be further from the truth. Unless *kaizen* is carried out concurrently, the ensuing standards with much variability due to a lack of good housekeeping and *muda* elimination will be just a piece of paperwork far removed from *gemba* and rarely practiced in daily work, and will give no positive impact to the improvement of the company's performance.

Thus, *gemba kaizen* should become an integral part of getting international certification, and after having received it, *gemba kaizen* should be a means to upgrade such standards on a continual basis.

One of the *kaizen* consultants once shared his first encounter with the magic power of standardization as follows:

In 1961, I was a manager for a large electronics company in Europe. I was responsible for transferring know-how and delivering machines from our factory to a Japanese electronics company with which we had a joint venture agreement. Before we delivered the equipment, the Japanese company sent four operators into our factory to study our production process, where 20 fully-automated lines were running on three shifts. Each line produced 2000 semiconductor diodes per hour, with a yield of 98 percent.

About six months after the Japanese plant had begun operations, we received a letter from them thanking us for our cooperation and for the precision of our machinery. They also noted that their yield was 99.2 percent.

As a result, we went to Japan to study what had been done, asking our Japanese colleague, "What changes did you make to realize this higher yield?" His answer: "We made a study of your *gemba* and observed that you are following 60 different procedures (20 lines working on three shifts). We discussed this and, with mutual consent from the *gemba* observers who had gone to your country, we decided on the best way to standardize the process."

THE 5S's: THE FIVE STEPS OF HOUSEKEEPING

The 5S's, the five steps of housekeeping, were developed through intensive work in a manufacturing context. Service-oriented companies can readily see parallel circumstances in their own "production lines"—whether they come in the form of a request for proposal (RFP), the closing of a financial report, an application for a life insurance policy, or a potential client's request for legal services. Whatever triggers the process of work in the service company, conditions that exist in the work process *complicate* the work unnecessarily (are there too many forms?); *impede* progress toward satisfying the customer (does the size of contract require sign-off by three officers?); actually prohibit the possibility of satisfying the customer (does the company's overhead make it impossible to bid on the job?).

As Figure 2-3 shows, standardization, 5S (housekeeping), and *muda* elimination are the three pillars of *gemba kaizen* in the commonsense, low-cost approach to improvement. *Kaizen* at any company—whether it be involved in a manufacturing or a service industry—should start with three activities: standardization, 5S, and *muda* elimination.

These activities involve no new management technologies and theories. In fact, words like *housekeeping* and *muda* do not appear in management textbooks. They therefore do not excite the imagination of managers, who are accustomed to keeping abreast of the latest technologies. Those who attend my lectures sometimes wonder why these subjects have to be brought up. However, once they understand the implications of these three pillars, they become excited at the prospect of the tremendous benefits these activities can bring to *gemba*.

GOOD HOUSEKEEPING IN FIVE STEPS

The five steps of housekeeping, with their Japanese names, are as follows:

1. *Seiri:*   Distinguish between necessary and unnecessary items in *gemba* and discard the latter.
2. *Seiton:*   Arrange all items remaining after *seiri* in an orderly manner.
3. *Seiso:*   Keep machines and working environments clean.
4. *Seiketsu:*   Extend the concept of cleanliness to oneself and continuously practice the above three steps.
5. *Shitsuke:*   Build self-discipline and make a habit of engaging in 5S by establishing standards.

In introducing housekeeping, Western companies often prefer to use English equivalents of the five Japanese S's—as in a "Five-S's Campaign" or a "Five-C's Campaign."

A Five-S's Campaign

1. *Sort:*   Separate out all that is unnecessary and eliminate it.
2. *Straighten:*   Put essential things in order so that they can be easily accessed.
3. *Scrub:*   Clean everything—tools and workplaces—removing stains, spots, and debris and eradicating sources of dirt.
4. *Systematize:*   Make cleaning and checking routine.
5. *Standardize:*   Standardize the previous four steps to make the process one that never ends and can be improved upon.

A Five-C's Campaign

1. *Clear out:*   Determine what is necessary and unnecessary and dispose of the latter.

2. *Configure:*   Provide a convenient, safe, and orderly place for everything and keep it there.

3. *Clean and check:*   Monitor and restore the condition of working areas during cleaning.

4. *Conform:*   Set the standard, train and maintain.

5. *Custom and practice:*   Develop the habit of routine maintenance and strive for further improvement.

A DETAILED LOOK AT THE FIVE STEPS OF 5S

SEIRI (SORT)

The first step of housekeeping, *seiri*, entails classifying items in *gemba* into two categories—necessary and unnecessary—and discarding or removing the latter from *gemba*. A ceiling on the number of necessary items should be established. All sorts of objects can be found in *gemba*. A close look reveals that only a small number of them are needed in daily work; many others either will never be used or will only be needed in the distant future. *Gemba* is full of unused machines, jigs, dies and tools, rejects, work-in-process, raw materials, supplies and parts, shelves, containers, desks, workbenches, files of documents, carts, racks, pallets, and other items. An easy rule of thumb is to remove anything that will not be used within the next 30 days.

Seiri often begins with a red-tag campaign. Select one area of *gemba* as the site for *seiri*. Members of the designated 5S team go to *gemba* with handfuls of red tags and place them on items they believe are unnecessary. The larger the red tags and the greater their number, the better. When it is unclear whether or not a particular item is needed, a red tag should be placed on it. By the end of the campaign, the area may be covered with hundreds of red tags, inviting comparison to a grove of maple trees in the fall.

Sometimes *gemba* employees may find red tags on items they actually need. In order to keep these items, employees must demonstrate the necessity of doing so. Otherwise, everything with a red tag on it is removed from *gemba*. Things that have no reason to stay in *gemba*, no apparent future usage, and no intrinsic value are thrown away. Things that will not be needed within the next 30 days but may be needed at some point in the future, are moved to their rightful places (such as the warehouse, in the case of supplies). Work in process that exceeds the needs of *gemba* should be sent either to the warehouse or back to the process responsible for producing the surplus.

In the process of *seiri*, one can obtain valuable insights on how the company conducts its business. The red-tag campaign leaves in its wake a mountain of unnecessary *gembutsu*, and employees are confronted with uncomfortable questions, such as, "How much money is tied up in prematurely manufactured products?" People ask themselves how they could have acted so foolishly. At one company, a red-tag campaign unearthed enough supplies to last for 20 years!

Both managers and operators have to see such extravagance in *gemba* to believe it. This is a practical way for managers to get a glimpse at how people work. Upon finding a heap of supplies, for example, the manager should be asking, "What kind of system do we have for placing orders to suppliers? What kind of information do our purchasing people use in placing orders? What kind of communication is maintained between production scheduling and production? Or do the staff responsible for purchasing just place orders when they think it is about time to do so?"

Managers should be equally rigorous when they find work in process made well in advance: "Why do our people keep producing work in process for which we have no immediate need? Based on what kind of information do they start production?" Such a situation indicates fundamental deficiencies in the system, such as having insufficient control between production and purchasing in *gemba*. It also shows insufficient flexibility to cope with changes in production scheduling.

At the end of the red-tag campaign, all managers—including the president and plant manager as well as *gemba* managers—should get together and have a good look at the heap of supplies, work in process, and other *gembutsu* and start making *kaizen* to correct the system that made this waste possible.

Eliminating unnecessary items via the red-tag campaign also frees up space, enhancing flexibility in the use of the work area, because once unnecessary items have been discarded, only what is needed remains. At this stage, the maximum number of items to be left in *gemba*—parts and supplies, work in process, and so on—must be determined.

Seiri can be applied to individuals working in offices as well. For example, a typical desk has two or more drawers. Items are often placed in these drawers indiscriminately; side by side in a single drawer one may find not only pencils, ballpoint pens, erasers, writing pads, rubber bands, business cards, and scissors, but also toothbrushes, candy, perfume, aspirin, coins, matches, cigars, costume jewelry, Band-Aids, and other objects. These items must first be classified by use. In a desk with only two drawers, office supplies and personal items should each occupy one drawer.

Next, the maximum number of each item is determined. For instance, let's say we decide to place in the drawers only two pencils, one ballpoint pen, one eraser, one pad of paper, and so on. Any items beyond the maximum number are discarded—that is, removed from the drawer and taken to the office supply storage area in the corner of the room. Sometimes, this storage area is called a recycling bank. When supplies in the drawers are exhausted, the employee goes to the recycling bank to replenish them. In turn, the employee in charge of the bank watches the inventory and, when it drops to the designated minimum, orders more supplies.

By paring to a minimum the supplies in our office drawers, we eliminate the need to shuffle through the collection of pencils, papers, and cosmetics to reach a desired item. This process develops self-discipline as well as improving record keeping and enhancing employees' ability to work effectively.

SEITON (STRAIGHTEN)

Once *seiri* has been carried out, all unnecessary items have been removed from *gemba,* leaving only the minimum number needed. But these needed items, such as tools, can be of no use if they are stored too far from the workstation or in a place where they cannot be found. This brings us to the next stage of 5S, *seiton.*

Seiton means classifying items by use and arranging them accordingly to minimize search time and effort. To do this, each item must have a designated address, name, and volume. Not only the location, but also the maximum number of items allowed in *gemba* must be specified. For example, work in process cannot be produced in unlimited quantities. Instead, the floor space for the boxes containing the work must be delineated clearly (by painting a rectangle to mark off the area, etc.), and a maximum allowable number of boxes—say five—must be designated. A weight may be suspended from the ceiling above the boxes to make it impossible to stack more than five. When the maximum allowed level of inventory has been reached, the production in the previous process must stop; there is no need to produce more than what the following process can consume. In this manner, *seiton* assures the flow of a minimum number of items in *gemba* from station to station on a first-in, first-out basis.

Taiichi Ohno was once invited to visit the assembly line of another company. Asked to comment on the line, he said, "You have much too much work in process waiting by the line side. Leave a minimum number on the line side, and send back all the excessive items to the previous process." A mountain of pressed metal sheets had to be sent back to the press shop, and the workers there had to do their job surrounded by pressed metal sheets that created a prisonlike atmosphere. Ohno said, "This is the best way to show people that the harder they work, the more money the company will lose."

The items left in *gemba* should be placed in the designated area. In other words, each item should have its own address, and conversely, each space in *gemba* also should have its designated address. Each wall should be numbered, using designations such as Wall A-1 and Wall B-2. The location of such items as supplies, work-in-process, fire hydrants, tools, jigs, molds, and carts should be designated either by its address or by special markings. Markings on the floor or workstations indicate the proper locations of work-in-process, tools, and so on. Painting a rectangle on the floor to delineate the area for boxes containing work-in-process, for example, creates a space sufficient to store the maximum volume of items. At the same time, any deviation from the designated number of boxes shows up instantly. (Readers familiar with "just-in-time" will recognize that this is the first stage of introducing a "pull" production system.) Tools should be placed well within reach and be easy to pick up and put down. Their silhouettes might be painted on the surface where they are supposed to be stored. This makes it easy to tell when they are in use.

The hallway should also be marked clearly with paint. Just as other spaces are designated for supplies and work-in-process, the hallway is meant for transit: nothing should be left there. The hallway should be completely clear so that any object left there will stand out, allowing supervisors to notice the abnormality instantly and take remedial action.

SEISO (SCRUB)

Seiso means cleaning the working environment, including machines and tools, as well as the floors, walls, and other areas of the workplace. There is also an axiom that goes: *Seiso* is checking. An operator cleaning a machine can find many malfunctions. When the machine is covered with oil, soot, and dust, it is difficult to identify any problems that may be developing. While cleaning the machine, however, one can easily spot oil leakage, a crack developing on the cover, or loose nuts and bolts. Once these problems are recognized, they are easily fixed.

It is said that most machine breakdowns begin with vibration (due to loose nuts and bolts), with introduction of foreign particles such as dust (due to the crack on the cover, for instance), or with inadequate oiling and greasing. For this reason, *seiso* is a great learning experience for operators, since they can make many useful discoveries while cleaning machines.

I was once engaged in *seiso* activities at the plant of a wooden floor tile manufacturer which contained many woodworking machines such as power saws. All senior managers, including the president, joined in *seiso* with the operators. (This was said to have been the first time employees saw the president show up at *gemba* wearing overalls and holding a broom.) While they were cleaning the exterior of the machines, as well as the walls and beams on the ceiling, they said over and over, "I can't believe it!" Thick layers of wood chips and dust clung to the walls. On removing the debris, the director of finance discovered naked electrical wires running along the walls. The vinyl cover had long since deteriorated. He marveled at the fact that a fire had never broken out in the plant.

SEIKETSU (SYSTEMATIZE)

Seiketsu means keeping one's person clean, by such means as wearing proper working clothes, safety glasses, gloves, and shoes, as well as maintaining a clean, healthy working environment. Another interpretation of *seiketsu* is continuing to work on *seiri, seiton,* and *seiso* continually and every day.

For instance, it is easy to go through the process of *seiri* once and make some improvements, but without an effort to continue such activities, the situation will soon be back to where it started. To do *kaizen* just once in *gemba* is easy. To keep doing *kaizen* continuously, day in, day out, is an entirely different matter. Management must deploy systems and procedures that assure the continuity of *seiri, seiton,* and *seiso.* Management's commitment to, support of, and involvement in the five S's becomes essential. Managers must determine, for example, how often *seiri, seiton,* and *seiso* should take place, and who should be involved. This should become part of the annual planning schedule.

SHITSUKE (STANDARDIZE)

Shitsuke means self-discipline. People who practice *seiri, seiton, seiso,* and *seiketsu* continuously—people who have acquired the habit of making these activities part of their daily work—acquired self-discipline.

The five S's may be called a philosophy, a way of life in our daily work. The essence of 5S is to follow what has been agreed upon. It begins with discarding what we don't need in *gemba* (*seiri*) and then arranging all the necessary items in *gemba* in an orderly manner (*seiton*). Then a clean environment must be sustained so that we can readily identify abnormalities (*seiso*), and the above three steps must be maintained on a continuous basis (*shitsuke*). Employees must follow established and agreed-upon rules at each step, and by the time they arrive at *shitsuke* they will have the discipline to follow such rules in their daily work. This is why we call the last step of 5S self-discipline.

By this final stage, management should have established standards for each step of 5S, and made certain that *gemba* is following those standards. The standards should include ways to evaluate progress at each of the five steps.

A *gemba* manager of a chemical company once told me that when he asked his *gemba* operators to measure key parameters of the process and plot them on the control chart, the operators didn't take this task too seriously: the numbers always stayed in the center of the control chart. Once 5S was successfully implemented and everybody began to acquire self-discipline, however, the manager found that the operators' attitude had changed: the data on the control chart began to show deviations.

There are five ways to appraise the level of 5S at each stage:

1. Evaluation of self
2. Evaluation by an expert consultant
3. Evaluation by a superior
4. A combination of the above
5. Competition among *gemba* groups

The plant manager should set up a contest among the workers; the manager can then review the state of 5S in each *gemba*, and select the best and worst *gemba*. The best can receive some award or other recognition, while the worst receives a broom and bucket. The latter group will have an incentive to do a better job so that another group will get these items next time.

In order to review progress, evaluation must be conducted regularly by plant managers and *gemba* managers. Only after work on the first step has been approved can workers move on to the next step. This process lends a sense of accomplishment.

After *seiso* has been completed, management's attention should focus on a new horizon—namely, maintaining and ensuring momentum and enthusiasm. After working hard at *seiri, seiton,* and *seiso* and having seen improvements in *gemba,* employees begin to think, "We've made it!" and relax and take it easy for a while (or even worse, cease their efforts altogether). Strong forces at work in *gemba* try to push conditions back to their previous state, making it imperative for management to build a *system* to assure the continuity of five-S activities.

INTRODUCING 5S

Kaizen values the process as much as the result. In order to get people involved in *continuing* their *kaizen* effort, management must carefully plan, organize, and execute the project. Managers often wish to see the result too soon and skip a vital process. The 5S is not a fad, a flavor of the month, but an ongoing part of daily life. Any *kaizen* project therefore needs to include follow-up steps.

Because *kaizen* addresses people's resistance to change, the first step is to mentally prepare employees to accept 5S before the campaign gets started. As a preliminary to the five-S effort, time should be allocated to discuss the philosophy behind and the benefits of 5S.

- Creating clean, sanitary, pleasant, and safe working environments.
- Revitalizing *gemba* and greatly improving employee morale and motivation.
- Eliminating various kinds of *muda* by minimizing the need to search for tools, making operators' jobs easier, reducing physically strenuous work, and freeing up space.

Management should also understand the many benefits of 5S in *gemba* to the company overall:

- Helping employees acquire self-discipline; self-disciplined employees are always engaged in 5S, take positive interest in *kaizen,* and can be trusted to adhere to standards.
- Highlighting the many kinds of *muda* in *gemba;* recognizing problems is the first step in eliminating waste.
- Eliminating *muda* in *gemba* enhances the 5S process.
- Pinpointing abnormalities, such as rejects and inventory surplus.
- Reducing wasteful motion, such as walking and needlessly strenuous work.
- Allowing problems associated with shortage of materials, line imbalances, machine breakdowns, and delivery delays to be identified visually and thence to be solved.
- Resolving outstanding logistical problems in *gemba* in a simple manner.
- Making quality problems visible.
- Improving work efficiency and reducing costs of operation.
- Cutting down on industrial accidents by eliminating oily and slippery floors, dirty environments, rough clothing, and unsafe operations. *Seiso,* in particular, increases machine reliability, thus freeing maintenance engineers' time for working on machines that are prone to sudden breakdown. As a result, engineers can concentrate on more upstream issues, such as preventive maintenance, predictive maintenance, and the creation of maintenance-free equipment in cooperation with design departments.

Having both understood these benefits and made certain that employees understand them, management can then move forward with the *kaizen* project.

MUDA

One day, after attentively observing operators working in *gemba*, Taiichi Ohno said to the workers, "May I ask you to do at least one hour's worth of work every day?" Believing themselves to have been working hard all day long, the workers resented this remark. What Ohno actually meant, however, was, "Will you do your value-adding work for at least one hour a day?" He knew that most of the time the operators were moving around in *gemba* without adding any value. Any non-value-adding activity is classified as *muda* in Japan. Ohno was the first person to recognize the enormous amount of *muda* that existed in *gemba*.

The Japanese word *muda* means waste, but the word carries a much deeper connotation. Work is a series of processes or steps, starting with raw material and ending in a final product or service. At each process, value is added to the product (or, in the service sector, to the document or other piece of information), and then sent on to the next process. The resources at each process— people and machines—either do add value or do not add value. *Muda* refers to any activity that does not add value. Ohno classified *muda* in *gemba* according to the following seven categories:

1. *Muda* of overproduction
2. *Muda* of inventory
3. *Muda* of repair/rejects
4. *Muda* of motion
5. *Muda* of processing
6. *Muda* of waiting
7. *Muda* of transport

MUDA OF OVERPRODUCTION

Muda of overproduction is a function of the mentality of the line supervisor, who is worried about such problems as machine failures, rejects, and absenteeism, and who feels compelled to produce more than necessary just to be on the safe side. This type of *muda* results from getting ahead of the production schedule. When an expensive machine is involved, the requirement for the number of products is often disregarded in favor of efficient utilization of the machine.

In a just-in-time system, however, being ahead of the production schedule is regarded as worse than being behind it. Producing more than necessary results in tremendous waste: consumption of raw materials before they are needed; wasteful input of manpower and utilities; additions of machinery; increase in interest burdens; additional space to store excess inventory; added transportation and administrative costs. Of all *muda,* producing too much is the worst. It gives people a false sense of security, helps to cover up all sorts of problems, and obscures information that can provide clues for *kaizen* on the shop floor. It should be regarded as a crime to produce more than necessary. Overproduction stems from the following invalid assumptions or policies:

- Produce as many as we can in the process, disregarding the proper speed at which the next process or next line can operate.
- Give the operator enough elbow room to produce.
- Let each process or line have an interest in raising its own productivity.
- Speed up the go-straight ratio because of line failures. (*Go-straight ratio* refers to the percentage of products that are completed without rework.)
- Allow machines to produce more than needed because they have excess capacity.
- Introduce expensive machines because they cannot be depreciated unless the operation ratio is improved.

MUDA OF INVENTORY

Final products, semifinished products, or parts and supplies kept in inventory do not add any value. Rather, they add to the cost of operations by occupying space and by requiring additional equipment and facilities such as warehouses, forklifts, and computerized conveyer systems. In addition, a warehouse requires additional manpower for operation and administration.

While excess items stay in inventory and gather dust, no value is added. Their quality deteriorates over time. Even worse, they could be destroyed by a fire or other disaster. If *muda* of inventory did not exist, much waste could be avoided. Inventory results from overproduction. If overproduction is a crime, inventory should be regarded as an enemy to be destroyed. Unfortunately, we all know managers who cannot sleep at night when they don't have "good inventory." Inventory is often likened to the water level that hides problems. When an inventory level is high, nobody gets serious enough to deal with problems like quality, machine downtime, and absenteeism, and thus an opportunity for *kaizen* is lost.

Lower inventory levels help us to identify areas that need to be addressed and force us to deal with problems as they come up. This is exactly what just-in-time production system is after: When the inventory level goes down and finally reaches the one-piece flow line, it makes *kaizen* a mandatory daily activity.

MUDA OF REPAIR/REJECTS

Rejects interrupt production and require expensive rework. Often the rejects must be discarded—a great waste of resources and effort. In today's mass-production environment, a malfunctioning, high-speed automated machine can spew out a large number of defective products before the problem is arrested. The rejects may also themselves damage expensive jigs or machines. Attendants must therefore be assigned to high-speed machines, standing by to stop the machines as soon as a malfunction is identified. Having to dedicate an attendant to this task defeats the purpose of having a high-speed machine. Such machines should at least be equipped with mechanisms that shut them down as soon as a faulty product is produced.

Suppliers often complain of too much paperwork and too many design changes when dealing with their customers. In a broader sense, both problems involve *muda*. The excess-paperwork *muda* could be eliminated by reducing red tape, streamlining operations, eliminating unnecessary processes, and speeding up processing decision-making time. The problem of excessive design changes results in *muda* of reworks. If the designers did their work right the first time—if they had a better understanding of customer and supplier requirements as well as the requirement of their own *gemba*—they could eliminate the *muda* of design changes. *Kaizen* can be applied as effectively to engineering projects as to matters in *gemba*.

MUDA OF MOTION

Any motion of a person's body not directly related to adding value is unproductive. When a person is walking, for instance, he is not adding any value. In particular, any action that requires great physical exertion on the part of an operator, such as lifting or carrying a heavy object, should be avoided, not only because it is difficult but also because it represents *muda*. The need for an operator to carry a heavy object for a distance can be eliminated by rearranging the workplace. If you observe an operator at work, you will find that the actual value-adding moment takes only a few seconds; the remainder of his motions represent non-value-adding actions, such as picking up or putting down a work piece. Often, the same work piece is first picked up with the right hand and then held with the left hand. A person working at a sewing machine, for example, first picks up a few pieces of fabric from the supply box, then puts them down on the machine, and finally picks up one piece of fabric to feed into the sewing machine. This is *muda* of motion. The supply box should be relocated so that the operator can pick up a piece of fabric and feed it directly into the sewing machine.

To identify *muda* of motion, we need to have a good look at the way operators use their hands and legs. We then need to rearrange the placement of the parts and develop appropriate tools and jigs.

MUDA OF PROCESSING

Sometimes inadequate technology or design leads to *muda* in the processing work itself. An unduly long approach or over-run for machine processing, unproductive striking of the press, and deburring are all examples of processing *muda* that can be avoided. At every step in which a work piece or a piece of information is worked on, value is added and sent to the next process. *Processing* here refers to modifying such a work piece or piece of information. Elimination of *muda* in processing can frequently be achieved with a commonsense, low-cost technique. Some wasteful processing can be avoided by combining operations. For instance, at a plant where telephones are produced, the receiver and the body are assembled on separate lines and later put together on the assembly line. To protect the surfaces of the receivers from scratches as they are being transported to the final assembly line, each receiver is wrapped in a plastic bag. By connecting the receiver assembly line and the final assembly line, however, the company can eliminate the plastic wrapping operation.

Waste in processing also results, in many cases, from a failure to synchronize processes. Operators often try to engage in the processing work in much finer a degree than is necessary, which is another example of *muda* of processing.

MUDA OF WAITING

Muda of waiting occurs when the hands of the operator are idle; when an operator's work is put on hold because of line imbalances, lack of parts, or machine downtime; or when the operator is simply monitoring a machine as the machine performs a value-adding job. This kind of *muda* is easy to detect. More difficult to detect is the *muda* of waiting during machine processing or assembly work. Even if an operator appears to be working hard, a great deal of *muda* may exist in the form of the seconds or minutes the operator spends waiting for the next work piece to arrive. During this interval, the operator is simply watching the machine.

MUDA OF TRANSPORT

In *gemba,* one notices all sorts of transport by such means as trucks, forklifts, and conveyers. Transport is an essential part of operations, but moving materials or products adds no value. Even worse, damage often occurs during transport. Two separate processes require transport. In order to eliminate *muda* in this area, the so-called *isolated island*—any process physically distant from the main line—should be incorporated into the line if possible.

Together with excess inventory and needless waiting, transport *muda* is a highly visible form of waste. One of the most conspicuous features of most Western manufacturing *gemba* is a heavy reliance on conveyer belts. Such layouts sometimes make me wonder whether the engineer who designed them is a model-railway hobbyist. Whenever we notice a conveyer in *gemba,* our first question should be, "Can we eliminate it?" The best thing a company can do with its conveyers is to sell them to its competitor. Better yet, it should wrap them up in a gift package and send them to the competitor, free of charge!

Kaizen consultant Greg Back recalls his experience when he was consulting a well-known German automotive manufacturer. Back and his colleague were working at the press shop on a multidie press to reduce changeover and setup times.

At the start of the project, Back set a target of a 50 percent reduction in the setup time (which was then ten hours) by the end of the week, without any technological changes. Both the supervisor and workers reacted with disbelief and anger ("We have not been sleeping all these years!").

By the end of the week, however, the time had been reduced to 5.5 hours, mostly through changes in the way of working, such as incorporating the 5S, shifting from internal to external work for changeover, etc. By making additional minor technical changes and further standardizing procedures and practices in the following two months, the company, on its own, further reduced changeover time to 3.5 hours.

The press line foreman later confessed to Back: "When you people showed up and told me what possibilities you saw, I was very angry. After all, I'm an expert at these things and my people are very good. But then I said to myself, "OK, let these *kaizen* consultants embarrass themselves! Now I have seen the results and how you did it and I started thinking about why I hadn't seen all this *muda* before. And I thought about what I had been doing. When I was going through my line and saw that my people were busy and working hard, I was satisfied. I never really looked closely at *what* they were doing, *how* they were doing it, or *why* they were doing it that way! They were busy, complaining about the amount of work, the job was difficult and had always taken so long. I never really looked closely at the process in *gemba!*"

As anything that does not add value is *muda*, the list of *muda* can be extended almost indefinitely. At Canon Company, *muda* is classified according to the categories listed in the accompanying table.

WASTE CATEGORY	NATURE OF WASTE	HOW TO ELIMINATE
Work-in-Process	Stocking items not immediately needed.	Streamline inventory.
Rejection	Producing defective products.	Reduce rejects.
Facilities	Idle machinery; breakdowns; excessive setup time.	Increase capacity utilization ratio.
Expenses	Overinvesting for required output.	Curtail expenses.
Indirect Labor	Excess personnel due to poor indirect labor system.	Assign jobs efficiently.
Design	Producing products with more functions than necessary.	Reduce costs.
Talent	Employing people for jobs that can be mechanized or assigned to less skilled people.	Institute labor-saving or labor maximization measures.
Motion	Not working according to work standard.	Improve work standards.
New-Product Run-Up	Slow start in stabilizing the production of a new product.	Shift to full-line production more quickly.

SOURCE: *Kaizen: The Key to Japan's Competitive Success* by Masaaki Imai (New York: McGraw-Hill, Inc., 1986).

Serge LeBerre, Managing Director of the *Kaizen* Institute in France, once told me that engineering *muda* should be added to the list, because much *muda* can be seen in engineering work as well. For instance, engineers tend to design a complex structure even when a simple solution is readily available. Equipped with knowledge of the latest science and technology, engineers are eager to find a chance to employ them, and not to employ less complex means that meet the purposes. Such a mentality defeats the requirements of *gemba*, not to mention the requirements of the customer. Modern-day engineers always look for more complexity and sophistication, says LeBerre, but they should instead seek to cut waste.

Tomoo Sugiyama, director of Yamaha Engine Company, proposes *less* engineering in *gemba* and has devised a "List of

Less-Engineering Items" as a means of highlighting things that should be eliminated. (Sugiyama came up with the term *less engineering* when he was searching for a catch phrase that would help *gemba* people identify problems more easily. Although the phrase does not sound like authentic English, it captured the imagination of his employees. The popularity of "endless tapes" and "tubeless tires" in Japan has made "less" a very familiar word.)

Man (Worker)

> Look-less
> Walk-less
> Search-less
> Block-less

Machine

> Air-less
> Conveyer-less
> Air cut-less
> Air press-less

Material

> Bolt-less
> Burr-less
> Wait-less
> Stop-less

Methods

> Bottleneck-less
> Stock-less

Quality

> Reject-less

Careless mistake-less

Nonstandard-less

Sugiyama initiated *kaizen* activities in the name of "less engineering," and found that they were readily accepted. For example, the company developed the following three principles of air-less engineering:

1. Do not carry air.
2. Do not store air.
3. Eliminate space that does not create added value.

Upon determining that air constituted 93 percent of the company's packaging for motorcycle mufflers and exhaust pipes, Sugiyama targeted the waste for *kaizen* and achieved a great deal of savings. Later, airless engineering was also applied to utilizing warehouse space more efficiently. From this experience, Yamaha devised a formula for calculating space savings in monetary terms and embarked on a company-wide air-less campaign.

In Sugiyama's view, anybody can add to the List of "less" Engineering Items simply by taking the trouble to identify *muda*.

MUDA OF TIME

Another type of *muda* observed daily is the waste of time, although it was not included in Ohno's seven categories of *muda*. Poor utilization of time results in stagnation. Materials, products, information, and documents sit in one place without adding value. On the production floor, temporal *muda* takes the form of inventory. In office work, it happens when a document or piece of information sits on a desk or inside a computer awaiting a decision or signature. Wherever there is stagnation, *muda* follows. In the same manner, the seven categories of *muda* invariably lead to the waste of time.

This *muda* is far more prevalent in service sectors. By eliminating the aforementioned non-value-adding time bottlenecks, the service sector should be able to achieve substantial increases in both efficiency and customer satisfaction. Because it costs nothing, *muda* elimination is one of the easiest ways for a company to improve its operations. All we need to do is to go to *gemba*, observe what is going on, recognize *muda*, and take steps to eliminate it.

MUDA, MURA, MURI

The words, *muda*, *mura*, and *muri* are often used together and referred to as the three MU's in Japan. Just as *muda* offers a handy checklist to start *kaizen*, the words *mura* and *muri* are used as a handy reminder to start *kaizen* in *gemba*. *Mura* means irregularity and *muri* means strain. Anything strenuous or irregular indicates a problem. Furthermore, both *mura* and *muri* also constitute *muda* that needs to be eliminated.

MURA (IRREGULARITY)

Whenever a smooth flow of work is interrupted in an operator's work, the flow of parts and machines, or the production schedule, there is *mura*. For example, assume that operators are working on the line and each person is performing a given repetitive task before sending it to the next person. When one of them takes more time to do the job than the others, *mura* as well as *muda* results, since everybody's work must be adjusted to meet the slowest person's work. Looking for such irregularities becomes an easy way to start *gemba kaizen*.

MURI (STRENUOUS WORK)

Muri means strenuous conditions for both workers and machines as well as for the work processes. For instance, if a newly hired worker is assigned to do the job of a veteran worker without sufficient training, the job will be strenuous for him, and chances are that he will be slower in his work and may even make many mistakes, creating *muda*.

When we see an operator sweating profusely while doing a job, we must recognize that too much strain is required and remove it. When we hear a squeaking sound from a machine, we must recognize that a strain has developed, meaning that an abnormality is occurring. Thus, *muda, mura,* and *muri* combined are handy checks to identify abnormalities in *gemba*.

Of all *kaizen* activities, *muda* elimination is the easiest to start, as it is not too difficult to identify *muda* once one has acquired such a skill. *Muda* elimination usually refers to stopping something that we have been doing up until now, and therefore costs little to implement. For these reasons, management should take the initiative in starting *kaizen* with *muda* elimination wherever it exists—in *gemba*, in administration, and/or in the area of service-providing.

THE FOUNDATION OF THE HOUSE OF *GEMBA*

As shown in Chapter 2, the house of *gemba* rests on a solid foundation of employee involvement activities such as teamwork, morale enhancement, self-discipline, quality circles, suggestion making, and related pursuits—communication, empowerment, and skill development, as well as visual management.

Management must build a firm commitment to carrying out these activities continuously. Only when management demonstrates that it is highly motivated, self-disciplined, and *kaizen*-minded can *gemba* people do their job of maintaining and improving standards to satisfy customers by achieving the targets of quality, cost, and delivery (QCD).

Most companies that introduce *kaizen* unsuccessfully fail to build the necessary infrastructure first. Fortunately, we do not have to wait until the infrastructure is complete and everybody in *gemba* has made the transformation to see improvement. People can begin to change their thinking and behavior as soon as they begin working on *kaizen*. For instance, by the time the 5S is firmly established in *gemba,* people will have the self-discipline necessary to follow through on what has been agreed upon. *Gemba kaizen* yields such impressive results that *gemba* operators are the first to recognize its benefits.

Marina Calcagni, an operator at Giorgio Foods Company, offered the following comments on her personal experiences of *kaizen* in the company:

When *kaizen* began, it was something that shocked everybody. It was something different. People came here just to work, to get their regular paycheck, and go home. And now instead *kaizen* opened our eyes, I think it really did. And it makes you think twice when you're doing something. I think we learned that if we're doing something better, it's for us; it's not for anybody from the outside. Our place looks cleaner and neater, it's a safer place to work.

Personally, I think that *kaizen* helped me, not only here at work, but even at home. I think it makes me think twice, I want to do better every day. We don't have to wait until there's a problem. We have to do something to make things better in whatever area. Not because it's a problem, just to make it better, and that's what *kaizen* taught us.

A LEARNING ENTERPRISE

Bill Ford, a visiting honorary professor at the Industrial Relations Research Center, University of New South Wales, Australia, advocates the concept of a learning enterprise. He quotes a saying by Dick Dusseldorp: "Training is for cats and dogs. People learn." "A learning enterprise," says Ford, "is one where individuals, teams, and the enterprise itself are continually learning and sharing in the development, transfer, and use of knowledge and skills to produce continual improvement and the creation of a dynamic competitive advantage. Such enterprises are creating cooperative work environments in which the stakeholders in business—be they shareholders, managers or workforce—share in the development of common goals."

In building the foundation of *gemba kaizen,* we are pursuing the same goal—namely, building a learning enterprise involving both management and the workforce—to develop common goals and values. Here, improvement is a way of life and people take pride in their work, continually upgrade their skills, and are empowered to solve problems in *gemba.* The job is seen as a mission, a means to fulfillment and personal growth. Thus, *gemba* should become a citadel of learning. In order to build a learning organization, management must empower *gemba* employees by providing learning experiences. As mentioned earlier, the tools for learning in *gemba* rely heavily on common sense and simple checklists, such as asking "Why?" five times; the five steps of housekeeping; *muda, mura, muri*; and following the axiom "Don't get it. Don't make it. Don't send it." Learning experiences in *gemba* must be based on an appreciation of fundamental human values, such as respect for humanity, commitment, determination, economy (sensible use of resources), cleanliness, and order.

Learning here should be synonymous with *doing* it. Rather than being given too much teaching, *gemba* employees should be given opportunities to *learn by practicing and doing,* being physically involved, using their hands as well as their brains. After the introduction of 5S and standardization at Tokai Shin-ei, president Yoshihito Tanaka said: "In hindsight, we have learned that our job is to do what we are supposed to do—namely, to do what we have agreed to do. In other words, a good company is the one where everybody is doing what he/she is supposed to do. We also learned that the best learning experience you can get is the one you gain through practicing, using your body, and learning by doing. Providing the concept alone is not enough."

This is why *gemba kaizen* activities in Japan have always stressed action. The following are the ten basic rules for practicing *kaizen* in *gemba*:

1. Discard conventional rigid thinking about production.

2. Think of *how to do it,* not why it cannot be done.

3. Do not make excuses. Start by questioning current practices.

4. Do not seek perfection. Do it right away even if for only 50 percent of target.

5. Correct mistakes at once.

6. Do not spend money for *kaizen*.

7. Wisdom is brought out when faced with hardship.

8. Ask "Why?" five times and seek the root cause.

9. Seek the wisdom of ten people rather than the knowledge of one.

10. Remember that opportunities for *kaizen* are infinite.

People in *gemba* are deeply ingrained in their old habits of working. When *gemba kaizen* is first introduced, strong psychological resistance must be overcome. The above ten rules are employed by management as a guide to facilitate the introduction of *gemba kaizen*.

Just as Japanese companies faced obstacles in implementing *gemba kaizen*, Western management must be prepared for resistance and introduce *gemba kaizen* with firm determination.

Jim Crawford, vice president and managing director for value management and product research and development at Excel, offers the following observation on his personal transition through the *kaizen* process after several years of involvement in promoting *kaizen* at his company:

> The most profound personal change as a result of *kaizen* is understanding that our work processes are the delivery mechanisms for results. This understanding leads to the recognition that we can dramatically improve long-term results by improving our work processes.
>
> My past perspectives led me to believe that dramatic results could be achieved by working faster and harder. These efforts delivered disappointing results. Dramatic improvement was still elusive.
>
> Driven by the belief that quick, short-term dramatic improvement was still attainable, efforts were devised to approach the improvement of results by increasing manpower and capital resources. In retrospect, these efforts also fell short.
>
> The concept that we can only improve results by improving our work processes is a simple concept, yet it is often misunderstood. The key question is why do managers have

such difficulty with this concept? Hopefully, by sharing my personal observations we can find an answer.

I have found through benchmarking that successful companies have managers who are committed to the *kaizen* process. These managers embrace the concept that results are not improved by management over the short-term, but by managers who support the long-term efforts of others in managing their work processes.

Transforming an organization from darkness to light also takes patience and courage. This change at Excel is painfully slow. Courage from within to support long-term efforts is difficult to come by, given the pressure for dramatic improvements in results. The ability to lead and exhibit patience in order to achieve dramatic, long-term improvement only comes from understanding the concept that sustainable improvements in results come from long-term improvements in our work processes.

The case studies of both Leyland Trucks and Excel address the subject of how management went about building an internal structure to become a learning enterprise. According to one definition of the difference between *education* and *training,* education teaches what one does not yet know, while training teaches what one knows already—but teaches it in such a way that doing it right becomes almost second nature. In other words, in training, people learn by doing—by practicing repeatedly. Skills cannot be acquired simply by reading a book or listening to a lecture: they must be practiced.

SUGGESTION SYSTEM AND QUALITY CIRCLES

Important parts of the structure of the house of *gemba* are the suggestion system and quality circles—proof that employees are actively involved in *kaizen* and that management has been successful in building the *kaizen* infrastructure. There are marked differences between the suggestion systems practiced in Japan and those in the West.

Whereas the American-style suggestion system stressed the suggestion's economic benefits and provided financial incentives, the Japanese style stressed the morale-boosting benefits of positive employee participation. Over the years, the Japanese style has evolved into two segments: individual suggestions and group suggestions, including those generated by quality circles, JK (*Jishu Kanri* or autonomous management) groups, ZD (Zero Defect) groups, and other group-based activities.

Suggestion systems are currently in operation at most large manufacturing companies and at about half the small and medium-size companies. In addition to making employees *kaizen*-conscious, suggestion systems provide an opportunity for the workers to speak out with their supervisors as well as among themselves. At the same time, they provide an opportunity for management to help the workers deal with problems. Thus, suggestions are a valuable opportunity for two-way communication in the workshop as well as for worker self-development.

Generally speaking, Japanese managers have more leeway in implementing employee suggestions than their Western counterparts do. Japanese managers are willing to go along with a change if it contributes to any one of the following goals:

- Making the job easier.
- Removing drudgery from the job.
- Removing inconvenience from the job.
- Making the job safer.
- Making the job more productive.
- Improving product quality.
- Saving time and cost.

The outlook of Japanese management stands out in sharp contrast to the Western manager's almost exclusive concern with the cost of the change and its economic payback.

The implications of standardization have been mentioned often in this book. When *gemba* employees participate in *gemba kaizen* and come up with new and upgraded standards, they naturally develop a sense of ownership of these standards, and will therefore have the self-discipline to follow them.

If, on the other hand, the standards are imposed from above by management, *gemba* employees may show psychological resistance to following them. It becomes a "them versus us" issue. This is another reason why it is so crucial to involve *gemba* people in such *kaizen* activities as suggestion systems and quality circles.

BUILDING SELF-DISCIPLINE

Needless to say, self-discipline is a cornerstone of the house of *gemba* management. Self-disciplined employees can be trusted to report on time to work; to maintain clean, orderly, and safe environments; and to follow the existing standards to achieve QCD targets.

In my *kaizen* seminars, I often ask the participants to write down ways of helping employees acquire self-discipline. Here are some of the answers I have received:

1. Reward incremental steps.
2. Catch them doing it right.
3. Open yourself to questions.
4. Develop a culture that says it's okay.
5. Make the process known to improve standards.
6. Conduct assessment.
7. Encourage customer involvement.
8. Implement a suggestion system.
9. Establish quality circles.
10. Build in reward systems.
11. Communicate expectations clearly.
12. Conduct frequent reviews of the process.

13. Provide measurement feedback.
14. Foster a climate of cooperation.
15. Give specific instructions regarding criteria.
16. Be involved in setting standards.
17. Explain why.
18. Set a good example.
19. Teach how and why.
20. Make progress displays visible.
21. Remove barriers.
22. Encourage positive peer pressure.
23. Create a threat-free environment.

When employees in *gemba* participate in such activities as housekeeping, *muda* elimination, and review of standards, they immediately begin to see the many benefits brought about by these *kaizen* and they are the first to welcome such changes. Through such a process, their behaviors as well as attitudes begin to change.

For instance, as already mentioned in Chapter 5, the last step of 5S is *shitsuke* (self-discipline), and employees who have followed the five steps, up to the last step, are the ones who have acquired self-discipline. An employee who has participated in reviewing and upgrading the standard of his or her own work, naturally develops ownership of such a standard as a result and willingly follows such a new standard.

In the same manner, employees eventually come to develop self-discipline as they engage in other *kaizen* projects and learn by doing such things as elimination of *muda* and visual management. Thus, self-discipline translates into "everybody doing his or her own job according to the rules that have been agreed upon."

Self-discipline is a natural by-product of engaging in *gemba kaizen* activities.

Visual management is another key component of the foundation of the house of *gemba,* and it will be explained in detail in Chapter 8.

VISUAL
MANAGEMENT

In *gemba,* abnormalities of all sorts arise every day. Only two possible situations exist in *gemba:* either the process is under control, or it is out of control. The former situation means smooth operations; the latter spells trouble. The practice of visual management involves the clear display of *gembutsu,* charts, lists, and records of performance, so that both management and workers are continuously reminded of all the elements that make quality, cost, and delivery (QCD) successful—from a display of the overall strategy, to production figures, to a list of the latest employee suggestions. Thus, visual management constitutes an integral part of the foundation of the house of *gemba.*

MAKING PROBLEMS VISIBLE

Problems should be made visible in *gemba.* If an abnormality cannot be detected, nobody can manage the process. Thus, the first principle of visual management is to spotlight problems.

If rejects are being produced by a broken die on the press and nobody sees the rejects, there will soon be a mountain of rejects. A machine equipped with *jidohka* devices, however, will stop the moment a reject is produced. The machine stoppage makes the problem visible.

When a hotel guest comes to the reception desk and asks for an aspirin or a list of good restaurants nearby, the hotel's inability to fulfill these needs constitutes an abnormality. By posting a list of the most frequent requests received from guests, the hotel's management can gain an awareness of service deficiencies that need to be addressed. This is visual management: making abnormalities visible to all employees—managers, supervisors, and workers—so that corrective action can begin at once.

Most information originating from *gemba* goes through many managerial layers before reaching top management, and the information becomes increasingly abstract and remote from reality as it moves upward. Where visual management is practiced, however, a manager can see problems at a glance the moment he/she walks into *gemba*, and can thus give instructions on the spot in real time. Visual management techniques enable *gemba* employees to solve such problems.

The best thing that can happen in the *gemba* of a manufacturing company is for the line to stop when an abnormality is detected. Taiichi Ohno once said that an assembly line that never stops is either perfect (impossible, of course), or extremely bad. When a line is stopped, everyone recognizes that a problem has arisen, and seeks to ensure that the line will not stop for the same reason again. Line stoppage is one of the best examples of visual management in *gemba*.

STAYING IN TOUCH WITH REALITY

If the first reason for visual management's existence is to make problems visible, the second is to help both workers and supervisors stay in direct contact with the reality of *gemba*. Visual management is a practical method for determining when everything is under control and for sending a warning the moment an abnormality arises. When visual management functions, everybody in *gemba* can manage and improve processes to realize QCD.

VISUAL MANAGEMENT IN THE FIVE M's

In *gemba*, management must manage the five M's: manpower, machines, materials, methods, and measurements. Any abnormality related to the five M's must be displayed visually. What follows is a more detailed look at visual management in these five areas.

MANPOWER (OPERATORS)

- How is worker morale? This can be measured by the number of suggestions made, the extent of participation in quality circles, and figures on absenteeism. How do you know who is absent from the line today and who is taking their place? These items should be made visible at *gemba*.

- How do you know people's skill level? A display board in *gemba* can show who is trained to do what tasks, and who needs additional training.

- How do you know that the operator is doing the job right? Standards that show the right way to do the job—for example, the one-point standard and the standard worksheet—must be displayed.

MACHINES

- How do you know that the machine is producing good-quality products? If *jidohka* and *poka-yoke* (fail-safe) devices are attached, the machine stops immediately after something goes wrong. When we see a machine that is stopped, we have to know why. Is it stopped because of scheduled downtime? changeover and setup? quality problems? machine breakdown? preventive repair?

- Lubrication levels, the frequency of exchange, and the type of lubricant must be indicated.

- Metal housing should be replaced by transparent covers so that the operator can see when a malfunction occurs inside the machine.

MATERIALS

- How do you know the materials are flowing smoothly? How do you know whether you have more materials than you can handle and whether you are producing more products than you should? When a minimum inventory level is specified and *kanban*—attaching a note to a batch of work-in-process as a means of communicating orders between processes—is used, such anomalies become visible.

- The address where materials are stored must be shown, together with the stock level and parts numbers. Different colors should be used to prevent mistakes. Use signal lamps and audio signs to highlight abnormalities such as supply shortages.

METHODS

- How does a supervisor know if people are doing their jobs right? This is made clear by standard worksheets posted at each workstation. The worksheets should show sequence of work, cycle time, safety items, quality checkpoints, and what to do when variability occurs.

MEASUREMENTS

- How do you check whether the process is running smoothly? Gauges must be clearly marked to show safe operating ranges. Temperature-sensing tapes must be attached to motors to show whether they are generating excess heat.
- How do you know whether an improvement has been made and whether you are on the way to reaching the target?
- How do you find out whether precision equipment is properly gauged?

Trend charts should be displayed in *gemba* to show the number of suggestions, production schedules, targets for quality improvement, productivity improvement, setup-time reduction, and reduction in industrial accidents.

VISUAL MANAGEMENT IN THE FIVE S's

The reader has probably realized that visual management also has a lot to do with the five steps of housekeeping. When we engage in 5S, we find that its outcome is better visual management. Better housekeeping helps make abnormalities visible, so that they can be corrected.

The 5S methods can be organized from the perspective of visual management:

- *Seiri* (discarding unnecessary things): Everything in *gemba* should be there if, and only if, it is needed now or will be used in the immediate future. When you walk through *gemba,* do you find unused work-in-process, supplies, machines, tools, dies, shelves, carts, containers, documents, or personal belongings that are not in use? Throw them away so that only what is needed remains.

- *Seiton* (putting in order the things that remain): Everything in *gemba* must be in the right place, ready for use when you need it. Everything should have a specific address, and be placed there. Are the lines on the floor marked properly? Are the hallways free of obstacles? Once *seiton* is being practiced, it is easy to identify anything out of order.

- *Sieso* (thorough cleaning of equipment and the area): Are equipment, floors, and walls clean? Can you detect abnormalities (vibrations, oil leakage, etc.) in the equipment? Where *seiso* is practiced, any such abnormality should soon become apparent.

- *Seiketsu* (keeping oneself clean and working on the three items above daily): Do employees wear proper working clothes? Do they use safety glasses and gloves? Do they continue their work on *seiri, seiton,* and *seiso* as a part of their daily routine?

- *Shitsuke* (self-discipline): Each individual's 5S duties must be specified. Are they visible? Have you established standards for them? Do workers follow such standards? The workers must record data on graphs and check sheets on an hourly, daily, or weekly basis as requested. As a means of fostering self-discipline, management may request that workers fill in data each day before going home.

Good 5S in *gemba* means that as long as the machines are in operation, they are producing good-quality products.

POSTING STANDARDS

When we go to *gemba,* visual management provides performance measures. We see an abnormality when we find excessive boxes of supplies on the line side; when a cart carrying supplies is left outside its designed area; when a hallway is filled with boxes, ropes, rejects, and rugs. (A hallway is meant to serve only as a passage, not a storage area.)

Displaying work standards in front of the workstation is visual management. These work standards not only remind the worker of the right way to do the job, but more importantly, enable the manager to determine whether the work is being done according to standards. When operators leave their stations, we know there is an abnormality because the standards displayed in front of the workstation specify that the operators are supposed to stay there during working hours. When the operators do not finish their work within cycle time, we cannot expect to achieve the day's production target.

While standards delineate how workers should do their jobs, they often do not specify what action should be taken in the event of an abnormality. Standards should first define abnormalities, and then outline the steps to follow in response.

Daily production targets should also be visible. Hourly and daily targets should be displayed on a board alongside the actual figures. This information alerts the supervisor to take the measures necessary to achieve the target, such as shifting workers to the line that is behind the schedule.

All the walls in *gemba* can be turned into tools for visual management. The following information should be displayed on the walls and at the workstations to let everybody know the current status of QCD:

- *Quality information:* daily, weekly, and monthly reject figures and trend charts, as well as targets for improvement. *Gembutsu* of rejects should be displayed for all operators to see. (These *gembutsu* are sometimes referred to as *sarashi-kubi*—a word from medieval times meaning the severed head of a criminal on display in the village square.) These rejects are often used for training purposes.

- Cost information: productivity figures, trends, and targets.
- *Kosu* (see page 131).
- Delivery information: daily production charts.
- Machine downtime figures, trends, and targets.
- Overall equipment efficiency (OEE).
- Number of suggestions submitted.
- Quality-circle activities.

For each particular process, any number of additional items may be required.

SETTING TARGETS

The third purpose of visual management is to clarify targets for improvement. Suppose that external requirements have prompted a plant to reduce the setup time of a particular press within six months. In such a case, a display board is set up next to the machine. First, the current setup (for example, six hours as of January) is plotted on a graph. Next, the target value (one-half hour by June) is plotted. Then a straight line is drawn between the points, showing the target to aim for each month. Every time the press is set up, the time is measured and is plotted on the board. Special training must be provided to help the workers reach the target.

Over time, something incredible takes place. The actual setup time on the graph starts to follow the target line! This happens because the operators become conscious of the target and realize that management expects them to reach it. Whenever the number jumps above the target, they know that an abnormality (missing tools, etc.) has arisen, and take action to avoid such a mishap in the future. This is one of the most powerful effects of visual management. Numbers alone are not enough to motivate people. Without targets, numbers are dead.

Yuzuru Itoh, former director of the quality control center at Matsushita Electric, made the following comments (quoted in my book, *Kaizen: The Key to Japan's Competitive Success*, pages 64–65) about the power of targets to motivate people:

> One of the more interesting experiences I had involved the soldering workers at a television plant. On the average, each of our workers soldered 10 points per work piece, 400 work pieces per day, for a daily total of 4000 soldering connections. Assuming he works 20 days a month, that's 80,000 soldering connections per month. One color TV set requires about 1000 soldering connections. Of course, nowadays most soldering is done automatically, and soldering workers are required to maintain a very low defect rate of no more than one mistake per 500,000 to 1 million connections.
>
> Visitors to our TV factory are usually quite surprised to find workers doing such a monotonous job without any serious mistakes. But let's consider some of the other monotonous things humans do, like walking, for example. We've walked practically all our lives, repeating the same motion over and over again. It's an extremely monotonous movement, but there are people such as the Olympic athletes who are intensely devoted to walking faster than anyone has ever walked before. This is analogous to how we approach quality control in the factory
>
> Some jobs can be very monotonous, but if we can give workers a sense of mission or a goal to aim at, interest can be maintained even in a monotonous job.

The ultimate target of improvement is top management's policies. One of top management's roles is to establish long- and medium-term policies as well as annual policies and to visibly show them to employees. Often, such policies are shown at the entrance to the plant and in the dining room as well as in *gemba*. As these policies are broken down into subsequent levels of management that finally reach the shop floors, everybody will understand why it is necessary to engage in *kaizen* activities.

Kaizen activities become meaningful in the minds of *gemba* people as they realize that their activities relate to corporate strategies and a sense of mission is instilled. Visual management helps to identify problems and highlight discrepancies between targets and current realities. In other words, it is a means to stabilize the process (maintenance function) as well as to improve the process (improvement function). Visual management is a powerful tool for motivating *gemba* people to achieve managerial targets. It provides many opportunities for workers to reinforce their own performance through displays of targets reached and progress made toward goals.

SUPERVISORS' ROLES IN *GEMBA*

$\mathbf{F}$requently supervisors in *gemba* do not know exactly their responsibilities. They engage in such activities as firefighting, head counts, and achieving production quotas without regard to quality. Sometimes they don't even have daily production quotas in mind; they just try to produce as many pieces as possible while the process is under control—between the many interruptions caused by machine downtime, absenteeism, and quality problems. This situation arises when management does not clearly explain how to manage in *gemba* and has not given a precise description of supervisors' roles and accountability.

Supervisors' roles have evolved in Japan over the past five decades. Japan owes much to the Management Training Program (MTP) and the Training Within Industries (TWI) program. These programs came to Japan from the United States and were designed to help the Japanese develop their own managerial and supervisory training programs. The MTP program primarily trained middle managers, while the TWI programs trained supervisors.

The following is a summary of these programs' origins and development from "Training, Continuous Improvement, and Human Relations: The US TWI Programs and the Japanese Management Style," by Alan G. Robinson and Dean M. Schroaeder (*California Management Review*, Volume 35, 1993):*

W. Edwards Deming, Joseph Juran, and other American experts have rightfully earned their place in the history books for their significant contributions to the industrial development of Japan. However, the U.S. Training Within Industries (TWI) programs, installed in Japan by the occupation authorities after World War II, may well have been even more influential. At least ten million Japanese managers, supervisors, and workers are graduates of the TWI programs or one of their many derivative courses, all of which remain in wide use in Japan in 1992. TWI has indeed had a strong influence on Japanese management thought and practice: a number of management practices thought of as "Japanese" trace their roots to TWI.

The TWI programs were developed in the United States fifty years ago. They were designed to play a major role in boosting industrial production to the levels required to win the Second World War. Even though TWI did this very successfully, after the war the programs' usage dropped off until, in 1992, they are hardly used or even known in the United States.

The story is quite different in Japan. After the war, Japanese industry was running at less than 10 percent of its 1935 to 1937 levels. Faced with the threat of widespread unrest, starvation, and social disorder, it was only natural for the Occupation authorities to think of TWI, a set of programs specifically designed to boost productivity and quality on a national scale. While TWI had an impact on many countries around the world, it undoubtedly had its greatest effect on Japan. In 1992, even though the programs have changed little since their arrival in Japan, they are well-respected in Japanese management circles and are viewed as important enough to the national interest to be overseen by the Ministry of Labor, which licenses instructors and upholds training standards throughout the country.

TWI provided three standardized training programs for supervisors and foremen. The first, Job Instructional Training (JIT), taught supervisors the importance of proper training of their workforce and how to provide this training.

The second, Job Methods Training (JMT), focuses on how to generate and implement ideas for methods improvement. The third, Job Relations Training (JRT), was a course in supervisor-worker relations and in leadership.

The Japan Industrial Training Association and various professional organizations conducted these training programs. At the same time, many leading Japanese companies internalized the programs to meet their own requirements to train supervisors.

The United States Air Force (USAF) initiated, developed, and introduced MTP to Japan during the occupation period following World War II. Japan's Ministry of International Trade and Industry (MITI) and Nikkeiren, the Japan Federation of Employers' Associations, have jointly overseen the course for close to fifty years, strongly influencing Japanese management thought and practice. And yet, even though many of the management practices commonly thought of as Japanese trace their roots back to MTP, the course is hardly known in the West. As Alan G. Robinson and Sam Stern point out in "Strategic National HRD Initiations: Lessons from the Management Training Program of Japan" (*Human Resource Development Quarterly*, Volume 6, Number 2, 1995):

> By the end of 1994, more than three million Japanese managers will have graduated from the Management Training Program or one of its derivative courses. In many Japanese companies, successful completion of MTP has become mandatory for promotion into middle management.
>
> MTP taught a significant percentage of several generations of Japanese managers three things:
>
> 1. The importance of human relations and employee involvement
> 2. The methodology and value of *continuously improving* processes and products
> 3. The usefulness of a scientific and rational "plan-do-see" approach to managing people and operations

The first point—the importance of human relations and

employee involvement—bore fruit in Japan in the formation of quality circles; the development of internal facilitators such as big brothers, big sisters, and junior leaders and the like; and the organization of employee involvement programs such as sports clubs and book clubs to promote mutual self-enlightenment among employees.

The second point—the methodology and value of continuously improving processes and products—matched perfectly with the *kaizen* way of doing business that was emerging in Japan at the time, and helped managers and supervisors to review and improve their work processes.

The third point—the usefulness of a scientific and rational "plan-do-see" approach to managing people and operations—has come to be well known in Japan, together with the PDCA cycles of Deming's teachings, and has helped to instill deeply the mind-set of the plan-do-check-action cycle of never-ending improvement. Even to this day, many Japanese executives prefer to use the terms "plan-do-see" as a model.

The curriculums of MTP and TWI produced another forerunner of something that has come to be known and practiced by every Japanese manager even to this day: the so-called "five W's and one H"—why, what, where, when, who, and how—otherwise known as 5W1H. The 5W1H approach provides a widely used checklist when quality circle members go about solving problems, as well as when managers are engaged in a *kaizen* project.

While the original format of MTP and TWI have remained almost the same during the last fifty years, new subjects have been added or incorporated into the curriculum, particularly for those companies that have developed their own training programs. These subjects include the concepts of quality, cost, and delivery (QCD), standardization, visual management, *muda* elimination, 5S, and *takt* time (theoretical time it takes to produce a piece of product ordered by the customer), reflecting the transformation of Japanese management over the years as a result of various *kaizen* practices and the introduction of such new practices as total quality control (TQC), total productive maintenance (TPM), and just-in-time (JIT).

The transformation of the TWI program has firmly established the roles of a typical Japanese supervisor in *gemba*.

MANAGING INPUT (MANPOWER, MATERIALS, AND MACHINES)

The supervisor is a person who has a line responsibility for directly supervising 20 or so operators in *gemba* and has accountability for the outcome. The span of control of supervision may differ from industry to industry and from company to company. Also, the title of such a person's job may vary; the person may be called group leader, foreman, *hancho*, or (in Germany) *meister*. (By the way, *hancho*, originally a Japanese term meaning chief or boss, means supervisor when used in *gemba*.)

In *gemba* the supervisor manages inputs to produce outputs. The inputs are the so-called three M's—namely, manpower, materials, and machines. (Sometimes methods and measurements are added to these three, and the list is collectively referred to as the five M's.) The output is quality, cost, and delivery or QCD. (Sometimes morale and safety are added to these three, and the list is referred to as QCDMS.)

A company's supervisors are held accountable for achieving the outputs of QCD, but they must manage the basic three M's—manpower, materials, and machines—in order to do so.

First and foremost, supervisors must manage their people. Yet supervisors often say, "Yes, I know that I am supposed to make good products on schedule, but you see, our people are not motivated to do a good job; they are poorly trained, and they don't even follow established standards. That is my problem!"

No supervisor has any business making such a statement. If his or her people are not motivated, the supervisor must introduce various programs to motivate them. If people don't follow standards, countermeasures must be developed. Perhaps the current standards are outdated and impractical, or the operators lack the training to follow them. Or there may be too much *muda, mura,* and *muri* in the work environment, making standards too difficult to follow. Supervisors who blame their people are abdicating their role.

In a plant producing electronic devices that employs part-time housewives in the afternoon, management found that the part-timers made far more rejects than regular employees. Data revealed that most of their mistakes occurred around 3 p.m. When management asked the housewives what sorts of things were on their minds around that time of day, the typical answers were as follows:

"At about that time, I am suddenly reminded that it is time for our children to come home from school and I start wondering if they can find the cookies I left in the refrigerator."

"I start thinking about the dinner and wonder which nearby store I should go to in order to buy fish. I want to know which store offers the best loss leader. Ms. A on the next line is knowledgeable on such matters, and maybe I should go meet her after work."

The insights gleaned from interviewing these members of its part-time workforce prompted management to set aside a large meeting room for the employees' use during their 3 p.m. coffee breaks. Management told the employees that they could talk about cookies, fish, loss-leaders, or other subjects to their hearts' content, but after the break, they should concentrate on their work. Eventually, the company saw a dramatic reduction in its reject rate.

Figure 9-1 shows a cause-and-effect diagram of a supervisor's work. This type of diagram is called an Ishikawa diagram, after its developer, Professor Kaoru Ishikawa. Because of its shape, it is also called a fishbone diagram. The effect (result) is quality, cost, and delivery (QCD). The causes (processes) are materials, machines, manpower, measurements, and methods (the five M's). Depending on the circumstances, more causes (in this case, the environment) can be added to the diagram.

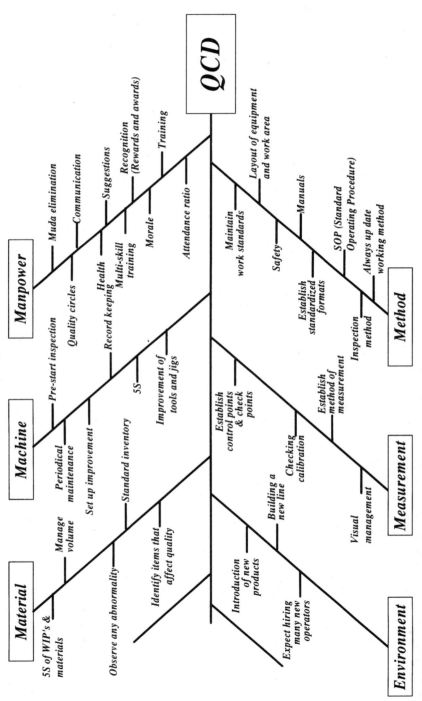

FIGURE 9-1. A cause-and-effect diagram of a supervisor's work.

111

By managing the causes, supervisors can realize the goal of their work: QCD.

The diagram shows that, just as supervisors must manage materials and machines in *gemba,* they must also manage manpower. To do that, they must manage several smaller "bones" of the fishbone: training, communication, quality circles, suggestions, rewards and awards, absenteeism, and morale. Whenever they find a human-related problem, they are supposed to find a solution.

Nissan Motor Company defines the two major tasks of the supervisor as follows: The first task is to achieve the target production volume. In this instance, it is assumed that the quality and cost targets are achieved together with the volume. The second major task is to develop and train subordinates. To do this, the supervisor must be able to transfer his or her technical and management skills by developing subordinates who can take over his or her role in the future and by training newly hired employees.

Kaizen consultant Shuichi Yoshida, managing director of the Kaizen Institute of Japan, attended MTP training courses before he was promoted to section manager in 1970 at the vehicle assembly plant of Nissan Motor in suburban Tokyo. Nissan Motor, like other Japanese companies, had modified MTP programs originally introduced from the United States to meet Nissan's own requirements and used the programs as one of the qualifications for employees' promotion to managerial ranks.

Yoshida was later chosen as one of the internal instructors for MTP within Nissan. As more than half of this ten-hour program consisted of the JIT, JMT, and JRT courses on TWI, Yoshida obtained a license to teach TWI courses later on, and would provide the training courses to the supervisors after he was transferred to the Tochigi plant of Nissan Motor in 1976. In those days, the Japanese auto industry depended to a great extent on unskilled seasonal workers to produce cars to meet rapidly expanding domestic and overseas demand. Just as was the case with the U.S. industry during World War II, the Japanese auto industry had to train unskilled workers in a short time, and found TWI methods very effective. Each course consisted of one week of two-hour lectures and practice sessions; after the lectures, participants returned to *gemba* to put into action what they had just learned.

Yoshida also volunteered to teach supervisors English, the language of the technical jargon used in the Japanese auto industry. Yoshida's classes were collectively referred to as the YES (Yoshida English School) Course. On pleasant days, Yoshida gave his classes outside of the plant on the lawns.

In Yoshida's view, supervisors should not act like prison wardens looking to find fault and administer punishment, but should act as tutors and look after subordinates. Whenever mistakes are found, supervisors should reflect where their teaching has failed and find out how to do it better. Supervisors need to use both heart and brain in dealing with their people, says Yoshida.

At Nissan, the roles of supervisors are defined as follows:

- Prepare work standards.
- Provide training and make certain that operators do their jobs according to standards. (This is the maintenance of management function.)
- Improve the status quo by improving standards. (This is the improvement of management function.)
- Take notice of abnormalities and address them right away.
- Create a good working environment.

Dealing with abnormalities at the worksite is a primary responsibility for a supervisor. The following are conditions that constitute abnormalities:

- Standard working procedure is not followed.
- Deviation is noticed in operators' work procedures, materials, or parts.
- Failure of equipment, tools, or jigs has occurred.
- A reject has been produced, or a symptom that may lead to a reject has been observed.

- The process is out of control, or an unusual distribution is shown on the control chart.

First, the supervisor must know what constitutes an abnormality. The standards should specify abnormal conditions and explain steps to be followed when such conditions occur. Most standards specify how to do the job right, but fail to define abnormalities and the proper procedures for addressing them.

If an abnormality occurs, the supervisor must go to *gemba* right away, confirm what has happened based on on-the-spot observation or on data, and take action promptly. To do this, he or she must follow the five *gemba* principles.

Some companies hold a three-minute meeting with operators in *gemba*. Supervisors explain recently noted abnormalities, the immediate corrective steps they took, and the measures adopted for permanent solution of the problem. Sometimes a manager at the meeting makes comments and offers guidance, which provides a good opportunity to train supervisors as well as to facilitate communication between supervisors and their superiors.

MORNING MARKET (*ASAICHI*)

Morning market (asaichi) is an activity employed in Japanese companies as a part of daily activities to reduce rejects in *gemba* by supervisors and operators on the line. Morning market derives its name from the markets where farmers bring their daily produce to sell. The Japanese word *asaichi* also means "the first thing in the morning." *Gemba*'s morning market displays rejects on the table the first thing in the morning of the day after they are made, so that countermeasures may be adopted on the spot and as soon as practicable, based on the *gemba-gembutsu* principles. All participants in this activity stand up. Morning market differs distinctly from other types of quality-related problem-solving activities involving staff, in that the supervisor and operators must play a leading role, with a commitment never to carry forward the same problem to the next day.

Nobody in *gemba* produces rejects out of a desire to do so. And yet they continue to occur. The causes are many, including the following:

- Abrupt breakdown of equipment
- Forced equipment deterioration that goes beyond the specified allowances
- Failure to follow standards
- Failure of materials and parts to meet specifications
- Failure to maintain 5S
- Careless and absentminded mistakes

Unless management determines the root causes of these problems one by one, *gemba* will soon be filled with a mountain of rejects.

Morning market in *gemba* consists of the following steps:

- An operator tags and places in a red box all rejects in a particular process and lists the rejects in the quality morning market report.
- The next morning, the supervisor in charge brings both the reports and *gembutsu* to the morning market corner and displays the rejects on the desk.
- The supervisor reviews the rejects with the operators and discusses countermeasures.
- The rejects are classified according to three categories (types A, B, and C), and countermeasures are adopted as soon as practicable (Fig. 9-2).

It is important that both the supervisor and the workforce touch and hold the *gembutsu* (in this case, the rejects) themselves. They should see them, smell them, taste them (if necessary), and discuss how they were made at the specific work site (*gemba*), and what equipment (also *gembutsu*) was used.

TYPE	NATURE	PERCENTAGE	EXAMPLES
Type A	Causes are clear. Countermeasures can be taken immediately.	70–80%	Standard was not followed. Out of spec materials and supplies.
Type B	Causes are known but countermeasures cannot be adopted.	15–20%	Occurs at the time of setup adjustment. Occurs during frequent stoppages of equipment.
Type C	Unidentified causes.	10–15%	Situation suddenly went out of control.

FIGURE 9-2.   How rejects can be sorted into three very distinct categories.

After Type A problems have been solved, countermeasures to prevent recurrence must be adopted. As for problems of Types B and C, the supervisor must report them to the section manager, who will hold a meeting later to devise solutions and will present the result to the plant manager.

When a company holds its first morning market, participants may find that there are too many rejects to fit on one table. But if morning market continues for three months, the rejects, as well as the time for the meeting, will be greatly reduced. In the meantime, plant productivity and profitability will also improve.

The plant manager should attend morning markets at different sites within the plant each day in order to become familiar with the problems encountered in each place. Figure 9-3 shows an example of a morning market report.

Plant	Dept.	Manager	Supervisor	Operator

1. *Date of occurrence*: October 9, 1995 14:00 PM

2. *Part number*: 123456-G1002

3. *Process & machine*: Key groove process (F-3214)

4. *Number of occurrences*: 4 pieces
   —*Number of processed pieces for the day*: 920
   —*Reject rate*: 0.43%

5. *Description of the reject*: [Draw sketches whenever possible.]

6. *Causes (confirmed/assured/not identified)*:
   One out of four bolts in the machine was loosened, causing vibrations.

7. *Countermeasures*:
   Tightened the four bolts with the right torque. Have not seen occurrences of the same problem since.

8. *Prevention of recurrences*:
   Requested the preset group to add a new standard. "Confirm the torque of tightening bolts of_____equipment."

FIGURE 9-3.   An example of a morning market report.

At Toyoda Automatic Loom Works, a booklet containing all relevant standards is handed to each operator shortly before the operator begins tasks of mass production. The booklet—used for training at first, and as a reference after production has started—contains the following standards:

- Organization chart and layout
- Operational safety rules (which also show what happens if the rules are not followed)

- Information on how to build quality into the process
- Work sequence table
- Standard operation procedures (SOP)
- Abnormality-handling procedures (which include a definition of abnormality, and instructions on how to detect abnormality and whom to report abnormality to)
- Definition of rejects (quality-related problems)
- Rules on the use of *kanban*

At one time, *gemba kaizen* activities were promoted uniformly at all factories of Toyoda Automatic Loom Works. Later, management realized that it should live up to the philosophy behind the Pareto diagram (graphical tool used for solving problems): establish priorities in selecting the *kaizen* projects. Thus, instead of promoting *gemba kaizen* indiscriminately throughout all areas in the plant, management decided to select one line as a model and provide the line with all the help and resources it needed from the corporate office as well as from plant management. Once visible progress had been made, improvements were extended to other lines. Top management visited the model line once a month to review daily management and *kaizen* activities. The review covered the following major points:

- What kind of standards are installed?
- How are standards adhered to?
- Who manages the standards?
- Who is engaged in *kaizen*?
- What roles do the line managers play?

As the managerial hierarchy included foremen, supervisors, and group leaders in the factory, top management also monitored the roles of these managers and the items for which they were responsible.

BEST-LINE QUALITY-ASSURANCE CERTIFICATION

For more than 20 years now, the so-called acceptable quality level (AQL) approach has not been followed in Japan. AQL is a system of quality assurance that allows suppliers to deliver a certain percentage of rejects to customers. For example, a customer might allow a supplier to deliver rejects at a rate of up to 1 percent, provided that the supplier compensated the customer according to terms previously agreed upon.

However, major Japanese companies have long since discarded this approach to quality assurance. Except for the first lot, companies accept supplies without inspection. During that initial inspection, if even one reject is found, the whole lot is returned to the supplier.

Since the 1980s, when highly automated equipment such as industrial robots came to be used on a large scale, the emergence of even a single reject in the process has meant serious consequences for production lines and, in turn, large economic losses for companies. The Japanese automobile manufacturers have therefore stepped up quality requirements—from the previous 0.1 percent to between 30 and 50 ppm (parts per million). In order to achieve this level of quality, it was essential to eliminate defects in the process itself.

Suppliers were thus obliged to review the quality-assurance practices of their production lines. The line supervisors took on the challenge of improving the process capability of their lines to the levels requested by their customers. The real test of the success of these efforts was the in-process rejects rate and customer returns. This system is known among Nissan's suppliers as best-line quality assurance, or QA Best Line.

After a line has reached a certain level of quality, the supervisor decides to apply for best-line certification. Toward this end, the supervisor and production manager together conduct a diagnosis of the line. The supervisor also asks the corporate director in charge of the corporate quality-assurance department to visit and diagnose the line, based on certain preestablished criteria, including various statistics on rejects and customer returns.

Figure 9-4 shows a certification awarded for QA best lines in one supplier to Nissan Motor Company. The idea behind QA best-line certification is that first one line achieves the necessary improvements, and then the process is extended to other lines, until every line in the plant has attained the same level of quality assurance and received certification to that effect.

Chart 1 Requirements for Approval

QA PERFORMANCE		GRADE		
		C	B	A
CUSTOMER RETURNS		No. of Returns/ 3 months	No. of Returns/ 6 months	No. of Returns/ 12 Months
FINAL INSPECTION REJECTS p.p.m.		<500	<50	<10
IN-PROCESS REJECTS %	REPAIRS	<0.5	<0.1	<0.01
	SCRAPS	<0.1	<0.05	0

Chart 2 Evaluation Items for Certification of QA System

Standardization	55 check points
Work to Standards	34 check points
Quality Confirmation of Designing/Process Changes	16 check points
5S	31 check points
Education & Training	6 check points
Problems Solved	7 check points

FIGURE 9-4.   Certification system for QA Best Lines.

Chart 3 Approval Steps

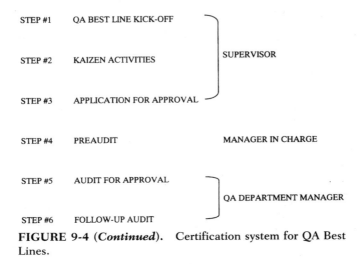

STEP #1	QA BEST LINE KICK-OFF	
STEP #2	KAIZEN ACTIVITIES	SUPERVISOR
STEP #3	APPLICATION FOR APPROVAL	
STEP #4	PREAUDIT	MANAGER IN CHARGE
STEP #5	AUDIT FOR APPROVAL	QA DEPARTMENT MANAGER
STEP #6	FOLLOW-UP AUDIT	

FIGURE 9-4 (*Continued*).   Certification system for QA Best Lines.

DEFINING CHALLENGES

In today's dynamic and competitive environment, management faces increasingly stringent requirements from customers who want better quality, a lower price, and prompt delivery. Only a clear management plan for improving on QCD all the time will keep up with this demand. Management must therefore keep setting higher QCD targets and challenging subordinates to attain them. As soon as a new target has been achieved, management must establish the next one, thus continuously urging subordinates along the never-ending road of improvement. Successful companies continue their success because managers lead subordinates in this manner and build a corporate culture of challenge. Such companies also know that once they lose this spirit, particularly at the *gemba* level, there will be no future for them. In today's companies, whether or not management possesses a spirit of challenge makes the difference between success and failure. Such a spirit of challenge should be the backbone of *gemba*.

However, a majority of managers today have lost the enthusiasm to challenge. In particular, many *gemba* supervisors settle for trying to maintain the status quo and working hard and loud and running around throughout the day without having any clear idea where they are going.

Setting challenges is the key element of a successful supervisor's job. The supervisor must possess sufficient understanding of the current process to establish appropriately challenging targets.

PSEUDO-MANAGERIAL FUNCTIONS OF SUPERVISORS IN *GEMBA*

As stated earlier, managers' jobs boil down to two major functions in *gemba*: maintenance and improvement.

Maintenance refers to preserving the status quo—that is, to make certain that subordinates follow current standards to achieve expected results. The objective of maintenance—to making certain that things do not go out of control—takes a lot of effort. Without maintenance, everything in *gemba* will deteriorate over time.

Improvement, meanwhile, refers to enhancing and upgrading current standards by continually establishing new and higher targets. Improvement can be further broken down into *kaizen* and innovation. Simply stated, *kaizen* means making better use of the existing internal resources of the five M's of manpower, machines, materials, methods, and measurements. *Kaizen* is accomplished by changing the way people do their jobs rather than by spending large amounts of money. It takes a challenging spirit to bring about *kaizen,* as people are always more comfortable with the way they have been doing their job in the past.

I believe that a surfeit of resources has unforeseen drawbacks: There is no impetus for *kaizen*; no incentive to rack our brains and look within for ways to improve—and before we know it, the competition has passed us.

In the context of *kaizen* philosophy, supervisors' jobs should also be broken down into two functions: (1) maintenance, the task of stabilizing and preserving the current process, and whenever an abnormality is detected, bringing the process back under control; and (2) improvement, which is as important as maintenance. In the improvement function, management must check to determine whether supervisors have attained management-imposed targets. Maintenance is sometimes referred to as "daily activities" and improvement, as "*kaizen* activities."

Supervisors must carry out all these activities in order to realize QCD. Chapter 3 points out the real challenge for management is to manage quality, cost, and delivery simultaneously. Supervisors should not confine their concern to meeting production volume nor sacrifice quality and/or cost to meet those production targets. The supervisor in *gemba* should always strive to realize QCD by attaining targets set by management and demanded by customers.

The properly trained Japanese supervisor participates in policy deployment by always keeping in mind two or three annual targets for *kaizen,* such as halving rejects and reducing inventory. In the process of assuming responsibility of this kind, supervisors come to regard themselves as members of the management team—in spirit, if not in fact.

GEMBA MANAGERS' ROLES AND ACCOUNTABILITY

KAIZEN AT TOYOTA ASTRA MOTOR COMPANY

The preceding chapter outlined the *roles* of a supervisor. Another crucial subject is the *accountability* of a supervisor. Every large industrial complex has several management layers in *gemba,* and defining their respective roles and accountabilities is often an issue. The following case study of *kaisen* at Toyota Astra Motor Company vividly illustrates the value of clarifying *gemba* managers' areas of accountability.

Toyota Astra Motor Company, a joint venture of Toyota Motor Company and P. T. Astra International, produces passenger and commercial cars in Indonesia. It began operations in 1971 and today has 5000 employees.

Although it had been operating in Indonesia for many years, Toyota Astra Motor recognized an acute need to clarify the roles of its *gemba* managers around 1991. The company had such *gemba* managers as supervisors, foremen, and group leaders, but confusion often arose as to their respective roles. When a given problem arose, the question often asked was who among these managers should address this particular issue. Who should devise a temporary countermeasure and standardize the new method to prevent the problem from recurring?

In addition, many other issues needed attention—there were problems with systems and procedures and problems concerning human resources—and many different areas required managing—among them quality, safety, cost reduction, 5S, and productivity.

Toyota Astra Motor Company (TAM) had sent many *gemba* trainee managers of different ranks to Toyota Motor Company (TMC) in Japan. However, when the managers came back to Indonesia and tried to implement what they had learned, the ambiguity of *gemba* managers' roles there remained unresolved. Finally, in 1992, the company began serious efforts to redefine the roles and accountability of each level of *gemba* managers. As a first step, Eddie Paino, manager of TAM's *kaizen* implementation office, went to TMC to learn in depth how TMC defined the roles of each level of manager.

TAM had the following managerial layers in *gemba*: group leaders, foremen, supervisors, and section managers. The ratio of subordinates to managers in each category was as follows:

Group Leader	One for every 8 operators
Foreman	One for every 2 group leaders
Supervisor	One for every 2 to 3 foremen
Section Manager	One for every 2 to 4 supervisors

One of the first tasks the company tackled was to clarify its various managers' roles and prioritize them in order to avoid conflicts and ambiguities. At that point, many of these managers took part in both pre- and post-promotion training courses, developed jointly by TAM's *kaizen* office and human resources division, as well as in problem-solving sessions and group discussions. All of this contributed greatly to clarifying the managers' roles. As a result, the prioritized roles of *gemba* managers at each level came to be defined as explained in Table 10-1.

TABLE 10-1 Roles Defined in Order of Priority at TAM

MANAGER	ROLES IN ORDER OF PRIORITY	QUALIFICATIONS
Group Leader	▪ Quality and defects oversight ▪ Line stops responsibility	▪ Must be able to help operators to follow standard operating procedure (SOP) and standard worksheet (SWS) in work area and assist foreman in developing and implementing work standard and quality standard. ▪ Must be responsible for preparing standard worksheet.
Foreman	▪ Productivity improvement ▪ Cost reduction	▪ Must be able to improve working conditions (productivity, cost, and quality) and increase subordinates' skills and capabilities. ▪ Must prepare activity plans for the above and discuss them with the supervisor.
Supervisor	▪ Human resources management ▪ People-related problem solving	▪ Must be able to assist section manager in improving a system of production control, standard operating procedure, quality control, safety, training, and development of multiskilled and thinking employees.
Section Manager	▪ Policy deployment ▪ Deal with specific problems brought up by subordinates ▪ People-related problem solving ▪ New product development coordination	▪ Must establish challenging enough target for quality, cost, delivery, safety, and morale (QCDSM). ▪ Must oversee line stop of more than 20 minutes, safety violation, accidents, and chronic defects.

ROLE MANUALS AT TAM

Once these roles were defined in order of their *priority*, management began to develop a system to evaluate the *performance* of managers at each level. To do this, the personnel division created and published pocket-size role manuals detailing the responsibilities of *gemba* managers of each rank, and distributed manuals to every manager.

As a general rule, the manuals divide managers' tasks into two parts: (1) the roles managers are expected to play (the activities they are expected to carry out) throughout the day; and (2) the items for which managers are held accountable. For both group leaders and foremen, the manuals provide a list of daily activities to be carried out during working hours. (The manuals contain no such list for supervisors and section managers because their daily activities cannot be defined in the same manner and detail as those of the group leaders and foremen. This means that the supervisors and section managers have more freedom for carrying out their daily responsibilities.)

The managerial roles/activities and accountabilities are also directly related to managers' performance appraisals and salaries. For instance, group leaders are requested to monitor defects and abnormalities, to keep records, to enter the data on certain checklists or graphs, and to post those checklists or graphs on a large display boards in *gemba*. Each group leader and foreman has his or her own display board, which is shared with the second and third shifts. (Often, operators' skill inventory tables and other tables and graphs are displayed on the same boards.)

The manuals clearly define the items to be monitored and the types of data to be collected, as well as the kinds of checklists to use. The items to be monitored for appraising purposes are not always the same for every process, but they always refer to such vital functions as quality, safety, productivity, cost reduction, training, and total productive maintenance (TPM).

By looking up and filling in data on such display boards daily, both group leaders and foremen can focus on the items requiring immediate attention. Their supervisors can in turn look at the display boards and instantly evaluate the initiatives, maintenance, and improvement of these items by their group leaders and foremen. The supervisors can then post a summary of the data obtained from their group leaders and foremen on their own display boards. Section managers have similar display boards. In effect, the series of checklists and graphs on the display boards serve as a *visual reporting system* among managers, allowing a quick identification of certain prioritized activities that need immediate attention. The display boards also serve as a *visual monitoring system* of the meeting of the minds of managers.

Before every shift starts, everybody gathers around the display boards for a five-minute talk in which group leaders can explain specific problems, drawing data from the display boards. (Similarly, the boards offer a means of telling visitors what is going on in *gemba*. When guests or senior managers conduct a *"gemba* walk," they can glance at the boards to find out what is going on or to update their knowledge of the various lines' progress.)

At the end of every month, the section managers and supervisors get together and evaluate the work of their subordinates (group leaders and foremen). Their evaluations are then posted on the display boards. The items to be evaluated are drawn from the role manual notebook and are categorized as *activities, initiatives, contributions,* or *efforts* related to maintaining and improving the items their subordinates are responsible for. The following are the major items to be evaluated in the case of a group leader, for example:

- Line stop due to cause
- Checking and identification of safety items
- Quality defects
- *Hiyari* (scare) reports
- Idea suggestions
- Quality circles
- 5S

For TAM foremen, the items to be evaluated are as follows:

- Safety awareness
- Absenteeism
- Line stop due to external cause
- Man-hours per unit
- Quality system
- Idea suggestions
- Quality circles
- *Hiyari* (scare) reports
- 5S
- Cost-down activities

TAM GROUP LEADERS' RESPONSIBILITIES

Group leaders are promoted from among the operators, and receive additional allowances for their work. If they have done a good job as group leader, they have a good chance of being promoted to a higher managerial level. The major responsibilities of the group leaders are maintaining quality and managing line stops. Group leaders are requested to have at least one quality circle in their group, and each quality circle must complete two themes per year. The circle members meet twice a month. Another of the group leaders' duties is taking care of absenteeism. If someone in the group is absent, the group leader either finds a replacement or takes the person's place himself or herself.

Group leaders must fill out checklists daily and, on critical items such as line stoppages, every hour. Group leaders hold a five-minute talk with their groups before each shift starts. The following subjects are discussed:

- Accidents that took place the day before
- Some problems encountered during the night shift

- Targets that were not achieved
- Any electrical or mechanical failures that took place

Group leaders must also manage line stops. Whenever a problem is found, operators are allowed to stop the line by pushing a nearby button. The moment the line is stopped, a clock showing aggregate stoppage time begins to tick. The group leader checks the clock every hour. He or she also checks for any problem or abnormality if line stoppages are higher than normal. Based on such data, the target for line stops for each month is determined. Needless to say, the total stoppage time affects the work-hour productivity for the group.

TAM FOREMEN'S RESPONSIBILITIES

A foreman's main job is improving productivity and reducing cost. To do this, a foreman is expected to reduce worker-hours (called *kosu* in Japanese), as well as eliminating all sorts of *muda*. *Kosu* is defined as total worker-hours in a particular process, multiplied by actual working time and divided by the units produced. For instance, if 10 people worked in one process for 9 hours, including overtime, and produced 200 units, the *kosu* would be calculated as follows:

$$\frac{10 \times 9}{200} = 0.45$$

Each working group must calculate the *kosu* per unit produced. Each group leader, foreman, and supervisor must set monthly targets for reducing *kosu*.

At TAM, a long time passed before *kosu* began to be used as a criterion of productivity improvement and cost reduction. But today, *kosu* is a very realistic indication of productivity improvement and cost reduction for each manager there, right down to the lowest-level group leader, and the relationship between *kosu* improvement and the available data is very clear to everyone at the company. At all levels, TAM employees can see how their actions contribute to *kosu* reduction.

TAM SUPERVISORS' RESPONSIBILITIES

Supervisors' main tasks are people-related:

- Developing multiskilled workers
- Quality circles
- Safety, etc.

Foremen and supervisors hold weekly meetings and discuss the following subjects:

- Safety
- Productivity
- Cost
- Quality
- Absenteeism
- Suggestions
- Quality circles

Every foreman and supervisor must submit weekly reports to his or her boss.

ITEMS THAT NEED TO BE MANAGED IN *GEMBA*

Generally speaking, items that need to be managed in *gemba* include the following:

- Productivity
- Cost reduction, including *kosu* reduction
- Safety

- Personnel training
- *Kaizen* activities
- 5S
- Improving employees' skills
- Quality
- Line stops

As already mentioned, TAM has developed a manual describing the roles and accountabilities of *gemba* managers. All the managers' jobs are broken down into two parts: (1) their daily activities; and (2) the specific actions for which they are held accountable. The daily activities column contains a detailed description of what managers are expected to do throughout the day, item by item. The items for which managers are accountable fall into the following categories:

- Production
- Cost
- Housekeeping
- Quality
- Personnel and training
- Safety

For each category, the manual provides a list of activities for the manager to perform. All these subjects are shared by the group leader, the foreman, and the supervisor, although the activities for each subject and the level of involvement differ among the three levels of management.

GROUP LEADERS' DAILY SCHEDULE OF ACTIVITIES: EXAMPLES FROM THE TAM MANUAL

A. Before Start of Work
 1. Enter factory and go to *gemba*.
 2. Review the report from the previous shift.
 3. Preparations before work:

      a. Prepare the work team and check the readiness of all equipment, jigs, tools, and other auxiliary material.

      b. If someone is absent, fill in the report and find a replacement through the foreman.

    4. Morning exercise and five-minute talk.

B. Morning Working Hours

    1. Start of work: Confirm that everybody has started working on time.

    2. Change of work procedures: Help foreman to teach newly developed work procedures.

    3. Check the production process: Lead the line operators in observing standard worksheets.

    4. During morning break:

      a. Perform sampling checks on several predetermined quality items.

      b. Lead and guide operators to counter any abnormalities during their work.

      c. Assist in or perform foreman's job when he is at a meeting.

    5. Conduct on-the-job training to develop multiskilled workers.

C. Afternoon Working Hours

    1. Check results of inspections:

      a. Check result of morning inspection by quality control people and ask for guidance on improvement from the foreman.

      b. As instructed by foreman, perform temporary countermeasures against problems and ask for further guidance for permanent solution.

    2. Help operators engage in repairs and rework, and check and evaluate results.

    3. Investigate the cause of line stoppage: propose temporary countermeasures and preventive measures to foreman.

    4. Give instructions for overtime work if necessary.

    5. Lead operators in performing 5S activities in *gemba*.

D. After Working Hours

    1. Write the shift report and leave any pertinent information for the next shift.

2. Lead quality-circle meetings: actively promote quality-circle activities and boost morale of workers.

Group Leaders' Activities: Production, Cost, and Quality Examples from the TAM Manual

The TAM manual also describes in detail the activities for which group leaders are accountable within the aforementioned categories—namely, production, cost, total productive maintenance (TPM), quality, personnel, training, and safety. As an example, the following are the group leaders' activities related to production, cost, and quality:

A. Production
1. Implement monthly production plan:
   a. Assign workers for smooth production flow.
   b. Train and assist new workers in their jobs.
2. Prepare for daily production:
   a. Check equipment, tools, parts, and materials.
   b. Perform the task as instructed by the foreman.
   c. Switch on the machines and confirm that they are functioning properly.
3. Follow Up:
   a. Investigate the cause of abnormalities.
   b. Report to the foreman.
   c. Take temporary actions.
   d. Devise permanent countermeasures.
   e. Report any action taken to the foreman.
   f. Help foreman as instructed.
4. After the operation:
   a. Prepare for the next shift; inform the next shift if any abnormalities have been found.
   b. Confirm that every switch is in "off" position.
   c. Assist superior in preparing daily reports.
5. Handle line stoppages:
   a. Investigate external line stoppages.
   b. Investigate internal line stoppages.
   c. Determine the causes and take countermeasures.

6. Prepare for the introduction of new models on the line:
   a. Help the foreman.
   b. Learn the new model and guide the operators.

B. Cost
   1. Plan cost improvements: voice opinions and suggestions on improvement plan to the foreman.
   2. Reduce labor costs: propose ideas and help superior in implementing labor cost reduction.
   3. Reduce direct costs:
      a. Record usage of materials.
      b. Study the cause of increase in material usage and propose countermeasures.
   4. Save energy:
      a. Identify any leakage, such as air and/or water.
      b. Upon identification, decide whether to act alone or seek help.
   5. Improve on a daily basis:
      a. Prepare for improvement.
      b. Assist foreman in guiding subordinates' improvement efforts.
   6. Other:
      a. Meet with subordinates to explain the results of cost reduction.
      b. Take every opportunity to enhance operators' cost awareness.

C. Quality
   1. Maintain and improve quality level:
      a. Clarify current quality levels versus targets for team members.
      b. Monitor and control the process of inputting quality data.
      c. Analyze cause and take countermeasures.
   2. Pursue daily "Built-in Quality":
      a. Inspect the first and last product of every working day.
      b. Perform scheduled inspection to prevent defects.
      c. Monitor workers to see that they perform their jobs according to work standards.

3. Take countermeasures when defects are found:
   a. For internally produced defects: Repair the defects and report to foreman while proposing countermeasures.
   b. For externally produced defects: Report to foreman and ask for instructions on repair.
4. Other: Meet daily with the team; inform members about quality problems and discuss with them; elevate the quality awareness of all members.

FOREMEN'S ACTIVITIES: COST-REDUCTION EXAMPLES FROM THE TAM MANUAL

The foreman's activities in the area of cost reduction are as follows:

1. Plan *kaizen*:
   a. Prepare the schedule of cost reduction programs after discussions with group leaders.
   b. Coordinate activities within sections and request specific *kaizen* items (new tools, etc.) from other sections.
   c. Monitor and follow up on progress of cost reduction schedule.
2. Reduce labor cost (*kosu*):
   a. Monitor monthly *kosu* reduction activities and follow up on progress.
   b. In case target was not met, study the cause and take action.
3. Reduce direct costs:
   a. Monitor actual usage of material, consumable tools, supplies, oil, etc. against planned usage.
   b. If usage is greater than planned, study the cause of the increase and take countermeasures.
4. Save energy:
   a. Identify leakage of such items as pressurized air and water, and institute action programs to stop it.
   b. Train and motivate workers to always switch off any equipment after use.

5. Daily *kaizen:*
   a. Prepare charts and monitor *kosu* for *kaizen* activities.
   b. Give instructions for *kaizen* activities based on problems identified.
6. Other:
   a. Lead group meetings and explain progress of cost reduction activities.
   b. Encourage everyone to increase cost-consciousness.

SUPERVISORS' ACTIVITIES: PERSONNEL AND TRAINING EXAMPLES FROM THE TAM MANUAL

Supervisors' activities in the personnel and training areas are as follows:

1. Train and develop subordinates:
   a. Inform all subsection members of the current status of the company, its environment, and its management policies. Subordinates should also be informed of such important matters as new market development and new products.
   b. Prepare long-term training programs for individual members.
   c. Maintain and update records of staffing capabilities and improvement status.
2. Develop multiskill workers:
   a. Monitor training schedules and programs to train multiskill workers.
   b. Monitor the way the multiskill training program is carried out and follow up on it.
3. Teach skills:
   a. Provide skills training through on-the-job training (OJT).
   b. Lead and guide the process of skill standardization required for each workstation, based on past experience and practices.
4. Enhance knowledge of equipment:
   a. Gain better understanding of equipment structures, functions, and manual of operations.
   b. Guide foreman and group leader to better understanding of equipment.

    c. Check and revise operation manuals as needed.

5. Guide new workers and transferees:

    a. Explain organization of the subsection to the newly recruited or transferred workers.

    b. Give guidance on job items in the subsection.

    c. Evaluate, prepare, and revise "new worker guide" to be used by foreman.

    d. Monitor and follow up on orientations of new workers based on the manual guide.

6. Pursue human-relations activities:

    a. Follow up and advise on informal activities such as personal touch activities (PTA) [each group is entitled to hold a meeting during working hours every month to enhance human relations, recreation, and free talk].

7. Pursue quality-circle activities:

    a. Act as senior facilitator and assist and give advice on quality-circle activities.

    b. Assist and give guidance in quality-control meetings, seminars, and training sessions.

    c. Give advice and follow up on smooth advance of quality-circle activities within subsection.

    d. Conduct activities to further enhance understanding of quality-circle activities.

8. Encourage suggestions:

    a. Promote and guide idea suggestion programs to meet the target of number of suggestions in each group.

    b. Monitor development and give guidance.

    c. Provide individual counseling for less active members.

    d. Review suggestions.

9. Build work discipline:

    a. Organize meetings and provide counseling to build a more positive working atmosphere.

    b. Confirm if all rules and regulations are observed. Give feedback if nonconformance is observed.

    c. Provide individual counseling to members who routinely violate rules and regulations.

    d. Check implementation status of rules and regulations within subsection.

10. Other:
    a. Give approval and instructions to engage in overtime work.
    b. Monitor and follow up on annual leave status.
    c. Provide individual counseling to operators with special problems.

SECTION MANAGERS' ROLES AND ACCOUNTABILITY AT TAM: EXAMPLES FROM THE TAM MANUAL

While the roles of group leader, foreman, and supervisor can be spelled out in specific action programs, the role of the section manager—building better internal systems and procedures—is less concretely defined. For instance, the section manager on quality at TAM is expected to shoulder the following responsibilities:

1. Policy and target setting:
   a. Define, and relay to each foreman, targets for quality improvement on each item.
   b. Devise strategies to achieve the targets.
2. Follow up on the progress toward targets:
   a. Conduct periodical review of section targets.
   b. Take problem-solving countermeasures.
   c. Follow up on the results of countermeasures.
   d. Support subordinates if results are unsatisfactory.
   e. Take up serious problems directly under section manager's authority.
3. Improve quality-assurance system: Build quality into the process and achieve 100% assurance.

THE CONDITIONS NECESSARY FOR SUCCESSFULLY DEFINING ROLES AND ACCOUNTABILITY AT TAM

The TAM manuals clearly outline the roles and accountability of the various *gemba* managers at Toyota Astra Motor in Indonesia. But in order for the manuals to be effective, two fundamental conditions must be satisfied:

1. There must be training programs to help managers to acquire the necessary skills to perform their respective roles.
2. There must be systems and procedures to manage such items as quality, cost, and delivery so that every manager knows exactly what he or she is supposed to do.

A group leader accountable for reducing quality problems or a foreman who has to reduce *kosu* must know exactly what to measure, using what kind of checklists, and must know how to calculate and report the data. Group leaders must also be equipped with problem-solving capabilities.

TAM's 25 years of effort in building its internal systems and procedures have enabled the company to define the respective roles of managers successfully. The managerial training programs that achieved this success have been closely related to the elimination of the *muda* (waste), *mura* (irregularity) and *muri* (strain) that are often associated with *kaizen* activities on the shop floor. When these three elements are applied to staff development, *muri* may be understood to mean human strain on the job. Workers not equipped with enough skills to perform their jobs, will feel strained. When such workers do not have sufficient and timely information about their jobs, they will probably make mistakes. When the workers do not understand the value they are adding for their customers, they will create more waste and cost. To eliminate *muri,* workers as well as managers should be trained to perform their jobs. In particular, the ability to adapt to changes in the business environment is regarded as one of the most important traits. Toyota believes that staff development is so important that it should be carried out continuously.

STAFF DEVELOPMENT

ON-THE-JOB TRAINING

The mainstay of Toyota's training is on-the-job training (OJT), which builds the *skills* of the worker. For its OJT program, Toyota developed a program called Toyota job instruction (TJI).

The training materials were initially derived from Training Within Industries (TWI), which includes job relations, job improvement (*kaizen*), and job instructions.

FORMAL CLASSROOM TRAINING

Various subjects are taught by certified trainers within Toyota. The TJI program, for example, is taught by a certified trainer in the classroom. Other examples of formal classroom training at the company are the Toyota production system (TPS), problem solving, pre- and post-promotion training, safety training, technical training, etc.

VOLUNTARY ACTIVITIES

These training activities are less structured than the other two, and participation is not compulsory. Activities falling into this category are quality circles, suggestion systems, and *hiyari* (scare) reports, quality *hiyari* reports, etc. Management feels that these activities stimulate employees' minds and teach them something of great value. Following is a description of one area of voluntary activities, *hiyari* reports.

THE IDENTIFICATION OF POTENTIAL PROBLEMS

HIYARI REPORTS

TAM has two special programs directed at anticipating problems in advance. One is called the *hiyari* (scare) report, and the other is called the quality *hiyari*, or *kiken-yochi* training—anticipating danger in advance, report. The *hiyari* (scare) report points out unsafe conditions or actions that could eventually lead to accidents in the workplace, while the quality *hiyari* report anticipates conditions that could lead to such quality problems as defects.

The two *hiyari* report forms are regularly used in conjunction with the submission of suggestions identifying potential problems. Such suggestions are more likely to receive a positive evaluation if a *hiyari* report form or a quality-*hiyari* report form is attached to them. In other words, management rewards the efforts of employees to anticipate or detect problems in advance and solve them before they become a reality. Management regards such an approach to problem solving as more valuable than addressing the problem *after* it has become a reality. *In one such case, an operator in the paint shop worried that the hoist might strike his head. He suggested removing the visual blockage so that he could see the incoming hoist chain more clearly. Another case concerned detection of defects during trial production of a new model (land cruisers). A metal finish worker had identified the possibility of dents when the operator opened the back door of the vehicle. The proposal was to install a door stopper for both side doors.*

Training in the Anticipation of Problems

TAM has a special training program devoted to anticipating dangers in which such subjects as safety, identification of potential problems, and *hiyari* reports are dealt with. The program elevates workers' awareness of unsafe conditions and behaviors, enhances their sensitivity about safety matters, and helps to increase the number of *hiyari* reports.

THE BENEFITS OF KAIZEN AT TOYOTA ASTRA MOTOR

After 25 years in operation, it appears that the *kaizen* culture has been firmly established at Toyota Astra Motor in Indonesia. In 1995, the average number of suggestions was seven per person per month, which was better than most Japanese companies. Management estimates that savings made by the suggestions were $5 million for the year. Since 1990, the target for *kosu* reduction or productivity improvement has been 10 percent every year, and this has been successfully achieved every year. In the early 1980s, Astra had a "car hospital" on-site housing as many as 400 current "car patients." *Today, all finished cars are delivered directly to the customer and an average inventory of finished cars at the factory is six hours.* *Kaizen* consultant, Kristianto Jahja, who used to work at TAM, remembers that in the early days he used to carry a plastic bag in his hand when he went to *gemba* and pick up the nuts and bolts that littered the floors. Nuts and bolts—and even machine part labels and soft-drink bottles—were sometimes found inside fully assembled cars as well! Today, such conditions are a thing of the past. Obviously, it takes many years of firm determination of management to bring about such a change, but it has been done at TAM—and with workers who typically earn as little as $150 per month.

Today, manufacturing companies are seeking new horizons outside their own countries. After Singapore, Indonesia, Malaysia, and Thailand, these companies are looking to Vietnam, Myanmar (Burma), China, and India, where workplace cultural transformations like the one achieved at Toyota's Astra Motor plant in Indonesia are not unlikely. This is bound to present a real challenge to companies in North America, Europe, and other industrial regions, where workers earn ten times more and are deeply imbued with traditional Western approaches to supervision and management.

JUST-IN-TIME

THE ULTIMATE PRODUCTION SYSTEM

In order to achieve successful quality, cost, and delivery (QCD) and satisfy the customer as well as itself, a manufacturing company must have three major systems in place: (1) total quality control (TQC) or total quality management (TQM); (2) total productive maintenance (TPM); and (3) just-in-time (JIT) production. Under Taiichi Ohno, the Toyota Motor Company originated JIT. Because of this, JIT is often referred to as the Toyota Production System. For obvious reasons, however, many companies prefer to use "JIT Production System," "Lean Production," or some other term. This book will use *JIT production system*.

Each of the three major systems necessary for achieving QCD has different targets: TQC has overall quality as its major target, while TPM addresses quality of equipment. JIT, meanwhile, deals with the other top priorities of management—namely, cost and delivery. Top management must firmly establish both TQC and TPM before JIT production is introduced. Many people have misinterpreted JIT. In one of the most common misunderstandings, a company expects its suppliers to deliver just-in-time. In order to benefit from a supplier's just-in-time delivery, a company must first establish the best possible efficiencies in its own internal processes. JIT is a revolutionary way to reduce cost while at the same time meeting the customer's delivery needs.

JUST-IN-TIME AT AISIN SEIKI'S ANJO PLANT

A visit to Aisin Seiki's Anjo plant in Japan will help the reader understand JIT. This plant produces such products as bed mattresses, industrial sewing machines, gas heating pumps, and air-conditioners. On entering the mattress production area, one would expect to find a huge space where many employees—surrounded by stacks of frames, springs, and fabrics—assemble mattresses. However, what the visitor sees instead is a compact scale of operations. In a space no larger than a high-school basketball court, seven dedicated lines produce mattresses of 750 different colors, styles, and sizes per day.

The machines in each line, except for quilting machines, are laid out in the order of processing. The major processes include spring-coil forming, spring-coil assembly, multineedle quilting, cutting, flange-sewing, padding, border-sewing, tape-edge sewing, and packaging. Each process connects to the next, allowing no room to place extra work-in-processes. Only one work piece at a time flows between the processes. The quilting process makes only one piece of cloth for one mattress at a time. Each work piece moves through the workstations while being processed. Twenty minutes after the weaving machine starts weaving the mattress cover, the mattress is completed and ready to be shipped to the customer, one of about 2000 furniture stores scattered throughout Japan that serve the company's dealers.

For the most popular models, a small storeroom at the end of the line holds a standard inventory of between three and forty mattresses (the number depends on daily sales), each placed in a given location and with a *kanban* tag (production order slip) attached. Every time an order comes in and a mattress is shipped, the *kanban* that had been attached to that mattress is sent back to the starting point of the line and serves as an order to start the production. This system ensures that the minimum required number of the popular models is always in stock. For nonstandard types of mattresses, no storeroom exists, as the mattresses are shipped directly from the production line to the furniture store that placed the order.

Aisin Seiki begins producing a mattress the day after receiving an order from a dealer; this is made possible by the very short lead time of production (two hours). Sometimes the company receives large orders from hotels and vacation resorts; when this happens, the company spreads the production, manufacturing a given number of mattresses each day. It fits this production evenly in between the production of other models so that the normal production schedule is not disturbed. This is called leveling. Large orders of this kind require the company to secure outside storage space until the shipping date. Although JIT is sometimes referred to as a nonstock production system, it is not always either possible or practical to keep a zero inventory.

Such a production system yields many insights. First, one can sense an invisible line connecting the customer and the production process. The short lead time allows the production to begin *after* an order has been received, and *gemba* employees can keep the customer in mind while making the product. It is almost as if the customer is waiting in the next room to receive the finished mattress.

Second, this system allows great flexibility to meet customer needs. With the use of *kanban,* popular models are replenished as soon as they are sold, thus minimizing inventory.

Third, this kind of production system can quickly respond to abnormalities on the line. If a reject is produced, the whole line must be stopped, as there will be no replacement. In other words, management has to make a concerted effort to address problems on the line so that the line never stops. Every quality problem, every equipment malfunction, every problem related to human error must be dealt with and settled so that the line is not stopped. JIT necessitates ongoing *kaizen* activities in *gemba* and calls for rigid self-discipline on the part of both management and workers. The fact that Aisin Seiki has received both the Deming Prize and the Japan Quality Control Award attests to the company's commitment to quality.

Fourth, JIT permits flexible production scheduling. Aisin Seiki produces only as many mattresses as are ordered by the customer. Even for the most popular models, they do not start production in anticipation of future demand, and the daily minimum allowable inventory is determined. On the other hand, once production begins, stagnation in the form of work-in-process is not allowed, and the product must be finished within the shortest possible time and shipped directly to the customer right away. For most products, a warehouse is not needed, and the truck running on the street serves as a warehouse.

Fifth, this kind of production system helps companies forecast the market more accurately. In the ideal world, production would not begin until all the orders had been received. However, this is not possible in reality. Because Aisin Seiki has learned from experience that the daily demand for the most popular model is about forty, that is the number of mattresses kept in inventory for that particular type. Depending on the popularity of each model, the daily inventory ranges between three and forty. The *kanban* system is used to make only as many as have been sold every day. For other types of mattresses, the company only starts production after the order has been received. Bear in mind that one of the definitions of JIT is "making only as many products, and in the same sequence, as ordered."

These are some of the visible features that we can readily identify by observing Aisin Seiki or any other JIT-based operation. Some additional features, which may not be as visible but are present nonetheless, include:

- *Takt* time versus cycle time (theoretical time versus actual time for completing one work piece)
- Pull production versus push production (producing only as many items as the next process needs versus producing as many as can be produced)
- Establishing production flow (rearranging equipment layout according to work sequence)

TAKT TIME VERSUS CYCLE TIME

Takt time is the total production time divided by the number of units required by the customer. The figure is expressed in seconds for mass-produced items. For slower-moving items, the *takt* time may be expressed in minutes, or even hours, as is the case in shipbuilding, for example. If Line A produces 80 mattresses in one day and the workers work for eight hours, the *takt* time is calculated as follows:

$$(8 \text{ hours} \times 60 \text{ minutes}) \div 80 = 6 \text{ minutes}$$

This means that if each process within Line A completes its work every 6 minutes, the finished mattresses go out the door every 6 minutes, and 80 mattresses will have been produced by the end of the day.

The word *takt* comes from the German word for the baton used by an orchestra conductor. The *takt* time is a magic number, as it is the pulse of the market. This is the number everybody in the company must live by. Just as a conductor's baton sways between andante and crescendo, the *takt* of the market keeps changing, and *gemba* must respond accordingly. If each process exceeds the *takt* time, a shortage of products will result; if it is faster, a surplus will occur. When *takt* time is properly observed, *gemba* is moving ahead with the same pulse as that of the market. Once management has achieved sufficient flexibility, *gemba* can respond instantaneously to changes in the pulse of the market, producing only as many pieces as are ordered.

Takt time is a *theoretical figure* that tells us how much time is needed to make one product at each process. Cycle time, on the other hand, is the *actual time* required for each operator to complete the operation. In *gemba*, abnormalities are a fact of life, and each time they arise, the cycle time is prolonged. The idea behind JIT is to bring the cycle time as close as possible to the *takt* time.

To achieve this ideal, abnormalities of all types must be addressed. When the cycle time is compared with the *takt* time in a company that has not adopted JIT, the cycle time is much shorter—in many cases half the *takt* time—producing a buildup of work-in-process and finished products that become surplus inventory.

The lines should also be reviewed for uniformity of cycle times. No matter how quickly a particular line may produce, total efficiency will not improve if the other lines operate at slower cycle times.

PUSH PRODUCTION VERSUS PULL PRODUCTION

Most manufacturing companies today are engaged in push production. Every process produces just as many units as it can and sends them to the next process whether the next process needs them or not. This stems in part from the following line of thinking: "As long as the processes are in order, let's make as many units as we can, since we never know when things might go wrong again."

In a mattress company, this way of thinking translates into weaving as many mattress covers as possible at the weaving machine, or making as many springs as possible at the spring-making machine. In a conventional company, such processes are usually located separately from the assembly line. Chances are that there are several weaving machines or spring-making machines located in one corner of the plant—far removed from the final assembly line—and that they continuously produce WIPs which are sent first to the warehouse, and later to the final assembly line.

Operators in such an environment do not know, and do not need to know, the volume and time requirements of their customer. This is a typical example of a push production system. At the final assembly, too, chances are that operators are assembling as many products as the line can churn out; the finished products find their way to the warehouse and wait for the order to arrive. A push system necessitates batch production, creating *muda* of transport and inventory.

Production at Aisin Seiki's Anjo plant, in contrast, is based on the pull of the market; the entire plant springs into action with the receipt of an order from a customer. Rather than build up inventory in anticipation of orders, the company makes every effort to anticipate customer demand for the immediate future and to build flexibility within the plant to cope with fluctuations.

Toshihiko Mitsuya, project general manager at Aisin Seiki's Anjo plant, says that mattress production is quite different from automotive production in that there are no fixed daily production volumes. In other words, there is no production planning; the only planning for mattresses is the orders received from the customers. For automobiles, daily production volumes are at least uniform.

A customer who comes to one of the 2000 furniture stores wants a mattress and wants it right away. Unlike a person shopping for an automobile, a person shopping for a mattress is not willing to wait long. Although the furniture stores carry the competitive models, Aisin Seiki's production method gives the company the flexibility to offer its full range of products in the shortest possible lead time. Today, a customer at any one of the 2000 furniture stores can select any of the 750 different models and have it delivered the next day, as long as the customer lives within 100 kilometers of the plant. If Aisin had not developed such a production system, the alternative would have been to build a large inventory.

ESTABLISHING PRODUCTION FLOW

In pull production, all processes should be rearranged so that the work piece flows through the workstations in the order in which the processes take place. Because some equipment is too large or too heavy or is used for multiple purposes, it is not always possible or practical to rearrange the equipment into exact work-flow order. However, isolated machines should be moved and incorporated into the line as much as is practicable.

Once the line is formed, the next step is to start a one-piece flow, allowing only one piece at a time to flow from process to process. This shortens lead time and makes it difficult for the line to build up inventory between processes.

An aircraft component plant conducted a simulation of such a one-piece flow, assuming that all processes were connected and that only one piece would flow between the processes according to *takt* time. At the time the plant conducted this simulation, its total lead time was eight weeks from start of production until the finished product went out the door. The simulation revealed that the lead time should take no more than four hours. The layout has since been changed to accommodate one-piece flow, and *kaizen* activities have solved many bottleneck problems.

Before starting a production line with one-piece flow, however, such problems as quality, machine downtime, and absenteeism must be addressed. One-piece flow production cannot begin until these problems are resolved, because each time a problem arises, the line must be stopped, and the problems that up to now have been regarded lightly become visible. The company loses money when the line is stopped. Precisely for this reason, management has to address the problem, and thus a line with one-piece flow makes it mandatory to identify and solve problems.

Besides shortening lead times and cutting excess inventory, one-piece flow also helps workers identify quality problems right away, because any problem in the previous process can be detected in the next process. One-piece flow also allows 100 percent inspection, since every piece goes through the hand of every operator.

Yet another positive merit of the one-piece flow line is that it does not require large equipment. A machine needs only to be large enough to process one piece at a time within the *takt* time. Conventional production processes based on the batch concept, meanwhile, require large machines to process large batches of work pieces at a time. Furnaces and painting units are a good example. In one plant, I saw a heating furnace as large as an indoor swimming pool.

At one of the plants of Matsushita Electric Works a large oven was used for treating micro switches on the main line. When a one-piece flow line was introduced, however, the company found that a toaster purchased at a nearby supermarket was sufficient for this purpose. As I mentioned earlier, machines are usually working too fast. A machine in a one-piece flow line can be much smaller than a machine used in conventional batch production. It also operates more slowly, making it suitable for a slower *takt* time. Such a machine may be purchased at a much lower price; even better, the company itself may be able to design and produce the machine. If a company with an expensive high-speed line producing a large quantity of products wishes to increase flexibility, it is often possible for the company to create, at little cost, an additional line to accommodate small or urgent orders. As such additional lines do not require much investment, management can afford to dedicate them to small or urgent orders while using the existing main line for large production runs. This minimizes the need for frequent setup changes on the main line. Often it is possible to arrange these small new lines in a U shape; the operator working inside the U can readily move from one process to the next. This arrangement makes it possible to manufacture products according to cycle time when needed, giving the manufacturer more flexibility to cope with diversified customer requirements.

THE INTRODUCTION OF JIT AT AISIN SEIKI

Until the mid-1980s, each of the eight sales offices of Aisin Seiki kept its own inventory of mattresses and delivered them to furniture stores. In those days, the company offered 220 different types of mattresses and required 30 days' inventory. The factory produced 160 mattresses per day with 20 operators, and the *kosu* (work hours) of production per mattress was 75 minutes.

"Salespeople," said Toshihiko Mitsuya, "gave us monthly sales projections, but they never turned out to be accurate. It resembled looking into a crystal ball. The plan changed all the time, giving our suppliers a difficult time keeping up with our changing orders as well. We had shortages of some supplies on the line all the time, and yet we had a mountain of inventory."

In those days, the plant had a warehouse with a capacity of 2200 square meters to meet fluctuations in sales as well as shortages of special types of mattresses. The company's production system, based on market projections, had the following shortcomings:

- It was difficult to estimate demands accurately. Due to a long lead time, it was necessary to venture a long-term forecast, and the plan was not very reliable.

- Production schedules had to be changed frequently. Responding to the changing information was difficult because it involved changes in production planning in many processes.

- Much *muda* was created in *gemba*. As *gemba* people did not want to be accused of being short of inventory, they tended to plan monthly productions in a large lot.

- A warehouse was necessary to avoid shortages of WIPs; managing the warehouse entailed additional costs.

THE FIRST STEP OF *KAIZEN* AT AISIN SEIKI

In 1988, Aisin Seiki decided to produce mattresses only in response to orders, rather than in anticipation of orders. The first step eliminated the warehouse. The question at that time was which type of inventory to address first: finished mattresses or WIPs. The company chose to start with the finished products, which included the accumulation of all costs incurred, such as labor, materials, processing, and utilities.

Kanban was introduced to maintain only the number of mattresses typically ordered every day. This meant carrying inventory for the popular models only—in proportion to their daily sales. For storage of the most popular mattresses (those with sales of over three units a day), a "store" was created immediately adjacent to the end of the production line. When popular models left the store, the *kanban* (production order slip) attached to each mattress went back to the start of the line in preparation for production of the units just sold to begin the next day.

Until Aisin implemented *kanban*, it had produced different types of mattresses, such as single, double, and semidouble models, on a weekly schedule. But under the new system, what had once been a weekly cycle of production was reduced to a daily cycle. Today, the cycle has been further reduced to two hours.

The key point at this first stage of *kaizen* was to start producing the different models of mattresses in the same sequence as the orders were received. To do this, shortening the setup time became a critical task. By shortening the setup time, the company increased by sixtyfold the number of setup changes needed for the quilting machines.

In 1986—two years before the first phase of its *kaizen* effort—Aisin Seiki made 220 different types of mattresses. After the first phase of *kaizen* the number jumped to 335. Yet finished product inventory was reduced to 2.5 days, compared with 30 days before. Although the company has grown by only one employee during this time, it now produces 70 more mattresses per day than before. And the *kosu* per mattress dropped to 54 minutes, from the previous 75 minutes.

THE SECOND STEP OF *KAIZEN* AT AISIN SEIKI

The use of *kanban* eliminated inventory at both the factory and the furniture stores in 1988. In 1992, Aisin Seiki was ready to tackle the second step of *kaizen:* eliminating excess inventory within the plant.

In an effort to reduce WIPs, the company developed a tool it called assembly-initiation sequence table, which specified the sequence in which to initiate production of 750 different types of mattresses to meet delivery dates. Customer orders are sent to the plant on line from Aisin Seiki's 2000 dealers and eight sales offices throughout Japan. The production line receives urethane, cotton, felt, and textiles just in time from the suppliers and assembles them into mattresses. Each of the seven lines has been arranged in such a way as to produce any type and size of mattress in a one-piece flow.

The plant has five quilting machines serving seven lines. The orders received and delivery dates specified determine the quilting sequence and the quilting machine follows the sequence, producing only one quilt unit for each mattress. As 750 different types of quilting must be produced, the system does not function without the sequence table, which allows the quilting process to keep two hours' worth of inventory. In other words, the quilting process is allowed to do only two hours advance production; it does not know what other types of quilts will be required by the assembly line after that.

The daily production schedule, including the number and types of units to be produced, is not provided to *gemba* in order to keep the *gemba* people from producing the mattresses at their own convenience rather than to accommodate customer orders. The system provides *gemba* with two hours' advance notice—a sufficient amount of time to cope with any urgent orders. One part-time worker using a PC prepares the sequence tables based on the day's orders.

Aisin's Anjo plant has introduced many other features of just-in-time production, such as leveling, in its mattress manufacturing. The plant has achieved its great flexibility to meet customer needs while reducing cost to a minimum.

SPREADING THE BENEFITS OF JIT TO OTHER INDUSTRIES

Aisin Seiki has been successful in introducing JIT in mattress manufacturing, a business that is highly seasonal and characterized by diverse demand. The company has taken on the challenge of delivering product just-in-time, immediately after receiving orders, and starting many *kaizen* activities. Today, Aisin Seiki has two approaches to production: (1) producing only those items that replace inventory; and (2) producing only in response to orders. The latter approach can be further broken down into two components: (1) producing for the day; and (2) producing in response to advance orders. With zero inventory, daily production takes first priority in each day's schedule. Large advance orders from hotels and the like, meanwhile, take second priority. Because orders tend to be concentrated on weekends, large fluctuations in demand sometimes occur. By spreading out the additional production over a given period, the company maintains a steady production level, and thus avoids disrupting the production line.

Since 1986, when it introduced just-in-time production, Aisin Seiki has increased its productivity by a factor of 4.5 and its gross sales by a factor of 1.8. The number of different types of products it makes has grown from 220 to 750, while inventory turnover has plunged to 1.8 days, one-seventeenth of the original time. And the *kosu* per unit has dropped from 75 minutes to 42 minutes. To realize production in a small lot, the number of setup changes had to be increased 40 times, while the total setup time was reduced. This was made possible because *kaizen* was launched based on real need.

Just-in-time production has yielded other benefits as well. It has substantially reduced not only setup times, but also *kosu* and lead time. It has eliminated the warehouse. Mattresses can now be delivered immediately and the sales staff can offer customers a full range of choices. Furthermore, eliminating the need to store finished products for long periods of time has also eliminated such quality problems as stains, soiling, and color fading.

Aisin Seiki is one of the major suppliers of automotive parts and components to Toyota Motor Company and has been engaged in just-in-time production for its automotive products for many years. The fact that the company succeeded in realizing just-in-time in an unrelated field such as mattress manufacturing points out that JIT production techniques and know-how can be applied with equal success to many different types of production lines. Aisin Seiki has implemented just-in-time technology in its production of industrial sewing machines as well. The company also provides a consulting service, called Toyota Sewing Products Management System, that assists the apparel industry in solving plant design, operation, and management problems.

Those who ignore such new trends will soon find themselves left out of the competition as their competitors start to take advantage of this wonderful production system. They would do well to heed the following remarks made by Chie Takagi, supervisor at Matsushita Electric Works, after the company had introduced just-in-time production: "As I look back on those old days, I wonder how we could have conducted our business that way. The way we produced our products then was—almost a crime!"

CHAPTER
TWELVE

JUST-IN-TIME AT WIREMOLD

This chapter is a case study showing how one company, Wiremold, tackled the problem of building in flexibility by introducing just-in-time.

Wiremold is an approximately one-hundred-year-old company in West Hartford, Connecticut. Its two major product lines are wire management devices and power conditioning products. Under the leadership of Art Byrne, who arrived as the new president in September 1991, the company started an all-out effort to introduce *gemba kaizen* with particular emphasis on just-in-time.

I had an opportunity to visit the company five months after the introduction of *gemba kaizen* and had lengthy discussions with Art Byrne and Frank Giannattasio, vice president of operations. During the first five months, they had freed up approximately 40 percent of the floor space in one plant. The inventory level, including raw material, work-in-process, and finished goods, was down more than 20 percent. The working capital turns had been increased by 30 percent, and they were expecting a 25 to 30 percent productivity improvement by the end of the year. After five months, a lead time of approximately six weeks to make a product took one week. Clearly, introducing *gemba kaizen* had brought about enormous improvements in a very short period of time. My conversations with them provide a vivid picture of just-in-time in action:

IMAI: What kind of changes have taken place in the way you do your business since JIT was introduced?

GIANNATTASIO: Wiremold previously operated on the premise of a forecast. We would generate a presumed consumption level of our various products, at which point we would schedule batches and produce several months' consumable volume of various products, store them in a warehouse, and they would then be consumed over a period of time—some in line with our forecast, some at an amount in excess of our forecast, and some at a volume less than our forecast. The result was slow-moving, expensive inventories.

To begin just-in-time manufacturing, we looked more at near-term consumption levels. Looking at the past six months, and more specifically, the last ten days, we used the information to continuously adjust our daily product-mix schedule and were able to run most of our products at least every week, many every day. We utilized *kaizen* to improve setup times and eliminate waste, which gave us the flexibility to achieve those very rigorous daily schedules.

As we developed our daily product-mix schedules to meet customer demand as opposed to a forecast, we made several changes. First, after evaluating customer demand, we determined our *takt* time, or the demand frequency of each of our products. Based on that *takt* time, we then managed our production system cycles to meet *takt* time, whereas previously we would set up in batch production and build as much as we could of whatever product we had in production.

We really did not have a measurement of how efficiently we were producing. Now, with daily demand known and established cycle time, we evaluate our production against the expectation of building a predetermined or an expected quantity of each product. We gauge ourselves against our ability to produce the volume in the appropriate time based on our cycle time, and when we are unable to do that, we are very quick to identify what problems exist, either with our supplier's product quality or with downtime within our own production system. We are much quicker to identify problems that are affecting our output, and ultimately, our customer service.

IMAI: What kind of role did you play as president in making such a change?

BYRNE: I think the role of top management in making such a change is really to be the key driver for that change. I've often told companies that have asked me, "Gee, what should we do to start just-in-time?" First, they have to have total commitment from top management. If they don't, and they try to implement it from the bottom up, they're basically bound to fail. In our particular case, I was not only the driver and leader for change, but because I didn't have anybody else here when I came who really understood just-in-time, I was also the initial trainer. I wrote the manual and conducted the first training classes. I trained perhaps two hundred people in two-day sessions. But that certainly gave people the clear impression that this is what we're going to do, and that I was really very much behind it. It wasn't something that I tried to delegate to somebody else or hand off to a committee. I think the key is that senior management has to be leading it and has to be very involved, be willing to go out on the shop floor, be willing to work on *kaizen* teams themselves, be willing to pick up a machine and move it. It really needs total commitment from the top, or it'll never really happen.

IMAI: What kind of organizational changes were needed to introduce just-in-time *gemba kaizen*?

BYRNE: Well, before we started *kaizen*, we did do a number of organizational changes. First of all, we tried to flatten out the organization. We had a very traditional vertical organization that we flattened out by putting everybody on teams. Our old organization was typically based on a type of process, e.g., stamping, painting, etc. We organized the new teams based around a product, so that each team leader had all of the resources needed to make the complete product, plan that product, and get that product to market. That was our first step. To support that activity, we've created a fairly extensive just-in-time promotion office. We have about six of our brighter, high-potential people in the just-in-time promotion office, and their job basically is to teach just-in-time, to train it, to follow up on the *kaizen* that we do, and make sure that all the things that we said we were going to do get done. They also work with the team leaders on the shop floor, and help implement *kaizen*.

IMAI: How do you relate the *kaizen*/just-in-time approach to the conventional strategic planning?

BYRNE: One thing that struck me in my previous roles as a strategic planner was that many companies can put together really wonderful strategic plans; they have an awful lot of difficulty, however, in implementing those plans. The reason for this is that their fundamental delivery systems (the way they make a product, the way they design and introduce a product) don't function very well.

So, even though the strategic plan might have been good, the time it took to develop the product, the time it took to make the product, the quality of the product that came out, was such that the plan's implementation never really worked.

With just-in-time, it's really akin to building a house. If you're going to build a house, you want a really solid foundation. Just-in-time is the solid foundation that we want to put under Wiremold, where we can reduce our lead time from six weeks to six hours, where we have the flexibility to make every product every day, and do it with very little inventory. That's quite a task when you have over fourteen hundred products.

If we can build that foundation however, and then marry it with drastic reductions in the time it takes to design and introduce new products, then we're going to be able to service our customers much better than any of our competitors. We are going to be able to introduce products much faster, and I think the combination will give us strategic alternatives that we wouldn't have had if we'd started simply with strategy but without a solid foundation. So I see *kaizen* as being part of strategy. It's not just some manufacturing thing but is integral to your strategy.

IMAI: Why is it that it is taking such a long time before American businessmen begin to realize the challenge as well as the benefits of JIT/*kaizen*?

BYRNE: U.S. management has for the most part neglected this and tried to solve it with short-term things or strategic things, not really looking at the fundamentals of what makes the business go. As a result, we find ourselves way behind in a lot of areas. Despite this, it's still very difficult to get a lot of U.S. companies to change. Most feel that, well, we're already good enough, we're making money, we're holding our market share. All of that may be true until somebody comes along who plays by a different set of rules.

The U.S. auto companies thought that they were doing a great job until all of a sudden the Japanese auto companies came along and played by a different set of rules and they found themselves over a period of time way, way behind. Now they've caught up a lot in quality, but still trail in other areas, such as productivity. The area that they're really way behind in is in the speed that it takes to develop new cars. If your competitor can develop a product in two years and it takes you six, you have to guess pretty accurately in order to even have a chance of being competitive by the time your new car comes out.

The auto industry tends to get a lot of publicity because of its size, but the same thing is true in most other industries in the U.S. I think that Japan-bashing is unfortunate, because it tends to allow people to hide behind their current way of doing things and doesn't force them to change.

I think that about 90 percent of all U.S. businessmen don't understand the depth of the disparity in the Japanese versus American manufacturing system. Almost all U.S. manufacturing managers that you talk with today will tell you that they are doing just-in-time, but most of them are way off-track. Half of them think of just-in-time as some sort of inventory system that in turn means that what they should do is beat up their suppliers. Others have read enough books to understand they should be creating a *flow* system. Very few understand how fundamental you have to get and how detailed you have to get, and even fewer understand that it's really a people thing. You have to change people's attitude, and that takes time, a lot of commitment, and a lot of education. We tend to be a country that is oriented towards making this quarter or making this month. This in turn makes it difficult for long-term change to occur. We talk about it, we publicize it, but when it comes right down to actually doing it, most companies balk.

IMAI: How much money did you spend to achieve these results?

BYRNE: We really didn't spend any money in terms of capital investment. Perhaps some small things here and there, but for the most part, the money that was spent was people-time. People-time invested in training and invested in *kaizen* activities to change the factory around, change the flow, and improve the way that we work.

IMAI: Do you believe that just-in-time is a Japanese method?

BYRNE: It's a fallacy to say that just-in-time comes from Japan. When you listen to someone like Taiichi Ohno, who is given credit for developing just-in-time, and ask him where he got the idea for just-in-time, he'll tell you he got it from the United States. He got it from two things: one, Henry Ford, and two, the American supermarket. In fact, I think the better way of describing just-in-time is "just makes sense," not "just-in-time." And I think the simplicity of the system and the "just makes sense" aspects of it, really can't have boundaries of Japan, or the U.S. It's a question of whether companies are willing to seize the opportunity and do something about it. It turned out that the Japanese, following Ohno's lead at Toyota, were the only ones that had the discipline required to stay with this program. It took Ohno about thirty years to develop a good just-in-time system. In the U.S. and perhaps in Europe, we tend not to have the patience to stay with something like this. So just-in-time, as far as I'm concerned, is not a Japanese thing, it's something that anybody can do without a lot of investment.

These conversations with Art Byrne and Frank Giannattasio took place in 1992. Wiremold has continued to work on JIT/*gemba kaizen* ever since. In recent correspondence from Frank Giannattasio, he summarized the situation at Wiremold as follows:

We at Wiremold have been operating our method of just-in-time manufacturing for four years. We call our just-in-time process the Wiremold Production System. We have reduced our delivery lead time 67 percent in four years—from shipping our customer orders in 72 hours of receiving the order to shipping within 24 hours. At the same time we have increased our inventory turnover rate 367 percent—from 3 times per year to 14 times per year—while nearly doubling the size of our business. We have done this by practicing the three basic principles of our production system:

• Build to *takt* time
• Incorporate one-piece flow

- Use pull system

We implement the principles with a strategy of *kaizen* and teamwork. We try to sustain all improvements in standard work while evaluating our progress with various measurements.

We have changed our production system from that of material requirements planning (MRP)–driven batch production to one of customer-pull driven, one-piece flow in a series of phases:

1. *Phase one* consisted of first reorganizing the factory both physically and organizationally. We organized our plant into business units based on product similarity. We then cleaned up our factory, following the guidance of the Japanese 5S's. This made waste very evident.

2. *Phase two* focused on setup-time reduction and disciplined adherence to production schedules. The schedules are now based on recent sales instead of MRP forecasts. Our efforts in this phase were to develop flexibility and responsiveness. We knew we had to shorten the lead times with our production process and to improve operating dependability of those processes. The gains we made with each *kaizen* were generally to reduce the existing setup time by at least 50 percent and in many cases by as much as 90 percent. We repeated these gains with successive *kaizens,* improving our setup times from hours to minutes.

3. *Phase three* capitalized on our quick response as a result of reduced setup times and improved process dependability by fully implementing our pull system. We now build today what was sold yesterday for all moderate- to high-volume products. We utilize some inventory cushion on the level of customer demand from day to day.

These three phases, as conducted over the past four years, have resulted in 20 percent productivity gains each year, over a 40 percent reduction in defects each year (we now realize only 1.4 defects per 100 in-process audits), an increase of inventory turnover of 367 percent, and a 67 percent reduction in delivery lead times.

We continue to execute a hundred or more *kaizen* exercises every year, and we try to involve 100 percent of the organization. Our next phase will focus on associate development and teamwork. We feel our future gains will come from the creative problem-solving efforts of our associates. Our associates have to be able to identify waste even in what seems to be an acceptable operation by most traditional means of evaluation.

Frank Giannattasio also writes about Wiremold's activities in improving flexibility in the past 4 years as follows:

Our firm has been involved with pursuing continuous improvement and just-in-time delivery now for about 4 years. We've experienced large degrees of success in many areas. One example of this success is the Plugmold area. In the Plugmold area we make over 200 different end products.

We originally produced all of these 200 products in a batch mode, producing large quantities of each product at random and infrequent intervals. Our first approach to improving customer service and reducing inventory levels was to develop a daily product-mix schedule. To do this, we reviewed the daily consumption levels of all 200 products and developed a schedule that systematically scheduled each product to be assembled. We then ran most of those 200 products each week, many of them every single day. As a result of this production mix, we were able to assign workers to specific products, and we uncovered a multitude of problems. We found a variety of reasons why assemblers could not build products at the rate we anticipated each day. Problems such as bad vendor parts, cracked receptacles, cut wires and miscut or miscrimped wires that didn't assemble properly, and the list went on and on. We found in excess of 60 problems on just one assembly operation. In our efforts to resolve these problems, it was important to have daily follow-up and intensive measurements. After only 20 days we achieved our schedule on a daily basis in all operations. It was a culmination of efforts of many different team members.

One specific operation in the Plugmold area was a 3-wire table assembly operation. This was an operation where four workers independently assemble a variety of 3-wire products every day. As we embarked on a daily schedule on the table assembly operation, the associates targeted their average cycle time, or their best available cycle time, as the basis for our schedule. We found out during the process of assembling each part that different problems arose that made our assembly time vary. Some of these problems arose from the performance of a tool known as a squasher, which is a necessary instrument to assemble the receptacle front to the receptacle back that makes our Plugmold strip. We found that the squashers were constructed in a different fashion, one to another over all four tables, and they gave varying results, some good, some less good. We first moved to make all squashers identical, in which case we were able to, on a daily basis, repeat the best available performance.

Another problem that we found was various center line loops on our grounding wire. This is a long, stiff wire with crimps that was a necessary component of our Plugmold strip. We found that if the center line was not exactly the same for each assembled component, extra assembly time was required to customize the fit to the receptacle. We improved the center line crimping device so that we were consistent from wire to wire.

Another problem was our vendor cord quality. We had problems with dirty cords directly out of the box that required assembler attention to inspect and clean. We worked with our vendor to improve their quality and began to get clean wires, requiring no more inspection time or operator rework.

Another example of a problem was varying lengths of Plugmold strip or metal base. We went back and reviewed our specification, and we were able to develop standards and train our operators at the mill to sort these parts within the limit samples and as a result, deliver no variability to the assembly operators.

Again, eliminating unnecessary inspection time and sorting at the assembly, all contributing to our efforts to produce a daily schedule. Now 4 years later, following numerous projects, *kaizen* activities, and short-duration *kaizen* events, we have increased our volume on these assembly tables 67 percent. We can make every product every day, taking no time to change over the table from part to part. We have increased our turnover on this product line from 3 times to 14 times per year, and we rarely identify any poor quality issues.

Byrne also had his side of the story of Wiremold's achievements, which were published in an article titled "How Wiremold Reinvested Itself with *Kaizen*" (*Target* magazine, vol. II, no. 1, reprint January/February 1995)*:

> At the old Wiremold, a product might take as much as six weeks to make its way from raw material to finished product. We'd make huge quantities of a single component because our changeover took so long. Often a batch of components would sit gathering dust in our large work-in-process inventory areas before products could be assembled because the other parts weren't scheduled to be run that week. Finished goods were sent to our 70,000-square-foot warehouse down the road to wait until needed for shipping to a customer. We were cash poor, yet had such large in-process and finished goods inventories that we were shopping for more warehouse space.
>
> We've come a long way since then, reinventing ourselves into a vibrant, growing firm. In just three years, our sales have doubled and our profits have tripled. We've grown our base business by more than 50 percent and supplemented that internally generated growth with six acquisitions—five of which we were able to make without borrowing because we had freed up so much cash from inventory reductions.
>
> Our success is not the result of any complex business strategy. Nor is it the fruit of some intensive program of capital investment. Rather, we turned our company around by turning our manufacturing operation on its head: We adopted *kaizen*.

---

*This excerpt is printed with permission from the Association for Manufacturing Excellence, 380 West Palatine Road, Wheeling, IL, U.S.A.

We began to implement our *kaizen* program of continuous improvement in late 1991. In slightly less than three years, here are some of the changes we've made:

- Productivity has improved 20 percent in each of the last two years.
- Throughput time on products has dropped from four to six weeks to two days or less.
- The defect rate on our products fell by 42 percent in 1993, and by 50 percent in the first half of 1994.
- Inventories have been slashed by 80 percent, resulting in our space needs being cut in half.
- Profit sharing lay out for our employees has more than tripled.
- Equipment changeovers have been reduced dramatically—in some cases from as much as ten hours to less than ten minutes.
- New-product development time has been slashed from almost three years to under six months.
- Vendors have been cut from more than four hundred to fewer than one hundred.

One ingredient essential to our success has been the way we look at *kaizen*. At Wiremold, we believe it's a fundamental part of our business strategy. After all, our business delivery systems are what the customer sees.

If we fall behind in quality or on lead times, we disappoint our customer and we won't succeed no matter how good our strategy. On the other hand, if our systems can outperform the competition, then we can outrun them.

We've actually made *kaizen* part of our business strategy—to continually "fix" our base business. We believe that the minute we stop doing so, we'll fall behind.

In summary, here are three "tips" that anyone getting started needs to keep in mind:

1. Changing people's mind-set is a critical part of the job. People are naturally skeptical, and you have to take dramatic and sustained action to overcome objections. In

the long run, you must change the culture of the organization. The "concrete heads" must go.

2. Senior management must lead the "change." That means not only at the beginning but throughout, continually putting pressure on the organization. Lack of leadership attention is one of the major reasons that improvement programs die within a year to 18 months.

3. This is a long-term commitment. You have to acknowledge up-front that there's no end point. Be prepared for your people to ask, "Are we finished yet?" And be equally prepared to answer, "It's not good yet," even when you think it is.

GOING TO *GEMBA*

Two-Day *Gemba Kaizen* and Overall Corporate *Kaizen*

When you go to *gemba* and observe the way your people work, the way materials are moved, and the way equipment is laid out, do you take everything for granted and accept it as satisfactory, or do you regard what you see as a starting point for *kaizen* and continuously look for opportunities to improve? Some Japanese managers go as far as to say to their subordinates, "Regard whatever you do now as the 'worst' way to do your job!" Your attitude could make a big difference in *gemba* over the years.

The worst thing a manager can do is live in a world isolated from *gemba,* making all decisions from the office. But even managers who do visit *gemba* cannot make improvements if they fail to see problems. The manager's ability to recognize problems brings success in *gemba kaizen*. What does "going to *gemba*" really mean? Many people think that they know *gemba* because they work there. But being physically present in *gemba* is not the same as knowing *gemba*.

Akio Takahashi, author of a Japanese book whose English title would be *Line Kaizen Textbook,* has been engaged for many years in assisting Nissan's major suppliers in *gemba kaizen*. He says that simply going and looking at *gemba* is not enough. Truly knowing *gemba* means expressing oneself in terms of actual nouns and numbers.

Statements along the lines of "This plant is not operating well enough" do not lead anywhere. A manager should say,

"The operating ratio of Line A is 65 percent, but it must be brought up to 85 percent." In Takahashi's view, expressing ourselves in specific nouns and numbers enables us to reach common ground for discussions, makes it easier to solve problems, and helps fix in our minds an accurate picture of *gemba*. It also allows everybody to engage in a *kaizen* project with a common purpose. After nouns and numbers come questions such as who, how, and when. Once a target has been agreed upon, the person in charge of the *kaizen* project—namely, a person who has a stake in solving the problem—must be designated, the solution to the problem must be determined, and the deadline of the project must be specified.

Actually, the ability to identify problems in *gemba* requires no sophisticated technology. To start, the manager must understand some of *gemba kaizen* basics, such as *muda*, housekeeping, visual management, and standardization.

Gemba kaizen means going to *gemba*—observing, identifying, and solving any problems right on the spot in real time. Japanese manufacturers excel at delivering products of good quality at reasonable prices under favorable terms. *Gemba kaizen* practices, improved continuously during the past five decades, have contributed greatly to building this highly effective system.

After Toyota Motor Company had developed just-in-time practices within its premises, Taiichi Ohno extended those practices to Toyota's primary suppliers. Ohno organized a *jishuken* (autonomous) study group as a vehicle to spread his philosophy. The group consisted of several employees of the company's suppliers. One of Ohno's "disciples" at Toyota who had been implementing just-in-time practices led the group. Each month, the group visited a *gemba* of a different supplier and conducted *gemba kaizen* there for three or four days.

The *jishuken kaizen* activities invariably reduced the number of operators involved at a given process, cut inventory, and shortened lead times. Layout changes, such as eliminating conveyers and forming U-shaped lines, often took place as well. *Jishuken kaizen* proved to be such an effective way of spreading Toyota's JIT know-how and practices among its sup-

pliers that the primary suppliers soon began involving their sec-
ond-tier suppliers in the activities as well. Even to this day,
jishuken activities take place regularly among Toyota's group of
companies.

TWO-DAY *KAIZEN*

In 1977, Nissan Motor Company and its suppliers introduced
a process called two-day *kaizen,* in which a particular production line is targeted for improvements that must be completed
within two days. Two-day *gemba kaizen* starts with a clear
objective. For instance, a plant manager expects a 20 percent
increase in demand next month, but he wishes to achieve the
necessary 20 percent productivity increase with just one hour
of overtime per day per employee. He discusses the subject
with the line managers and agrees to conduct a two-day *gemba
kaizen* on Line A, a bottleneck process, and to improve the
layout and jigs of Line A as a means of achieving the target.

Thus two-day *gemba kaizen* starts with a clear target.
Sometimes, depending on the circumstances, the project may
take three days instead of two. In order not to stop the line, the
layout changes usually take place during the night between the
shifts. Two-day *gemba kaizen* usually involves key players in the
plant: the plant manager, line managers, supervisors, staff,
team leaders, and operators.

A typical two-day *kaizen* project is carried out in the following manner. By the time the team members arrive at *gemba,*
they have had several meetings to study how to approach *kaizen*
in that *gemba,* so they begin the morning session by explaining
to operators what is going to happen. Then the team members
take about an hour to observe and make notes on the operations. Afterward, they meet to discuss their observations, come
up with *kaizen* ideas, and devise ways of implementing them.
They record on designated sheets the data they have gathered,
and work out *kaizen* plans for each process of the line.

During discussions, the team members go back to *gemba*
whenever they need to confirm something. The team leader

must select from among several *kaizen* plans the items to implement the next day; this decision must be reached before 4 p.m. on the first day. Once the decision has been made, the team holds another meeting with line operators and explains the schedule for the next day. Another purpose of this meeting is to encourage operators to speak up about any difficulties they encounter in their work. Based on such input from the operators, the team finalizes the *kaizen* plans for implementation the next day. Then the team works with the maintenance people to explain the kind of tools, jigs, and equipment repairs that will be needed.

As *gemba kaizen* necessitates equipment change, maintenance people and/or personnel capable of making the necessary jigs and tools stand ready to assist during the two-day project. This session will be finished by 6 p.m. Based on the instructions, new jigs and tools are prepared, brought to *gemba,* and installed on the line. This phase usually lasts until 10 p.m. or even midnight. Installing the devices, the *kaizen* team and the supervisor start the line, process the work pieces, and confirm any difficulties, such as operational or quality-related problems. Only after confirming that the line is functioning properly do the project team members go home.

Work on the second day starts half an hour earlier than usual. The *kaizen* team explains to the operators the changes on the line and the new work procedures. For instance, the team leader may say, "Up to now, six people have been working on this process, but we made changes so that the same work can now be done by five people. So, may I ask Mr._____ to stand back and watch while the other five people do the work?" The operation gets started at 8 a.m. as usual. As the operators need coaching, *kaizen* team members stay with them until 10 a.m. to allow them time to get used to the new procedure. Between 10 a.m. and noon, the operators continue work on their own and the team members make up a list of all problems encountered during this period. If the tools and jigs need further adjustments, they are sent back for modification before noon.

As soon as any necessary modifications have been completed, the operators start working on the line, and the team observes and measures the effects of the *kaizen* project. The team prepares the summary of the two-day activities by 4 p.m., at which time it begins the wrap-up session.

Sometimes several teams may be involved in the activities; in this case, teams compete with one another at the wrap-up session. Often, the senior managers from the plant as well as those from the corporate office attend the wrap-up session. The session closes at 5 p.m., completing the two-day *gemba kaizen*.

It often happens that the team members have no time to sleep during the first night, particularly when the line has to undergo substantial changes. Much can be achieved in such a two-day workshop, as the people involved use various worksheets during the two days and have prepared themselves by attending several study meetings beforehand. Even after the session, many activities must follow, such as confirmation of the effects, revision of work standards, and sometimes, revision of engineering rules and standards.

According to Takahashi, the following six items will help to achieve the target more easily during the two-day session:

1. Build a line that can produce according to the *takt* time.
2. Build a line flexible enough to meet deviations from *takt* time.
3. Thoroughly eliminate *muri* (strain), *muda* (waste), and *mura* (irregularity) in operations.
4. Eliminate factors that disrupt a smooth rhythm of operations.
5. Develop work procedures that can be written into standardized work.
6. Minimize the number of operators on the line.

Takahashi suggests that the work standard (item 5, above) should include the following:

A. *Conditions of Work*
   1. How to place parts and jigs
   2. Where to place parts and jigs

B. Handling of Parts and Jigs

   1. How to hold parts and jigs

   2. Locating where operator holds parts and jigs

   3. Body parts to be used

C. Combination of Motion

   1. Sequence of work

   2. Routing of work

Other key items to be included are safety considerations, inspection, cycle time, and standard work-in-process.

CHECKLISTS AS A *KAIZEN* TOOL

As a tool for carrying out *gemba kaizen,* Nissan has developed detailed checklist sheets for use during projects. For instance, when the team members observe the operator's movement, they use a checklist of economy of motion that includes such points as the following:

A. Eliminate Unnecessary Movement.

   1. Can we eliminate the movement involved in looking for or selecting something?

   2. Can we eliminate the need for judgments and extra attention?

   3. Can we eliminate transferring the work piece from one hand to another (e.g., picking up a work piece with the right hand and then transferring it to the left hand)?

B. Reduce Eyeball Movement.

   1. Can we confirm what we need to know by listening instead of looking?

   2. Can we use lamps?

   3. Can we place items within the relevant operator's field of vision?

   4. Can we use different coloring?

   5. Can we use transparent containers?

C. Combine Operations.

   1. Can we process while carrying the work piece?

    2. Can we inspect while carrying the work piece?

D. Improve the Workplace.

    1. Can we place materials and tools in a given area in front of the operator?

    2. Can we place materials and tools in the same sequence as the work?

E. Improve Tools, Jigs, and Machines.

    1. Can we use containers that are easier to pick parts from?

    2. Can we combine two or more tools into one?

    3. Can we replace levers and handles with a button to operate a machine in one motion?

In addition to its checklist for economy of motion, Nissan provides guidelines for two-day *gemba kaizen* activities. The guidelines include the aims of the project, the schedule, and the major activities.

The guidelines for major activities cover the following:

1. How to set the target
2. How to select the leader
3. How to check the line in question beforehand
4. How to confirm the inventory
5. How to explain the purpose of the project
6. What tools are to be prepared
7. How to select *kaizen* plans
8. How to instruct the operators
9. How to prepare standards
10. How to prepare the summary report

Specific individuals and departments are put in charge of each item on the list and given checklists to follow. For item 3—how to check the line in question beforehand—for instance, the following factors are included:

A. Person/people in charge:

B. Items to be checked, as follows:

1. Name of the line:
2. Product type:
3. Volume of production during this month:
4. Hourly production volume (for one week): [This item is particularly important for purposes of confirming the effects of *kaizen* and follow-up activities.]
5. Number of operators on the line:
6. Do they have second shift?
7. Percentage of overtime:
8. Rate of operation (previous month's record):
9. Failure rate:
10. Required *takt* time:
11. Layout:

GEMBA KAIZEN AT THE KAIZEN INSTITUTE

The Kaizen Institute has been conducting *gemba kaizen* sessions in the United States, Europe, South America, and many other parts of the world since the 1980s. The institute's consultants work together with Japanese consultants at the *gemba* of clients.

Following a visit by members of the Kaizen Institute to a client's *gemba,* the institute and the company's management agree on a long-term schedule of consultations, which often covers a period of several years. Such consultations usually begin with a two-day lecture on *kaizen* basics to all managers, including top management, followed by *gemba kaizen* activities at one of the client's *gemba.* The type of consultation selected—just-in-time *gemba kaizen,* total productivity maintenance/5S, quality improvement, etc.—depends on the requirements of the *gemba* in question. (In most cases, JIT-type *gemba kaizen* is selected, the reason being that it offers a dramatic change within a few days and management can see how much room there is for improvement.)

Often, different locations within the same *gemba* are targeted for different kinds of *kaizen* efforts; the *gemba kaizen* sessions are held repeatedly to transfer know-how to the client's management. Engaging in *gemba kaizen* also identifies cross-functional (interdepartmental) problems in the company. For instance, *gemba kaizen* often shows that customers' quality requirements are not being properly communicated to *gemba* by its sales department because there is no formal communication channel between the sales staff and *gemba*. Identifying such inadequate internal procedures makes it possible for top management to address these problems and build better internal systems. Figure 13-1 shows an average of improvements by type among U.S. companies that have engaged in a weeklong *gemba kaizen* with the help of the Kaizen Institute of America.

One of the reasons the Kaizen Institute starts with *gemba kaizen* is that it helps to identify many inadequate upstream management systems in the company. *Gemba* is like a mirror that reflects the real capabilities of the company: the problems

Gemba Kaizen Results	
Setup Time	−66.4%
Lead Time	−55.7%
Cycle Time	−17.9%
Downtime	−52.1%
Operators Required	−32.0%
Work-in-Process	−59.3%
Final Goods Inventory	−43.5%
Distance-traveled/Part	−54.1%
Floor Space	−29.4%
Parts Required/Unit	−57.0%
Cost Quality Rejects	−95.0%
Rework	−71.7%
Scrap	−45.9%
Equipment Required	−34.0%

FIGURE 13-1.   Average of improvements by type, 1993 to 1995.

encountered in *gemba* are often the result of poor support by various departments. Some examples include the following:

A. Engineering Department
   1. Poor layout design
   2. Inadequate equipment
   3. Inadequate preparation for production

B. Inspection and Quality Department
   1. Not enough failure mode and effect analysis (FMEA) studies before production
   2. Insufficiently detailed analysis of rejects
   3. Poorly prepared inspection criteria
   4. Lack of feedback

C. Production Control Department
   1. Failure to understand process capabilities of the line
   2. No grasp of inventory level
   3. Changing plans, ignoring *gemba* conditions
   4. Insufficiently precise production plan

D. Purchasing Department
   1. Ignorance of supplier capacity
   2. Inability to provide technical guidance to suppliers
   3. Insufficient quality audit to suppliers
   4. Inadequate management of incoming supply

E. Sales Department
   1. Failure to understand *gemba's* capabilities
   2. Failure to provide vital customer information to *gemba*
   3. Insufficient liaison with customers

F. Accounting Department
   1. Requesting more information than actually needed
   2. Delayed monthly reports
   3. Inadequate cost analysis

G. Administrative Department
   1. Introducing flavor-of-the-month programs that bear little relevance to the needs of *gemba*
   2. Inadequate training programs

H. R&D and Product Development Department
  1. Designing products that fail to take into account the capabilities of *gemba*
  2. Failure to advise *gemba* of anticipated changes in advance

Thus, *gemba kaizen* becomes a starting point for highlighting inadequacies in other supporting departments and identifies internal systems and procedures that need to be improved.

As 85 percent of the total cost of production is determined at planning stages upstream from *gemba,* and as the conditions for quality and delivery are also determined in the planning stages, improvement in upstream management is the key to achieving successful quality, cost, and delivery. *Gemba kaizen,* therefore, is but a starting point for much more exciting, challenging, and beneficial change. However, unless the caliber of *gemba* is first elevated to internationally competitive, world-class standards, no matter what improvements are made upstream, *gemba* will not be able to reap the benefits.

CASE
STUDIES

MK ELECTRONICS COMPANY

This case shows how the *gemba-gembutsu* principle and employees' determination never to send rejects to the next process helped to improve quality dramatically.

When Toshio Hasegawa, a consultant on production and quality control, first visited MK Electronics Co., he found that the reject rate of their main product, printed circuit boards, was 3 percent. MK Electronics is a small company in the countryside 70 kilometers outside of Tokyo employing 17 people, all housewives from nearby farms. The employees manually insert various electronic devices into the printed circuit boards. The company delivers its products to the secondary supplier, which in turn supplies to original equipment manufacturer (OEM) customers.

Hasegawa asked MK's president Chieko Kurabayashi how the rejects were dealt with. The president said, "My wife and I start fixing the rejects after all operators have left at 5 p.m. and we normally work till 11 every night." Asked whether operators knew they were producing these rejects, and that the president's family was fixing the problems, the president said "no."

To this, Hasegawa said, "Nobody makes rejects on purpose. Every time *gemba* employees make rejects, you should give them feedback immediately by showing them *gembutsu*. If you don't tell them and show them the rejects, how will they know the outcome of their work?

The president answered, "We are afraid of hurting their feelings! If I told them that they were making many rejects, they would feel persecuted, and might even quit the job. As we have a shortage of labor, we are afraid to do anything that may offend them."

Hasegawa held a series of meetings on quality issues with MK employees. He persuaded the workers to accept that henceforth, every time a reject was found, the *gembutsu* (defective circuit board) would be returned to whomsoever had made it and would be fixed right away, instead of being sent on to the next process in its defective state.

A popular catch phrase used in Japanese *gemba* is, "Don't get it. Don't make it. Don't send it." In other words, don't accept rejects from the previous process, don't make rejects in your own process, and don't send rejects to the next process. The modus operandi at MK up until then had failed to follow this maxim. In order to put an end to the vicious cycle in which the president and his wife secretly fixed rejects and the workers remained ignorant of their own mistakes—and thus produced more rejects—everybody had to become an inspector of her own work and assure the quality of the item being passed to the next process. Hasegawa was simply urging the workers to follow the three principles of the quality maxim.

Hasegawa also visited the secondary supplier to see how MK's products were received. He returned to MK with a suitcase full of rejects.

To remedy this situation, every MK operator was told to inspect each piece immediately after processing it, a procedure that became a new standard. If an operator found a mistake, she had to fix it before sending the item to the next person. Hasegawa had the operators get together, observe the *gembutsu* among themselves, and discuss how to handle the problem based on their observations. Operators would often say things like, "How could I have made such a mistake?" or, "I cannot believe I overlooked such a simple thing!" In cases where the same problems kept recurring, operators discussed changing procedures. As aids to quality control, the operators constructed some simple devices—a handmade jig to bend the wire at the correct angle and length, for example.

Another step MK took to enhance quality control was to

invest in training. Because soldering is an important part of the job at MK, the company sent half its employees to an outside course to gain soldering qualifications. The president took the course with them. The company also began using the consulting services of a soldering expert dispatched by one of its major customers every month.

Two major problems at *gemba* that MK worked aggressively to combat were spattering and dust. The company took the trouble to find out which type of brush would most effectively sweep away spatters and dust. After trying out a variety of materials, from metal to pig's hair, the company settled on brass brushes. However, the brushing work was later discontinued when the company changed the flux contents and thus eliminated spattering altogether.

MK's president Kurabayashi says, "I used to think that making some rejects was inevitable and that, according to our given processes, a 5 percent reject rate should be acceptable, since spending additional money to improve the process further would probably not pay off. But thanks to Mr. Hasegawa, we are now striving for zero defect, and if we strive for zero defect, we can attain a much higher level of quality. Our employees here are all farm people. They did not like school; that's why they work here. But they like the job. And they have guts. They are determined that they will never pass rejects to the next process."

Hasegawa told me that none of the company's employees, including the president, had ever heard of such things as statistical quality control, control charts, and cause-and-effect diagrams. Yet the company is achieving a 50 ppm (parts per million) range of quality.

According to Hasegawa, "There are three major requirements for good quality management. First, there must be quality of design. If the design is bad to start with, there is nothing much else we can do in *gemba*."

"Second, there must be quality of components from outside suppliers. It was found that the printed boards that they received from the supplier were giving them lots of trouble and were one of the major causes of their quality problems. This is the reason why I changed the supplier immediately after I started my consultations, as I was appalled by the quality of circuit boards MK was purchasing from the supplier, which could not keep up with their determination to improve quality."

"Third, there must be quality of workmanship, which means that the operators must be committed never to make or send rejects. Quality is not a theory but a practice!"

The MK employees' faithful adherence to the *gemba-gembutsu* principle and the credo, "Don't get it. Don't make it. Don't send it." stands out in sharp contrast to a story I have heard of a different company in a different country, where a student took a summertime job assembling engines. One day the student dropped a wrench inside an engine by mistake. A veteran operator working alongside him advised, "Don't worry. We have an inspector at the end of the line who will fix it anyway. So send it along!" Subscribing to this line of reasoning opens up the risk that a reject may escape the inspection network and eventually find its way to the end user.

Four years have passed since MK started to work in the new ways. In August 1994, the company delivered 80,000 printed circuit boards to their customers without a single reject. During these four years, the company has made no personnel changes and no investment in equipment. All it has done is change the way its workers do their job.

"Since the bursting of the economic bubble," says the president Kurabayashi, "the business climate has changed drastically, and many companies around here have gone bankrupt. The former supplier of circuit boards also went bankrupt. These are the companies that have failed to meet the increasingly stringent requirements for better quality and lower cost. I am glad we started our effort for zero defect and have survived the difficult times."

EXCEEDING CUSTOMER EXPECTATIONS AT WALT DISNEY WORLD

At Walt Disney World, *gemba kaizen* spirit is alive and well. *Gemba* employees at Disney are placed at the top of the organization. Walt Disney once said, "You can dream, create, design, and build the most wonderful place in the world, but it requires people to make the dream a reality." This case of Walt Disney World shows how Disney management's faithful adherence to housekeeping and standardization contributed to the success of the business.

Forty-one years after the opening of Disneyland in California in 1955, and 25 years after Walt Disney World was opened in Florida in 1971, the frontline cast members are still the most important in the company. At Walt Disney World, employees in the park are called cast members and customers are called guests. The guests' satisfaction is Walt Disney World's top priority, and housekeeping and standardization are the two major means to this end. Many visitors to the Walt Disney World Resort make repeat visits because they are so impressed with its clean and safe environment.

A FLAWLESS PERFORMANCE

On careful observation, guests will find that waste disposal containers are installed everywhere in the park. On my recent visit, I could count six such containers from the spot where I was standing. Walt Disney believed that no guest should have to walk more than 25 steps to discard litter. The containers are designed to blend unobtrusively into their surroundings. During the procession of Mickey Mouse and his gang on Main Street in the afternoon, I found many guests leaning against the containers or sitting next to them; some were even sitting on top of them munching snacks.

At regular intervals, the waste bins inside the containers are replaced in a swift, efficient manner. A cart carrying several empty bins is brought to the site and the bin inside the waste container is replaced with an empty bin. A cast member host makes a circuit of the park every 10 or 15 minutes with an elongated pan and a broom, picking up trash on the streets, under the benches, and in the shrubbery. Any Walt Disney World cast member walking through the park who happens to find litter is expected to pick it up. "If Mr. Michael Eisner were there, he would be doing the same," I was told. The collected trash is speedily conveyed to an underground station and sent to the processing plant through vacuum tubes. Thus guests are spared the sight and odor of garbage.

Another reason cited by guests for wishing to come back to Walt Disney World is the friendly and well-groomed Disney cast members. Walt Disney's dream was to provide services which not only satisfy the guests but also "exceed their expectations consistently." Walt Disney World is a place where guests are brought to the stage. The cast members are supposed to play their roles on the stage to entertain the guests. The cast must pay attention to safety and cleanliness and wear proper costumes at all times. Just as in film or onstage, imperfection (in this case, litter on the street, unpleasant odors, and the like) is not allowed. Therefore, every task, every movement of the cast, every building, every facility, every event, and every attraction must become a means of richly satisfying the guests. To do this, every newly hired cast member, including part-timers, must go through a two-day orientation program that instructs trainees in Disney's philosophy, the company's history, and the details of the job.

Cast members consist of full-time, part-time, and seasonal workers, and their jobs fall into about 1500 different categories. Every job has its own job description and standard operating procedures (SOP), and the 37,000 people working in the park are expected to follow the standards. If no such standards were provided and each of 37,000 cast members were to start working in his or her own way, management would soon find that there was no way to manage the cast members' behavior and the business, and therefore no way to ensure the satisfaction of the guests.

Each new cast member receives the following list of guidelines for serving the guests:

1. Make eye contact and smile.
2. Greet and welcome each and every guest.
3. Seek out contact with guests.
4. Provide immediate service recovery.
5. Display appropriate body language at all times.
6. Preserve the magical guest experience.
7. Thank each and every guest.

The cast members selling tickets at the entrance are told that their job is not to sell the tickets but to communicate with the guests. As the first Walt Disney World cast members to meet the guests, the ticket sellers are taught to make eye contact, smile, and greet the guests. These cast members are supposed to be well informed about the day's events.

A cast member selling balloons to children is expected to kneel so as to place himself or herself at the same eye level as the children—body language that demonstrates friendliness and intimacy. A cast member who finds a guest taking a snapshot of other guests is expected to volunteer to take the photo for the group.

The housekeeping hosts or hostesses also have their own job descriptions and SOP. They are reminded that their primary role is as stage players who entertain guests; the sweeping task is a secondary responsibility. Rather than stoop inelegantly to pick up litter, these cast members are expected to use a long-handled pan and broom, or a long stick with a scoop on the tip, to retrieve the trash and place it in the pan gracefully. Management must provide special training for performances of this kind. Often, guests do not notice the housekeeping cast members as such because they mingle with the crowd so naturally.

GIVING CAST MEMBERS DISCRETIONARY POWERS

Walt Disney would say that everything we do now is imperfect, and we must therefore constantly strive to do a better job; the moment we believe we have reached perfection, we stop improving. Cast members are empowered to take initiatives whenever necessary to exceed the guests' expectations.

For example, when a newlywed couple arrived at a Disney hotel, a receptionist cast member noticed that the bride was feeling ill. As soon as the guests were shown into their room, there was a knock on the door and hot chicken soup was delivered. The cast member was able to make this gesture because she had been given discretionary powers that allowed her to order the soup. The guests were so pleased and grateful that they later wrote a letter of praise to the management.

While cleaning a Disney hotel room being used by guests with children, a housekeeping cast member came up with the idea of arranging a menagerie of stuffed animals on the table in the room to look as if they had been having a party while the children were away. Imagine how enchanted the children were upon returning to the room.

AN EYE FOR STANDARDS

Each cast member is provided, during his or her job interview, with a booklet called *The Disney Look* that stipulates the importance of appearance; before a job offer is made, the cast member must agree to comply with the dress and grooming policies described in the booklet. *The Disney Look* specifies rules to be followed on such items as:

- Aftershave, perfume, and deodorant
- Costumes
- Hair coloring
- Pins and decorations
- Sunglasses
- Tattoos
- Hairstyle
- Mustaches, beards, and sideburns
- Fingernails
- Jewelry
- Shoes and hosiery
- Makeup
- Skirt length

Some examples of acceptable and unacceptable practices defined in the booklet are:

- *Sideburns (for men):* Sideburns should be neatly trimmed and may be permitted to extend to the bottom of the earlobe, following their natural contour. Flares or mutton chops are unacceptable.

- *Jewelry (for women):* Rings such as class rings and wedding rings, earrings, and conservative business-style wristwatches are permitted. Necklaces, bracelets, and ankle bracelets are unacceptable. Earrings must be a simple, matched pair in gold, silver, or a color that blends with the costume. A single earring in each ear is acceptable. Earrings can be clip-on or pierced and must be worn at the bottom of the earlobe. Their diameter must not exceed one inch.

The booklet also describes the procedures for supervisory cast members to follow in disciplining cast members for infractions of the appearance policies. For instance, the booklet stipulates that, should a cast member need to be reminded of the policies, the supervising cast member should do this coaching in private.

Because of the popularity of the Disney Approach to human resources development, Disney University professional programs are offered at Walt Disney World, enabling participants to actually view examples in the theme park on field trips and learn about Walt Disney World's strategies for people management, quality service, leadership, creativity, orientation, and standardization firsthand.

"THE PRESS CAME DOWN TWICE!": 5S AND SAFETY AT A PRESS SHOP

This case shows how safety and housekeeping are closely interrelated.

It happened one rainy day in June at a press shop in Japan. A young operator dashed, panting, into the supervisor's office. Using a 1300-ton press, he had been conducting a trial operation of a new die for an automobile panel. The purpose of this operation was to check whether the new die could produce the designed configurations. If it did not, the operator's job was to grind the die with a portable grinder while the die was mounted on the press.

"When I pushed the operation button," said the worker, "the press came down twice! But I had positioned the selector switch to the one-stroke position!" (For the safety of the operator, when the switch is in this position the press stops after each stroke).

The supervisor said, "We have been using this press for two years and this has never happened before. Are you sure you set the switch to the one-stroke position?" The young operator insisted that he had. As the incident concerned safety, the supervisor and the operator immediately went to *gemba* and conducted reproduction tests. However, they failed to reproduce the condition described by the operator. The supervisor concluded that the young man must have started the operation without setting the switch to the one-stroke mode, although the operator insisted that he had not made this mistake. Since a battery of reproduction tests failed to yield the results the operator had described, the operator had to accept, however reluctantly, the supervisor's conclusion.

This story later reached the ears of the union leader, who proposed that management conduct a thorough investigation of the case and stop the press until the results were known. A project team was organized which included an engineering manager, a production manager, and a union representative. The team performed various reproduction tests, but still failed to make the press come down twice.

At the same time, the engineering manager instructed both the maintenance department and the manufacturer of the press to review the electrical circuits of the press. The press manufacturer sent its engineer to review the electrical circuitry, which was ten centimeters thick. Although the engineer stayed for three days, no fault could be found in the circuits.

The results of the reproduction tests in *gemba* and the reports on the electrical circuits were sent to management and the union. The production manager decided to start up the press again. One rainy day, after a week had passed, the young operator ran into the supervisor's room, looking very upset. "The press dropped twice again!" said the operator. "This time, there can be absolutely no mistake. People told me last time that I must have made a mistake. But this time, there's no way it's my fault. I was extra careful with the selector switch!"

The supervisor reported this incident to the section manager, who in turn reported it to the department manager, who ordered reproduction tests. Again, the press did not come down twice. During the tests, one of the operators said to another, "By the way, the last time this happened, it was also raining, wasn't it?" Another responded, "Hey, maybe there's a current leakage somewhere!"

These comments prompted the supervisor to initiate a brainstorming session with the operators on the effect of weak current. With the help of the maintenance people, the supervisor and the operators inspected several spots on the press where electrical current might be leaking. On the side of the press, they found two electrical outlets located close together. One of these was the outlet for the electrical tools; the operator was using this outlet for his portable grinder. The iron powder produced by the grinder had fallen over these two electrical outlets, forming a cluster that looked very much like an electrical wire connecting the outlets. The employees suspected that high humidity might increase the electrical activity of this iron powder, causing the machine to switch into continuous mode without the operator's knowledge.

To confirm their hypothesis, the employees put more iron powder between the plugs and continued the reproduction tests. Sure enough, they saw that even though the operator had placed the selector switch in the one-stroke position, the press came down twice when the operation button was pushed. The production manager asked the manufacturer of the machine whether the press could drop twice in the event of a short circuit between these two plugs. The answer: Yes, it could happen.

To address the problem, the press shop took the following steps:

- The press was cleaned thoroughly (*seiso*). Particular attention was devoted to the two plugs and their vicinity, an area that tends to become dirty from the oil and iron powder produced by grinding. It was decided that the operator would clean this area every day with a dry cloth and vacuum up the iron powder. (The use of a blower was strictly prohibited, as this would simply scatter iron powder throughout the area.)
- With the help of the press maker, electric circuits were redesigned so that, even if the current were to run between the two electric outlets, the press would not come down twice.

To solve its problem, the press shop approached *kaizen* from two different standpoints: managerial technology, which includes such things as conducting *seiso* and establishing new standards; and proprietary technology, which was necessary for modifying the electrical circuits. The employees learned several lessons from this experience:

- The importance of 5S. In this instance, there was a direct relationship between it and safety.
- In probing the root causes of a problem, patience and tenacity are essential, and even factors seemingly unconnected to the situation must be taken into account.
- Brainstorming needs to involve everyone, including the operators.
- Countermeasures should focus on both managerial and proprietary technology.

HOUSEKEEPING, SELF-DISCIPLINE, AND STANDARDS: TOKAI SHIN-EI ELECTRONICS

This case shows how quality can be dramatically improved when the two pillars of *gemba kaizen* activities—housekeeping and standardization—are introduced.

Tokai Shin-ei, an electronics firm with slightly more than a hundred employees, started out as the sole supplier of printed circuit boards to one company. Initially, the company had no R&D capabilities in-house, and depended entirely on its customer to provide engineering drawings.

It was difficult for Tokai Shin-ei president Yoshihito Tanaka to find qualified workers in Shin-ei's hometown, a country town located about 150 kilometers north of Nagoya, Japan. The issue that haunted Tanaka was education. Since he was unable to hire employees with good educational backgrounds, he felt that the employees needed to be taught subjects such as statistical quality control and electronics. He asked a local high-school teacher to lecture his employees on the principles of electricity. However, the classes proved too difficult for the employees, so Tanaka invited a middle-school teacher to the company. This teacher, too, gave up after only a few lessons. Tanaka then invited a consultant on quality control to give a series of lectures. But this consultant soon ceased visiting *gemba*, preferring instead to come to Tanaka's office for chats because nobody in *gemba* could understand his lectures.

Thus Tanaka repeatedly found himself frustrated in his efforts to use outside resources for employee education. Suddenly one day, it dawned on him that he had been expecting a third party to teach his people, when such education should be the job of the president himself. He had neglected to share with employees his aspirations and visions for the company, as well as what he considered the company's problems. Realizing that he needed to take the initiative of teaching and sharing his ideas, he decided to hold a series of meetings with his employees.

In 1988 a mutual learning session was instituted, with Tanaka as the leader. The learning sessions were two-day programs held on the first weekend of every month. Employees took turns participating in the sessions, and every employee was required to do so at least once a year.

Saturdays were devoted to discussing issues of common concern. Tanaka saw that when employees were discussing issues of direct interest to themselves, they became much more excited and involved than they had during their lessons on electricity and quality control. Employees were involved, developed a sense of responsibility about the problems they were discussing, and came up with many possible solutions. On Sundays, the employees cooked and ate together at the nearby picnic ground, activities that greatly enhanced camaraderie.

The plant has been rebuilt since these sessions began, and a classroom specifically for the learning sessions has been added. Guest lecturers are invited to share their ideas, and the sessions are open to members of the community at large.

Currently, discussion subjects at the learning sessions include management plans, equipment purchase, recruitment, and bonuses. The company's financial reports and monthly performance figures are also reported. Other subjects addressed at the sessions include recreation, safety, communication, and financial management.

Hidesaburo Kagiyama, president of a local automobile parts supplier with a very successful nationwide network, was invited to speak at one session. Kagiyama has a unique management philosophy—management should start with housekeeping and end with housekeeping. He is a particularly firm believer in cleaning toilets—and does so himself every day.

Tanaka was so impressed with Kagiyama's lecture that he decided to put his ideas into practice right away. The next morning, he arose early and went to clean up the grounds of the shrine in his neighborhood. The shrine has a candy store on its premises, and the ground is carpeted with wrappers discarded by children. After cleaning up this litter, Tanaka set about cleaning the public toilets, which were so dirty the township had decided to close them. Tanaka went to the town hall and persuaded the local authorities to reopen the facilities, promising that he himself would clean them every morning.

Tanaka had heard Kagiyama say that housekeeping causes people to change their behavior, and to his surprise, he found this to be true. He enlisted his children's help in cleaning the toilets. The children would say, "Today the toilets were really dirty. It was wonderful!" What they meant was that they were gratified by the knowledge that people were using the toilets they had cleaned, and that they were happy to make them clean again. Tanaka realized that pleasing other people is the starting point of pleasing oneself.

Tanaka found that once the candy wrappers had been picked up and the toilets were being cleaned, children stopped throwing litter and people began trying to keep the toilets from getting dirty. Tanaka learned from this experience that self-discipline does not arise spontaneously, but as a result of participation in some beneficial activity such as cleaning the environment.

Aside from employee education, another issue that had been haunting Tanaka for a long time was employee self-discipline. In the company's early days, management had difficulty hiring workers who could be expected to carry out their appointed tasks. An operator was once found smoking when he should have been working. When reprimanded by a supervisor, he became so angry that he began striking the machine with a hammer. Tanaka realized that education in technologies and skills was utterly useless if there were fundamental problems in human relations and self-discipline. Tanaka came to believe that self-discipline should be the starting point of all activities taking place in his company. He came up with three activities to serve as the pillars of self-discipline: housekeeping, greeting each other, and etiquette.

Once Tanaka introduced employees to these three pillars of self-discipline, he was amazed to see how greatly they improved human relations, enhanced employee awareness of other quality issues, reduced equipment breakdown, and changed employees' attitude toward customers. Community relations also improved. In other words, an awareness revolution was taking place among employees. As yet another benefit of self-discipline, the reject rate dropped by half.

Tanaka launched a full-scale housekeeping project, and now the working day at Shin-ei Electronics starts at 7:30 a.m., when all the employees roll up their sleeves and join in cleaning the factory floor, offices, hallways, toilets, and even the cars in the parking lot and the roads within a one-kilometer radius of the company. Everyone concentrates on housekeeping for 15 minutes before regular work begins.

When I visited the plant in July 1995, the first thing I noticed was the parking lot, which was so immaculate that it looked like an automobile dealership's lot. The sales personnel in particular wanted their cars to look neat, since they use them when calling on customers. I also found *gemba* spotless. Although chemicals such as sulfuric acid are used in Shin-ei's operations, not a drop of liquid could be found on the floor. Before the cleanup, operators worked in boots and aprons because the floor was covered with chemical liquids. Now the employees wear slippers and normal working clothes.

Employees offered the following comments on this, the first housekeeping experience in which they had been directly involved:

- "By working with others in cleaning up the premises, I was able to communicate with people whom I had never had a chance to talk with before, and have come to feel much closer to them."

- "In the beginning, I just took pride in finding my own place neater than others'. But now, whenever I find other areas dirtier, I volunteer to pitch in and help. I used to think that what I was doing was best, but now I am ashamed I was so naive. I have grown as a human being as a result of cleaning. Cleaning is indeed a marvelous thing."

- "I have learned that in order to improve myself, I must help others to improve. I have come to believe that whatever I can do to help others, I should, though it is not always easy. I think I have become more patient."

- "When sales and production personnel cleaned together, we were able to communicate and understand each others' troubles."

- "I have become much more attached to and affectionate toward tangible items such as machines and buildings, and readily notice abnormalities, such as which spot on the machine gets dirtier sooner than other spots."

- "This experience has made possible joint work among sales, engineering, and production, which used to regard each other as adversaries before."

- I expect that these positive results that come out of cleaning together not only help our work but also benefit our family life."

Even after these housekeeping and other activities to enhance self-discipline had taken root in his company, Tanaka felt that something was missing. In late 1994, Tanaka told a *kaizen* consultant that, aside from quality, one of his major problems was that employees started work very slowly in the morning, getting busier as the day went on and becoming busiest toward the end of the day. He said the same was true for monthly production—that is, production started slowly at the beginning of each month and picked up at the end of the month to meet customers' orders.

The consultant's advice was as follows: "You have invested a sizable amount of money in your equipment. You hire a given number of people. Both equipment and people should be available to work at full capacity at all times. The uneven distribution of workload must be costing the company a lot of money. The reason for the uneven workload distribution lies in some inappropriate systems or work procedures in the company. So, why don't you address this problem? The biggest problem is that you have accepted such uneven distribution as something unavoidable and never questioned the situation. The first thing you need to do is to go through an awareness revolution.

"For instance," the consultant continued, "why does work start so slowly in the morning? It must be because the machines are slow to start due to inadequate setup preparations. Why can't you change the work procedure so that machine setup is completed before the end of the day? In other words, the existing standards and work procedures must be reviewed. In particular, if workers' operations are not standardized, there is no way to establish proper line balancing."

Tanaka decided to carry out the consultant's advice, and declared that a review of the existing standards would take place right away. The company had many work standards in place, but the standards had been prepared by engineering staff; *gemba* workers were expected to follow them unquestioningly. Often, engineers prepared standards without checking beforehand how they would affect *gemba*.

On Saturday and Sunday of the same week in which Tanaka had met with the consultant, all the employees were summoned for a review of the standards. (Employees were used to attending weekend discussion sessions.) The employees showed up at *gemba* bringing with them existing standards (work-sequence sheets) together with past records of problems. In order to review the work sequence, methods, and tools used for a given task, employees formed teams of three or more. A veteran operator performed a task according to the usual procedure while other operators looked on. Referring to the standard sheet, the onlookers corrected the veteran's actions when necessary. A second operator then tried to follow the sequence of work as demonstrated by the first operator. If the second operator encountered difficulty, employees discussed how the procedures might be made easier, and revised the standard accordingly.

At each process, there are several key points which must be observed for technical reasons; these points were incorporated into the new standards. Thus, the new standards specified the point that had to be observed at all times. Another feature of the new standards was that parameters previously left to individual discretion were quantified to the greatest extent possible. Processes were also simplified so that operators had only to push buttons on the machines.

These standards-review meetings carried over to Sunday, and involved managers, engineers, and veteran operators. The two-day session enabled employees to identify existing operational problems. The workers learned that making problems visible is the starting point of *kaizen*. They also found that although initial standards were written by engineers or line management, the nature of some tasks had changed considerably over the years, as had operators' understanding of the work procedures. Furthermore, operators often changed hands. The standards review showed employees that work speed differed from product to product, as well as from person to person. They found that adopting a uniform speed greatly increased efficiency and improved line balancing.

In the following weeks, the employees began implementing the new standards. Three months later, they held a two-hour standards-review session during normal work hours. This time, part-time employees were also involved. The review sessions helped to reduce careless mistakes, and operators became much more confident in their jobs. The sessions also promoted the "awareness revolution" among employees.

The engineers, who had once assumed that their role was to teach and guide employees in *gemba*, now work with those employees in establishing standards that are practical. Following are summaries of comments from operators who participated in the standards-review sessions:

- "Today, I wrote a work-sequence standard. I have been working here for ten years, and up to now, I have relied on my personal experience and hunches to do my job. It was not easy for me to write down what I do in my job. There were some *kanji* (Chinese) characters I couldn't write. I could not put into words what I was doing. I felt so helpless that I got a headache."

- "As I look at my daily work, I find that I have practically no work to do in the morning. Then, at about 4 p.m., there is an onrush of work. So, we need to distribute the workload evenly. As I am engaged in inspection, I can only stand to work until 5 p.m., since it is very tiring to inspect tiny pieces. Please arrange the workload in such a way that I can return home on time. Thank you for giving me a chance to review my own work."

- "I feel that I have been doing my job in such a way that I am the only person who knows how to do it. As a result of today's session, I learned that if I do my job according to a set procedure, someone else can do it even when I am absent."

- "No matter what kind of a job we do, I believe the most important thing is our attitude. I realized the importance of morale in doing my job."

- "I used to think that I knew what I was doing. But once I started writing it down, I was surprised to find many items that have slipped out of my mind or items I have newly recognized. I was surprised to find that some coworkers did not know enough *kanji* characters to write their comments. We helped each other write and found it a wonderful opportunity for communication."

- "All the participants forgot about the time and put their full efforts into the task. It was a wonderful learning experience."

- "We labeled the machine switches so that anybody can operate the machines. For those who don't know how to operate the machines outside their job area, the work sequence sheet and the switch labels were very helpful, and I believe even newly hired employees can easily use these machines."

A supervisor offered the following comment:

- "Today's theme was how to write a work standard to eliminate *muda, mura,* and *muri* (waste, irregularity, and strain). I realized that, until now, I had let the operators do the job the way they wanted to do it. Every time operators changed hands, there were deviations in product quality and the key parameters were not observed. When the operator in charge was absent, nobody else could do the job. For these reasons, I realized how important it was to prepare work standards. I also realized how difficult it was to communicate the right procedure to our own people. From now on, I will stick to the work standard as the basic rule of work, and each time there is a problem, I should look for the root cause; I should check whether it arose because the worker did not follow the standard or because the standard was inadequate; and also whether the standard included important control points. Thus, the work standard should be the starting point of *kaizen.*"

Six months after the first weekend standards-review session at Tokai Shin-ei, the reject rate had dropped to one-quarter of its previous level. Overtime had also gone down. More important, although sales had dropped during this period, profits had improved because some work formerly performed by veteran employees had been transferred to part-time employees. Many night-shift jobs were also transferred to part-timers. What enabled this transfer of labor? The standardization of work procedures. Tokai Shin-ei had achieved all these improvements without investing in any new equipment and without hiring any new employees.

THE ANSWER WAS IN THE FILES: *GEMBA KAIZEN* IN R&D

By Désiré Demeulenaere, *Kaizen* Consultant

A *kaizen* project in the R&D department of an automotive parts manufacturer in Italy yielded an amusing (but very educational) experience that shows the power of 5S in streamlining business processes and improving productivity while saving much space needed in *gemba*.

Most of the participants in this *gemba kaizen* effort were R&D engineers, but employees from other offices were also involved. On the first day, the employees were divided into three groups. Two of the groups were assigned to documentation, while the third was tasked with 5S in the laboratory. One of the groups working on documentation was sitting in the meeting room trying to decide where to start the *kaizen* process. I noticed that they were engaged in a very heated discussion.

I went to one of the cabinets in the room, opened it and, at random, took out one of the files. "What is in here?" I asked. Although the file bore no heading, one of the group members immediately replied that it contained documents on all office supplies, such as small tools, nuts and bolts, etc., purchased for R&D activities. This group member was the R&D engineer in charge, and one of his jobs was to coordinate and follow up on purchases. The file was crammed with papers, letters, offers, price lists, purchase requests, confirmations, and copies of invoices. There was no room for any additional documents. Upon seeing the file, the engineer looked sheepish and said that he was aware of the need for a new file but had had no time to prepare one. He said he would do so as soon as he could find time.

The documents in the file were arranged in reverse chronological order. To our surprise, the first sheet we found was more than ten years old! The last sheet, just a few days old, was a copy of a reminder to a supplier that had failed to deliver on time. This was the only "live" piece of paper in the file.

After some discussion about what to do with the file, we concluded that only four documents in it were worth keeping: the current order, the reminder, the previous order, and its confirmation of receipt. We agreed to keep orders and related documents on file until the R&D projects for which the items had been purchased were completed, since extra items sometimes need to be ordered or the R&D people have complaints about items received. After the engineers learned that the purchase department kept the complete originals of all orders, all other documents were destroyed at once. Within two days, the volume of documents had been reduced to less than one-third its previous level.

We also devised color codes for easy access to documents, and developed documentation standards and manuals. We structured the standards to suit the department's work flow. The new manual gave specific instructions for handling paperwork, including how to fill out forms and prepare documents, who should do so, which code numbers needed to be assigned to drawings and what to do in case corrections or modifications were required, which documents had to be filed in a given situation, and what to do when documents were taken out.

A month later, when the group measured the impact of their *kaizen* actions, their estimates showed that each of the 12 employees in the department was saving at least an hour per week. Furthermore, because getting rid of the superfluous paper made it easier to find the right document when they were needed, they found that their job had become more pleasant.

HOW 5S AT A DIE PLANT ELIMINATED THE NEED TO RELOCATE

By Désiré Demeulenaere, *Kaizen* Consultant

This is the story of a 5S program in a tire manufacturing company. As in the previous case, it too will show the power of 5S in streamlining business processes and improving productivity while saving much space needed in *gemba*. At this factory, about 1500 different types of tires are produced in a small lot and delivered to test drivers each year. One of the departments within this factory is engaged in designing, machining, testing, and delivering the dies used for the rubber extruders for the tires.

Six employees at this department complained that they lacked adequate space to do their jobs. When I visited, I found them working in cramped quarters indeed. The closely placed work tables were covered with papers, documents, drawings, measuring instruments, dies under preparation, computer monitors, and keyboards. Around the work tables and against the walls were five large filing cabinets of different dimensions and colors, each housing documents pertaining to the dies in storage. When a cabinet door was opened, it blocked the passage; nobody could walk around the office until the door was closed.

Next to the office was a small die-making machine shop. The finished dies were stored outside this department, along the wall next to the extrusion machine. There, too, the storage cabinets for dies and other materials were of different colors and dimensions.

I was invited by management to examine their proposal to move to a more spacious location. Management found it difficult to accept the proposal for two reasons: the relocation project would cost a lot of money, and the area claimed by the group was already occupied by another group.

After listening to their complaints, I suggested a two-phase approach. I told them they should first try a 5S program, and only after that should we discuss relocation. They insisted that relocation was the only alternative, but finally accepted my proposal and agreed to try 5S first.

We began the housekeeping process with the storage cabinets in the die preparation office. We found nearly 14,000 sets of documents, each pertaining to a different type of tire and die. Of these, only 1500 sets of documents were used every year. There were also 14,000 old dies gathering dust, despite the fact that the company manufactures only 1500 dies each year and of those, 500 are newly made.

We told the managers that the starting point of 5S was getting rid of unnecessary items. "But it is impossible for us to eliminate the documents and the old dies," they told me. "We have no idea which type of die will be requested next time and when. Most of the time, we have to work in a big hurry after we receive an order. Therefore, we must look for an existing die that's similar in design.

"If we keep the old dies, we only have to select the old one that comes close to the newly ordered die and make adjustments, instead of designing and making an entirely new one. For making a new die, much more designing and machining time is needed, and it's also expensive, since a new metal plate must be ordered each time."

This department stored the old dies, but was not authorized to dispose of them. That decision rested with tire development engineers located in a separate building—of whom the people in this *gemba* said, "Those guys are impossible to communicate with." As a result, the departments had not decided among themselves any rules for discarding old dies.

"Anyway," I said, "You are selecting each year 1000 dies to adapt to the new specifications out of the 14,000 in stock. So your stock of existing dies would last for at least 14 years! Is it not possible to make a list of all the dies that have not been used for more than three years? With such a list, you could then discuss your problem with the engineers."

On my return visit a month later, I found the employees very enthusiastic. Discarding unneeded documents had already enabled them to remove one cabinet from the office. The employees also said that they had sold more than 2000 old dies—a full cubic meter of metal—to a scrap-iron dealer. The workers were also happy with the positive relationships they had built with the tire development engineers. Together, the departments were able to arrive at rules on eliminating old dies. Furthermore, the employees found that fewer dies and documents meant less time lost in searching for needed articles.

These results were only the first fruits of a 5S program that later led to many more improvements. Subsequent actions included developing a system for scheduling die preparations, rearranging the office layout, repositioning machines in the machine shop to match the sequence of operations, and installing better lighting and ventilation systems.

In the end, the company has cut its delivery lead time for extrusion dies from three days to two. And the working environment has become so orderly and pleasant that the employees do not seem to remember ever having insisted on the need to relocate their *gemba*.

CLEANLINESS IS KEY AT DAIWA JITSUGYO

Daiwa Jitsugyo has more than two hundred Esquire Clubs throughout Japan that are practicing *kaizen* and have active quality circles. Esquire Clubs operate in much the same way as Playboy Clubs, with bunnies serving the guests.

As one *kaizen* activity, each club is asked to report the number of complaints from the guests to the head office. If a particular problem has been solved in one club, the solution is horizontally deployed to others, as many of these complaints are common among the clubs. In order to encourage clubs to submit reports, management presents an award to the club reporting the greatest number of complaints. This case is an example of housekeeping applied in the service sector.

The following article by Masanori Okazaki, manager of the Esprit Gaza club, is an excerpt from Daiwa Jitsugyo's in-house monthly magazine, *The Mate*:

Hello everybody! How are you doing on 5S?

At our establishment, we are scrubbing off the dirt of the past two years. Two years may sound short. Well, every day we receive one hundred guests in the daytime and two hundred in the evening inside a room of just 120 square meters. I must say the dirt we had to tackle was formidable.

For instance, take the speaker cover made of metal. Ever since I was transferred to this store, I thought that its color was dark brown. We started to scrub it with a steel scrubber using diluted detergent and lo and behold! We found that its original color was white! When we sprayed the solution on the wall, the dirt came off the wall as if we were rubbing the cosmetic foundation off a woman's face.

Think about it. Three hundred customers a day, many of whom are smoking, and multiply by two years! Getting dirty is the most natural thing to happen. Not cleaning the room is the most unnatural thing to do.

Once we were finished with the walls, we began to take notice of the brass hooks on the wall. Now that the walls had become shining clean, we found that the colors did not match the color of the brass hooks. We took one hook off the wall and started to clean it. Wow! How shiny it had become, and how beautifully it matched the color of the wall!

Now that we have started the business of cleaning, we cannot stop the momentum. We began to notice dirty spots everywhere and started to clean the room every day as long as we had time available. Thus, we found that the store has become much, much cleaner than before.

Now, the next challenge is how to keep on doing it and maintain the cleanliness.

For instance, one day we shined the restroom doorknob and it became much cleaner. Since three hundred customers touch the doorknob daily, it will be soiled in one day. The problem is that we have little time to devote to cleaning. We have some time while the store is closed to customers between daytime and evening work, but such time is used for setting the tables and dishes, etc., and no time is available to devote to cleaning.

"If these conditions persist," I thought, "it will be impossible to maintain cleanliness." I had to think about how we could do it without increasing the number of employees.

We discussed among ourselves what are really necessary things to do before receiving customers at 5 p.m. With their help, we made a list of all activities that we do between 4 and 5 p.m. and checked how much time it takes to finish each item.

As a result, we identified many tasks which could better be performed while the customers are in the store, such as not producing lemon juice during this period but rather after the customers have arrived, since we can serve fresher juice in this way. Thus, we changed our working schedule to make time available to do the cleaning. We are not there yet, but soon we should be able to make a schedule which allows a small number of people to work on 5S continuously.

Let's join forces and make a better and pleasant establishment!

STAMPING OUT *MUDA* AT SUNCLIPSE

Based in Commerce City, California, U.S.A., Sunclipse sells and distributes industrial packaging and corrugated shipping containers. The company's president, Gene Shelton, says, "We are not in a high-tech business; we are, however, in a high-energy business. Ours is a low-capital business. Anybody with good connections with customers can start the distribution business as long as he or she has a telephone and a desk. They don't even need to own a truck to transport products, because they can lease the truck. We recently had a new entry into our market from Taiwan. That's why we must work harder, think smarter, and keep satisfying our customers better than anybody else."

This case shows various ways, including *muda* elimination, introduced by Sunclipse to improve its competitive edge.

RELYING ON COWORKER INPUT

Over the years, the company has introduced various *kaizen* activities involving coworkers. (Sunclipse prefers the term *coworkers* to *employees* because of the latter's connotation of management-labor confrontation.) There are two major vehicles for coworker input for *kaizen* at Sunclipse. One is the opportunity-for-improvement sheet (OFI) (see Figure A) whereby coworkers can write down any idea for improvement on an OFI form and submit it to their supervisors. If the supervisor is unable to solve the problem, the subject is

O.F.I.
OPPORTUNITY FOR IMPROVEMENT

DATE: _____   REPORTED BY: _____

The following situation is making it difficult for me to do my job right the first time: _____

_____

_____

_____

_____

_____

_____

_____

_____

_____

_____

_____

_____

_____

OPTIONAL:

What has already been done: _____

_____

_____

_____

_____

What could be done: _____

_____

_____

_____

_____

LOG #: _____

FIGURE A.   An example of an opportunity-for-improvement sheet.

brought before the problem-solving team. The other vehicle for coworker input is the customer satisfaction form, on which coworkers can report any customer complaint or other problem. (See Figure B.)

KENT H. LANDSBERG CO.
PAPERLAND

CUSTOMER SATISFACTION
FORM

LOG #: _____

DATE: _____

CUSTOMER: _____

ADDRESS: _____

PHONE#: _____ ACCT #: _____

CONTACT: _____ SALES REP.#: _____

CUSTOMER CALLED FOR:

- ☐ LATE DELIVERY
- ☐ CUST. RET. PRODUCT -9
- ☐ ON HOLD TOO LONG
- ☐ NO RESPONSE BACK ON QUOTE/PROBLEM
- ☐ SAMPLE DELAY
- ☐ ATTITUDE (GOOD/BAD)

- ☐ WRONG QUANTITY
- ☐ TAX VS. RESALE
- ☐ WRONG PRODUCT
- ☐ BACKORDER
- ☐ INVOICE NOT REC'D OR WRONG
- ☐ COMPLIMENT

- ☐ WRONG PRICE
- ☐ PROD. NOT TO SPECS.
- ☐ NOT GIVEN FOLLOW-UP
- ☐ WRONG ADDRESS
- ☐ MISSED APPOINTMENT
- ☐ OTHER (SPECIFY BELOW)

EXPLICIT DESCRIPTION: _____

_____

_____

_____

ACTION REQUESTED: _____

_____

ISSUED BY: _____

ROOT CAUSE OF PROBLEM: _____

CORRECTIVE ACTION TO BE TAKEN: _____

_____

_____

_____

_____

_____

COMPLETED BY: _____ DATE: _____

FIGURE B. An example of a customer satisfaction form.

CONTINUING IMPROVEMENTS

Each Sunclipse division has a facilitator who devises various programs to ensure coworkers' support for continuous improvements. Each division also has a quality improvement team (QIT), which meets once every two weeks to go over unresolved problems and discuss how to carry out programs.

MUDA MILES

At Sunclipse's St. Hart Division in California, which produces corrugated paper products (and which places particular emphasis on eliminating *muda* or non-value-adding activities), facilitator Pat Arnold introduced "*Muda* Miles" as a way to visually display improvements made by coworkers. A map of the United States is posted in a prominent place, and each time a worker's suggestion helps reduce *muda*, the improvement is converted to a mileage value and plotted on the map. The object is to "travel" across the country, with St. Hart as the starting point of the journey. Alongside the map is a list of *kaizen* projects that have been implemented and their corresponding mileage.

THE WISH TREE

At the Orange Division of Sunclipse's Kent H. Landsberg operation, the major activities are administration, distribution, warehousing, and sales. When the division first introduced the suggestion system, coworkers were very interested and enthusiastic and there was a deluge of new ideas. A few months later, however, facilitator Stacey Snyder found that the initial burst of enthusiasm had given way to inertia. Realizing that a more accessible program was needed, Snyder came up with "The Wish Tree." She developed a form with a simple structure that allowed coworkers free expression of their wishes.

An orange tree (in keeping with the division's name) was placed in Snyder's office. For every idea submitted, a white ribbon attached to the "I wish..." form was detached from the form and placed on the tree. When people began working on the idea, the white ribbon on the tree was replaced with an orange flower; and when the problem was solved, the flower was replaced with an orange. The quality team is now considering the next step for involving coworkers in *kaizen* projects.

Each supervisor at this division is asked to submit a monthly report to management on how *muda* was handled in his or her area during the previous month. At bimonthly meetings, supervisors read their reports and exchange information on the current status of *muda* elimination.

GETTING THE SALES FORCE INVOLVED IN *KAIZEN*

The Kent H. Landsberg operation of Sunclipse, tasked with selling not only Sunclipse products but also the products of other manufacturers, is pivotal to the company's success. Nevertheless, management had a difficult time getting salespeople to participate in continuous improvement.

The sales representatives maintained that since their job was to increase sales, they were already involved in continuous improvement. The reps offered every excuse for not attending problem-solving meetings: they were too busy; they had their hands full just getting orders into the system and products to customers; they were not, to the best of their knowledge, causing any quality-related problems in the company. At times, the salespeople seemed to believe that the earth revolved around them.

Finally, management decided to get back to basics—to start with the voice of the internal customer and use data to convince the sales force. Managers learned that a large number of voice-mail messages from salespeople lacked one or more of the following pieces of information:

- Customer name
- Purchase order

- Buyer name
- Purchase quantity
- Method of transportation

At the next biweekly sales meeting, the 80 sales reps present were told that some seven hundred incomplete orders had been received from them in the previous month. Still, every salesperson believed that "Somebody else must have done it." Each salesperson was then handed a sealed envelope containing a record of the incomplete orders he or she had issued. The sales representatives opened their envelopes and a long silence followed. For the first time, the sales reps realized that they, too, had to change. By the next month, the number of incomplete orders had dropped to 289.

Today, the information systems department is working with the sales force to develop a digital paging system, including a mechanism for taking remedial action immediately when the system fails. They have developed an on-line fax monitoring system. Again, corrective action will be taken the moment mistakes are found.

The coworkers in these departments have also developed a data collection system that allows them to handle customer orders proactively. When a machine producing a particular product for a customer goes down, for example, the revised delivery date will be relayed to the sales representative through the digital paging system. The salesperson can then inform the customer of the change.

RECOGNIZING EMPLOYEE EFFORTS: Q BUCKS

Another feature of *kaizen* at Sunclipse is an employee recognition system called "Q Bucks." Q bucks may be awarded to coworkers who participate in the quality improvement process and participate in one or more of the following:

- Completion of a quality-related education or training session

- Submission of an OFI leading to corrective action
- Improvement of a work process
- Solution to a problem by the problem-solving team
- Performance of a measurement
- Achievement of a departmental goal
- Membership in the company's quality council, a corrective action team, a QIT, or some other quality-related committee like a quality-is-fun committee.
- Other quality-related contributions at the discretion of the divisional QIT.

Sunclipse has a contract with a merchandise redemption company that allows coworkers to redeem the Q bucks they have earned for products or services of their choice. The products and services, which coworkers choose from a catalog, range from $5 worth of merchandise to a two-week Caribbean cruise.

Greg Brower, Sunclipse's vice president, director of training, and head of the companywide *kaizen* project, told me the following story. One Sunclipse truck driver had to deliver products to a warehouse each day at the end of his day shift. Because the warehouse was never ready to receive the products when he arrived, the driver had to wait in the truck for a long time. By the time he began unloading, it was well into the night shift. Thus the driver was receiving an average of 20 hours' overtime pay per week. Troubled by this waste of resources, the driver made a suggestion. If he could arrange for a night-shift worker at the warehouse to do the unloading, he could leave the truck at the warehouse unattended and go home.

This suggestion earned the driver $380 in Q bucks. He and his family enjoyed perusing the catalog before finally settling on a 19-inch color TV. "He was very happy and we were delighted!" said Brower. "Once you get started in *kaizen*," Brower added, "it's difficult to stop. It just happens."

TRANSFORMING A CORPORATE CULTURE: EXCEL'S ORGANIZATION FOR EMPLOYEE EMPOWERMENT

Excel Industries, Inc., is a supplier of $600 million worth of goods to the ground transportation industry. Excel Industries supplies a broad customer base of automotive original equipment manufacturers (OEMs), such as heavy-truck, mass-transit, and recreational-vehicle manufacturers. The company is the leading supplier of window and door systems to the automotive OEMs. Excel has approximately 4000 employees and operates ten manufacturing facilities. Twenty-one percent of Excel's factory labor force is unionized.

This case addresses the issue of building a good, solid foundation for the house of *gemba*. It shows how Excel tackled the task of changing the corporate culture by clarifying the roles of managers vis-à-vis employees, providing training for employee empowerment, and building various infrastructures to carry out those tasks.

MEETING THE *KAIZEN* CHALLENGE

Excel Industries initially embarked on the *kaizen* process in March of 1992, with the assistance of the Kaizen Institute of America. The motivation for implementing *kaizen* was straightforward. Without a disciplined process to achieve continuous improvement, Excel's ability to remain an ongoing, independent entity was in jeopardy. Heightened global competition to meet customer demand for continuous improvement in quality, cost, and delivery demanded a response.

To address customer needs, Excel formed a corporate steering committee in March of 1993. This committee is cross-functional: Attending members include the company's president, three vice presidents of strategic business units, the vice president of human resources, three general managers of operations, the director of manufacturing operations, the director of corporate purchasing, and the vice president of value management.

After a year of *kaizen*, the committee saw impressive results in its 15 *gemba* workshops. The results included productivity gains of 57 percent, a 73 percent reduction of work-in-process (WIP), cycle-time reduction of 78 percent, and floor-space reduction of 44 percent. The *kaizen* committee recognized that *gemba* workshops were unlocking the human potential of Excel's employees. Excel wanted to find a way by which the potential and enthusiasm, generated by participation on a *gemba* team during a workshop, could be carried over to daily life within the company. The challenge was how to institutionalize the *gemba* workshop culture. The committee also wanted to ensure that Excel could sustain the *kaizen* process over the long term. To make sure this happened, the committee planned to use corporate and outside *kaizen* consulting resources on an ongoing basis to guide the process.

Following the plan-do-check-act (PDCA) process, Excel set out to benchmark companies with experience in the *kaizen* process in order to gain insight on whether these companies captured the potential and enthusiasm sparked by *gemba* workshops—and if so, how they did it. (See Figure C.) The

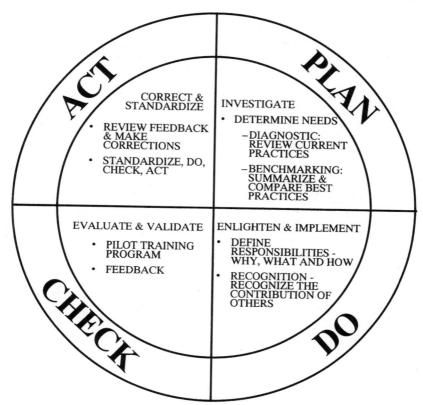

FIGURE C.   The PDCA process.

benchmark study revealed two factors as being key to sustaining *kaizen*: (1) strong management support for redefining responsibilities; and (2) empowered employees. Managers in companies whose *kaizen* efforts were successful found it necessary to change their corporate cultures from top-down driven to supportive.

Excel's new challenge was to define the steps or processes that would be required to help support a change in culture. The *kaizen* steering committee addressed this challenge by redefining the roles and responsibilities for the corporation. (See Figure D.)

The next step in changing the corporate culture was to redefine roles and responsibilities. The supportive process

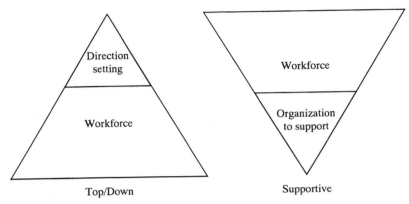

FIGURE D. Changing the corporate culture roles and responsibilities.

would require extensive training and education to help managers and other employees better understand their redefined roles and responsibilities. Senior management needed to know *why* change was necessary and to lead that change. Middle management needed to define *what* needed to be changed and support the change in culture. Employees needed to define *how* change should be implemented and accept responsibility for implementing same.

EMPLOYEE EMPOWERMENT TRAINING

Excel Industries brought together a dedicated group of professionals from the Kaizen Institute of America and Trinity Performance Systems, plus a team of Excel employees spanning several areas, to form the Excel 2000 Empowerment Team. It assembled a cross-functional empowerment team with professionals from every area, including administration, engineering, manufacturing, quality, and human resources. Two individuals from each of Excel's nine plants were asked to participate. Excel's *kaizen* steering committee team members were empowered to establish a training objective (empowerment), develop a budget for empowerment training for the next five years, draft a training curriculum, and serve as an advisory board for the format and presentation of materials.

The empowerment team met monthly for ten months; each meeting lasted three to four days.

Excel knew that its customers had reduced, and would continue to reduce, their supply base over the next few years. Customers with 1500 suppliers today will have only 700 suppliers in the year 2000. All suppliers use tools such as statistical process control (SPC). Some use value engineering and *kaizen,* but few utilize empowerment. Excel intends to be a leading supplier in the future and believes empowerment will enable it to accomplish this vision and attain a competitive advantage.

The understanding and definition of employee empowerment varies among organizations. At Excel, employee empowerment means that everyone has the authority and responsibility to improve their own work as long as they are part of the team, have the appropriate data, and follow a standardized improvement process. Employee empowerment is *not* synonymous with participative management, shared decision making, pushing decisions down, or "anything goes." Figure E illustrates the components of empowerment at Excel.

The Excel 2000 Empowerment Team's mission is to equip Excel Industries, Inc. with an educational system that pro-

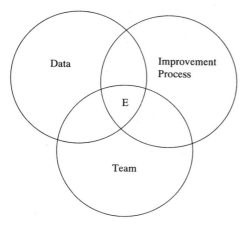

FIGURE E.   The components of empowerment. E represents employees working in teams using data to prioritize and direct improvements throughout the *kaizen* process.

vides all teams with the knowledge, skills, and behavior to willingly accept ownership for the continuous improvement of their standardized processes. The Excel 2000 team developed the following training modules to accomplish this task:

A. Team kickoff (team, staff, and support groups)
1. Define empowerment.
2. Define teamwork.
3. Speak with data.

B. Sponsor (staff)
1. Define team goals.
2. Determine the resources.
3. Commit to support team.

C. Standardize work team—standardize-do-check-act (SDCA)
1. Standardize the work process.
2. Map the process.
3. Develop the team.

D. Improve work processes—plan-do-check-act (PDCA)
1. Define value added.
2. Define waste (*muda*).
3. Conduct "*muda* walk."
4. Introduce data-gathering tools.
5. Identify process improvement by speaking with data.

In addition, there are nine modules designed to train the supervisor/coach to manage the process, develop people and teams, and integrate systems.

All of the above training promotes a shift within Excel toward a culture of incremental improvements. The company will accomplish its cultural change by establishing teams empowered to standardize, improve, solve problems, and be innovative in their work so that results better fit the customer's requirements. The SDCA and PDCA processes develop these teams both naturally and in a cross-functional manner. Excel has a totally committed and supportive management team, and this support and commitment is active, not passive. Empowerment teams are given a team sponsor. The sponsor for the company's first such team, the Excel 2000

Empowerment Team, is the plant general manager. Subsequent teams will be sponsored by members of the plant's managerial staff. Sponsors set team goals; allocate and ensure that resources are committed to support the process; mentor team coaches and future sponsors; "walk the talk." Figure F depicts the process of empowering employees at Excel.

THE NEED FOR ADDITIONAL TRAINING

As Excel's empowerment team was developing training materials for empowered shop-floor work teams, it became evident that additional training modules would be needed to support the vision of changing the corporate culture. Also, the team found that training shop-floor employees, first-line supervisors

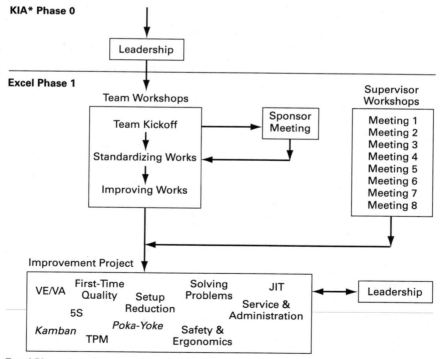

FIGURE F.   The process of empowering employees.

(coaches), and management staff personnel was just the first phase in the process. The team proposed a three-phase approach that would include every employee in the Excel organization. The team felt that additional training in support functions at both manufacturing sites and corporate headquarters would help focus the efforts of all employees to support the empowered shop-floor work cells and better serve the needs of Excel's customers.

The next step in the empowerment process will address Phase 2: training related to manufacturing plant support functions. This training will focus on training these functional groups to support the empowerment team. Roles and responsibilities will be clearly defined. The Excel 2000 Empowerment Team will develop a needs analysis for the support groups. Gaps will be defined and training will be developed to better support the shop-floor empowered teams and focus on customer needs. After Phase 2, a third phase will address training related to corporate support functions. This training will focus on the training of technical and administrative groups to support the empowered manufacturing plants.

ACTION AND ACCOUNTABILITY

Excel's senior management has clearly defined *why* a cultural change is necessary. Global competition is exerting pressure for continuous improvements in quality, cost, and delivery. Failure to comply with customer needs threatens Excel's ability to survive as an independent entity.

Middle management has clearly articulated *what* needs to change in the corporate culture. Through the efforts of the Excel 2000 Empowerment Team, middle management now possesses the process, skills, tools, and training necessary to unlock the human potential of Excel's employees.

Excel employees have gained the ability to define *how* to implement change and accept responsibility for change. Employees now have the authority and responsibility to improve their own work as part of a team working with data and following a standardized process.

The key to Excel's future success is directly related to the accountability between senior management, middle management, and all employees. The accountability of senior management will be measured by the ability to *lead* and *support* the process. Middle management will be assessed by its ability to *develop trust* by coaching and teaching the process and by providing support, and nonmanagerial employees' accountability will be measured by the extent to which they can *implement change* and *accept responsibility.*

THE JOURNEY TO *KAIZEN* AT LEYLAND TRUCKS

Leyland Trucks Ltd., Britain's leading commercial vehicle maker, designs, develops, and produces a range of civilian and military trucks sold throughout the world. The company was formed in 1993 when its management team led a buyout of the Leyland Assembly Plant in Lancashire, England, and of its associated businesses, from DAF BV.

The current managing director, John Oliver, who joined Leyland Trucks before DAF BV went into receivership, not only went through the management buyout process, but led the company through *kaizen* and into a new, "lean" production system to attain many dramatic improvements, including achieving the lowest cost of any European truck maker. As Oliver has vividly described Leyland's experiences, in his report submitted to me in 1995:

> In the 1980s, we invested an enormous amount in technology with little results. Now we emphasize building employee commitment, teamwork, slim organizational structure, and effective communication.
>
> The past five years have taught us that the most effective cost-reduction programs start without any intent to reduce costs at all. We have frequently seen initiatives designed for quality, whether quality of process, product, or people, generate highly welcome financial benefits. It may be far-

fetched to state that the more you ignore cost reduction, the bigger the eventual saving will be. However many occasions show that to be exactly the case.

As in the previous example of Excel, this case addresses the issue of building a good, solid foundation for the house of *gemba,* but Leyland used another approach. Leyland's management directed its efforts toward making organizational changes to meet the new challenges, delayering the management structure, improving systems efficiencies, and introducing new measures to change the cultures.

MAKING ORGANIZATIONAL CHANGES

To start the process of *kaizen* at Leyland Trucks, Oliver initiated three major changes to the company's organizational structure: (1) introducing business units; (2) cutting excess layers of bureaucracy; and (3) improving systems and procedures.

BUSINESS UNITS

When John Oliver arrived at the Leyland assembly plant in mid-1989 as operations director, he found the employees' morale very low. Their attitude toward Leyland DAF could best be described as grudging acquiescence. Some were downright hostile.

Oliver and the other managers resolved to improve the quality of working life. Improve an employee's job satisfaction, went the argument, and you would improve his self-esteem and eventually his affinity with the company. Management realized that the key to improving the quality of life was building infrastructure appropriate to employees' requirements—and *not* focusing on improving the design of individual jobs or assignments. "Our traditional hierarchical and functional structure was too remote, too slow, too impersonal, and too bureaucratic to meet employee needs," Oliver says. "If we were serious, then we had to find a new model."

Eventually management came up with the concept of the

business unit, a liaison team composed of employees representing each functional area (industrial engineers, planners,
quality technicians, logistic specialists, etc.). The members of
the business unit would work on the shop floor, next to the
lines—in direct and regular contact with the regular shop-
floor employees. The business unit members would be trained
in interpersonal skills, including team building. The objective
was simple Management 101 pursuits. As a result of these
efforts, quality defects dropped from 28 per vehicle in 1986 to
four in 1995. (See Figure G.)

"I am convinced that had we set out with the specific
objective of cost reduction we would have failed," says Oliver.
"The singleminded pursuit of quality of process and enhanced
employee affiliation brought these huge savings."

ORGANIZATIONAL DELAYERING

Traditional management structure presented many obstacles
to building an empowered organization. However, any move
toward a flatter, wider pyramid challenged the status quo. Any
organization resists radical change; there is never a "right"
time for such change. Nevertheless, management realized that
the traditional multilayered organization had to go.

The results, says Oliver, were well worth the effort: "Over
two years, 42 percent of senior and middle management positions disappeared. Loosening the chains of the old hierarchical bureaucracy improved the added value of the team by 30
percent to 50 percent. Increasing individual spheres of influence—at first feared and resisted by anxious managers—very
quickly led to improved self-confidence, self-esteem, and job
satisfaction. Colleagues who had spent the previous 20 years
doing largely the same thing day after day experienced a new
resurgence of spirit, a new level of energy."

BUILDING EFFECTIVE SYSTEMS

Management's third organizational change improved systems
and procedures. On this subject, Oliver offers the following
observations:

Memo on Signing for Replacement Tools and New Tools

When a tool broke on the assembly line the operator would look for his supervisor to make out a replacement note. This note was then taken to a store where it was exchanged for the new tool. The problem with the process was that the operator could not always find the supervisor and this could cause the following problems: the operator's work was not complete; tools were being shared; tools were being stolen; and in some cases the operator would request additional tools to ensure that he would not go through the same frustrations.

The results meant that everybody had a locker full of tools. To add to the problem, when the tooling budget costs got excessive, an instruction was passed to the managers that they had to sign for all replacement notes. Of course this caused more frustration because if people had difficulty finding the supervisor you can imagine how difficult it would be to find a manager.

So this was one of the first areas of empowerment which was developed down to the team.

Here's a story which made us realize the frustrations being caused:

One day when we were coming out of a meeting an operator met me and asked me to sign his note. I took the note from him, looked at the tool being requested, and when signing, mentioned that the tool cost the company £10. He replied very aggressively, "You have got it wrong, the tool has cost you £19." I asked why and he said, "Because I've been looking for you for one hour and 30 minutes at £6 per hour. Plus, I've not completed my operation." So, this gave us the incentive to empower the teams.

FIGURE G.   (1) Memo illustrating the frustrations and cost of doing things "the old way" at Leyland; (2) organizational charts showing old structure and new business unit concept.

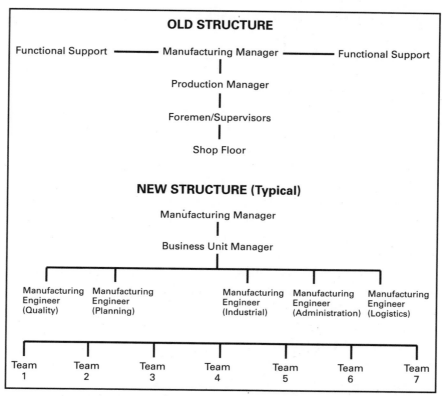

FIGURE G. (*Continued*)   (1) Memo illustrating the frustrations and cost of doing things "the old way" at Leyland; (2) organizational charts showing old structure and new business unit concept.

Many constraints prevent ideal empowerment. The problems associated with a multitiered structure, equally burdensome systems, processes and procedures, confuse instead of clarify, complicate instead of simplify. In most mature organizations, process development and proliferation have not been planned. New processes are added to compensate for weaknesses or nonconformance in old processes, but only rarely does the organization go back to root causes and start afresh. A hierarchical organization tolerates this state of affairs and further waste, never challenging or questioning the status quo. An empowered, minimum-tier organization cannot afford to be so charitable. Clarity of process logic is all-important. Customer processes have to have suppliers. Requirements must be understood—and the cost of meeting those requirements justified. Can the task be done better, more effectively or perhaps even eliminated?

An initiative called systems effectivity addressed this issue of process clarity. Again, the objectives contained nothing about cost reduction, but pointed toward some form of quality. We first employed a self-audit, designed to enhance involvement. For up to five days, groups of employees kept personal diaries describing everything they did. The participants and their colleagues analyzed the data to distinguish added-value activities from those which were consequences of nonconformance elsewhere in the system. People enjoyed both the novelty of self-assessment and the challenge of analysis.

Our expectations from the exercise were modest. We wanted a more transparent bureaucracy. We wanted to challenge the status quo. We got all that and more. Thirty percent of the paperwork from the operation disappeared—and along with that, a whole host of meetings, agendas, minutes, reports, and miscellaneous bumph [paperwork] which simply cluttered our daily lives and scarcely added any value whatsoever. In short, yet another example of almost inadvertent cost reduction on a very sizable scale.

When we started it, the objectives were improved perceptions of "ownership," simplicity of systems, clarity and availability of information, greater customer satisfaction and so on. But the final analysis showed a £1,000,000 annual saving on the conventional cost of quality performance—a staggering 83 percent reduction.

CHANGING THE CULTURE

There is a Japanese saying to the effect that a statue of Buddha will amount to nothing if the person who carves it fails to put a soul into it. Even after Leyland introduced the "hardware" aspects of business units, delayering, and system effectiveness, management found these measures insufficient to take the company where it wanted to go. Additional efforts to involve and empower employees were needed. Of these efforts, which came to be known collectively as Project "Bridging the Gap," Oliver writes:

> Small focus groups of representatives across a range of functions and levels addressed some of the more long-standing and vexatious questions. International visits to key competitors exposed representatives to benchmarking of work practices.
>
> All this took place while the above-mentioned activities were going on. In addition, a small experiment that introduced cell working in our machining area got very positive internal publicity. The local management of the area recruited the operators to work and involved them in the design of everything from plant layout to process design. This departure from previous practice drew attention as all the prospective members of the new cost center worked together planning their new world of work.
>
> The consequences of this experiment were startling. Quality levels improved sharply. Floor-to-floor times shrank by 80 percent. Inventories fell to previously unheard-of levels. Efficiencies improved significantly. And equally important, absentee levels in the same group of people fell from an exceptionally high 8 percent to less than 2 percent.
>
> We realized a dynamic at work which, if reproduced across the company, would transform its fortunes. The question was, *how?* Sadly, even after 18 months of successful business units, cellular manufacturing, organizational delayering, and so on, we had not achieved our fundamental requirements of winning the hearts and minds of the workforce at large. Things improved, but not sufficiently to remove the ancient barriers of mistrust and suspicion. Something had to weld the entire workforce into one coherent, mutually dependent and mutually supportive unit.

ENCOURAGING EMPLOYEE INITIATIVE

Realizing this, John Oliver decided to encourage *employees* to initiate changes in the company:

> With the help of local consultants, we offered every employee the opportunity to express his or her *real* views and concerns in a structured manner. The key benefits of the change initiation programs were:
>
> - Independently generated information—the key word being *independent.*
> - Quantifiable conclusions which gave an indication of relative importance.
> - A representative, cross-sectional sample size so that all groups felt involved.
> - Feedback facilitated by a consultant who was independent of the company to avoid bias and partiality.
> - But most important, ownership of both the problem and the solution by the workforce. It was important that they knew and understood that it was their *collective* view.
>
> Through this process, we were trying to (1) persuade the majority of the workforce that change is inevitable; (2) demonstrate that these changes are mutually beneficial; and (3) generate real ownership of the change process. To make it happen, the following six key stages were developed:
>
> - *Stage One: Presentation and communication of the program.* It was important that the trade unions were involved.
> - *Stage Two: Identification of needs through in-depth interviews and groups discussions.*
> - *Stage Three: Identification of priority and satisfaction.* This involved asking the workforce to take a view of an ideal job for themselves in an ideal world, identify 45-50 needs, and rank them according to their aspirations.
> - *Stage Four: Analysis.* This ended up in drawing a hierarchical picture of needs, priorities, and satisfaction from function to function and from department to department.
> - *Stage Five: Feedback of data to employee groups.*
> - *Stage Six: Diagnosis.* Various employee groups were organized to move into problem-solving mode.

Standard attitude surveys were often seen as solutions imposed on employees to problems defined by management, often with a hidden agenda suspected. In this process, change initiation, need, its priority, and the level of dissatisfaction, were *all* defined by the workforce, and therefore owned by them.

Recognizing a Job Well Done

The first step toward recognizing employee efforts happened in the area of idea generation. Overcomplexity, overbureaucracy, and wholesale dissatisfaction had defeated previous suggestion plans. Clearly, a new approach was needed. As John Oliver writes:

A brainstorming exercise on the plans concluded that the main objective behind suggestion plans was to get people to make suggestions! That's not quite as silly as it may seem. The lesson we learned was that success should be measured by the number of times employees thought positively, constructively, and imaginatively about the company, not how much successful suggestions could save us.

We devised the "Every Little Counts" plan, where every employee who makes a suggestion and submits it on a formal entry form gets a £1 voucher for a national chain store. It did not matter whether the suggestion saved 1 pence or £100,000. As long as it was done constructively, the voucher was handed over with a "Thank you."

The ELC scheme has mushroomed since, with its own self-managing infrastructure. Financial tradeoffs are avoided to ensure that the controversies over previous models are not repeated. Contribution levels are high by traditional standards and by current British best practice.

While ELC offered an organizational response to greater involvement, it also tested the relationship between the managers/supervisors and the workforce during the working day. After years of impersonal, task-oriented management, we needed a much more interactive style that demonstrated awareness of the social dimension of the working world. Managers had to learn to greet people at the start of shift, to use first names, to get to know the whole person—not just the work characteristics. This was not easy. To change these habits of a lifetime was a different proposition, and they needed a helping hand.

Accordingly the mouthful "informal individual recognition token" was created. For every 100 employees in a particular cost center or management area, the manager was given 25 tokens to hand out during the coming year for exceptional work, whether consistent or incidental. In year two, the token became a rather nice metallic tape measure. The tape measures, obviously useful in the world of work, became a source of some pride—a major step forward from the fear of being singled out. In year three, a rather large sports bag suitably embossed was chosen. Its size was important, to elevate the visibility of the recognition process. Recognition became a comfortable, mutually acceptable part of everyday life. In year four, the token is a company T-shirt. The only way anyone can lay their hands on this garment is to be singled out by a manager for exceptional performance. To wear one has become a matter of pride. Our key thrust within the area of recognition is, however, the acknowledgement of the contribution of the team. Every three months, nominations for the quarterly team awards are canvassed energetically. Care is taken again to avoid the financial tradeoff between recognition and reward. We have had enough experience to conclude that monetary gain demeans the process. Although teams who are commended receive only a simple certificate applauding their efforts, the level of pride is there for all to see. An informal but public ceremony is used to ceremonially acknowledge their contributions. The winning team has its name endorsed on a large shield. It is a very comfortable, very much accepted process which is now embedded into the culture.

WORKING AS A GROUP

Teamwork, says Oliver, has been a way of life at Leyland from the beginning:

When we started our journey in 1989, we visualized a company whose ethos was grounded on the concept of teamwork. It could be functional or multifunctional, formal or informal, horizontal, vertical or diagonal. What really counted was the spirit and the readiness to use the group as the core of the business.

Involvement and participation have come to life. The autonomous working groups on the tracks with their peer key operators have demonstrated efficiencies never previously encountered. Multifunctional project groups, properly sponsored, trained and facilitated, spring forth regularly and deliver remarkable results free of bureaucracy and senior management intervention. Ad hoc teams appear regularly and tackle issues in a structured fashion that overcomes functional barriers.

Involvement and participation can be talked about and can be encouraged. But the acid test is in the execution. Group working is the ideal vehicle to practice what we preach.

THE START OF A JOURNEY

Oliver concludes his remarks by saying:

The foregoing describes just a few of the mechanisms designed to foster involvement and participation. However, I believe the fundamental task is to keep pushing the barriers back, to keep on introducing new ideas to maintain the momentum. Leyland is only at the start of its journey.

ALWAYS LEARNING AT LÖBRO

Löhr & Bromkamp GmbH (Löbro) in Offenbach, Germany, is a GKN group member that produces constant velocity joints and shafts. Löbro, which has 1800 employees, has been engaged in various *kaizen* activities during the past few years.

This case shows how Löbro engaged in various *kaizen* activities until it reached the conclusion that, given their type of business, total productive maintenance (TPM) was the most urgent task for them. Löbro management realized that *gemba kaizen* is a long journey and that it takes a process of learning by doing for both managers and workers.

To comply with ever-more-demanding requirements from its automotive customers, Löbro reorganized its quality system in 1989 and shifted its emphasis from quality control to quality management. It beefed up its already strong internal training programs, increasing its number of internal trainers from 10 to 25 in 1992; it has 120 today.

In 1990, an employee suggestion system was reinstituted, and companywide visual management was introduced. More than 50 percent of Löbro's shop-floor workers are "guest workers" of 35 different nationalities, with different languages and religions. Management realized that taking this diversity into account in communicating with its employees would be one of the key issues for improving quality.

Visual management means displaying in a visual manner the current status of operations. Accordingly, the company posted various graphs and charts on the current status of *kaizen* activities on the walls and in every corner of the factory. In addition, video corners were installed so that operators could come in and watch video programs on topically relevant *kaizen*-related subjects. In the same year, the structure of production went through reappraisal.

In 1991, *gemba* was reorganized. The two factories were split into seven shop-floor units and the number of management levels was reduced from six to four. The small-factory concept was the guiding principle in creating shop-floor units. Each unit had a specific range of parts to produce, and each unit's customer was the assembly unit. Policy deployment was instituted and specific quantified company goals were set. Löbro's *gemba* went through various *kaizen* programs, such as total productive maintenance (TPM) and just-in-time (JIT). Outside consultants were invited in to give employees on-the-job training on these subjects.

Since 1992 Löbro has been engaged in a campaign to reduce absenteeism; as a result, the rate of absenteeism has dropped from 9.5 percent in 1992 to 4.7 percent in 1995. Also in 1992, the concept of units and teamwork was extended to administration and sales. Again, the idea was to improve service to customers by creating smaller units dedicated to providing sales and technical services. This was also the year in which the company sent 25 master craftsmen, setters, and engineers to Japan to visit world-class factories. At the cost of 10,000 deutsche marks per person, management showed its commitment to quality by encouraging employees to see and believe that they, too, could do it.

In 1993, a video-based monthly information system was introduced; thus far, ten different programs on important subjects such as visual management have been shown through this program. *Kaizen* activities involving operators in *gemba* began this year.

After having engaged in many *kaizen* activities, management decided to introduce TPM in 1994 throughout the company. Given its type of business, management came to the conclusion that TPM was an urgent priority, and created a dedicated organization to promote it. The TPM effort began with an all-out cleaning of the equipment, involving all employees. The company's organization to promote TPM is known as LÖMIS; the name comes from the initials of the following four words: Löbro, mitarbeiter (operators), instandhalt-nug (maintenance), and system.

TPM as it is being promoted by LÖMIS consists of the following six elements:

1. Autonomous maintenance
2. Elimination of six major sources of loss
3. 100 percent production quality
4. A planning system for new machines
5. Training for all operators
6. Increased office efficiency

LÖMIS has created a mascot, an operator with a gear in his hand. The mascot, whose name was chosen by popular vote by 60 *gemba* people who started the TPM project, appears on wall charts, in company magazines, brochures, and pamphlets; on key chains handed out for promotional purposes; and, of course, in a video program created to explain LÖMIS and the TPM project. Every employee receives a note pad bearing an outline of LÖMIS activities. (Figure H shows an example of LÖMIS instructional materials.)

Every month, one *kaizen* theme is designated as the LÖMIS project. One recent project involved reduction of air leakage in a particular *gemba*. Employees identified 293 air leaks in 96 equipment malfunctions; LÖMIS spearheaded 108 *kaizen* activities to solve the problems. By the end of the month, hourly air leakage at the *gemba* had been reduced from 16 cubic meters to 1 cubic meter. A subsequent LÖMIS project involved marking the floors as an aid to 5S.

THE NUMBERS SPEAK FOR THEMSELVES

Various *kaizen* activities at Löbro between 1990 and 1995—including 5S, JIT, and TPM—have yielded the following improvements:

Symbolic figure of our LÖMIS Program

May I introduce myself?

<u>My name is LÖMIS.</u>

In the forthcoming years we want to work together on the improvement of our workplaces and of our production equipment.
If you have any questions, please get in touch with my colleagues of the LÖMIS team.

<u>We help you by implementing the following measures:</u>

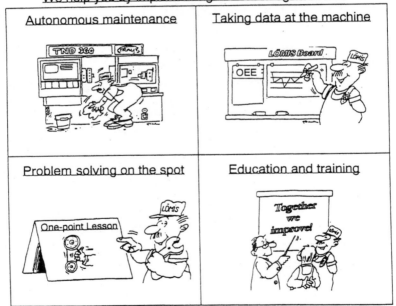

FIGURE H.   An example of LÖMIS instructional materials.

- *Absenteeism:*   Reduced by half.
- *Suggestion system:*   Increased from 0.15 to eight suggestions per employee per year. (Löbro is now counting suggestions actually implemented; its goal of six per person per year was achieved by the end of 1995.)
- *Scrap:*   Reduced by half.
- *Customer rejects:*   Reduced by 90 percent.
- *Training days:*   Increased from 0.8 days to five days per employee per year.
- *Setup:*   Reduced by half.
- *Throughput time:*   Reduced by 30 percent.
- *Inventory:*   Reduced by 40 percent.

Recalling *kaizen* experiences at Löbro, Managing Director Michael Beseler recently told me:

> In hindsight, I can say that although *kaizen* means changing for the better, that doesn't mean that everything we did in the past was wrong. Actually some of the practices of former days had to be reintroduced because they had been forgotten in recent times. Many people at first did not understand this. They felt that *kaizen* was something completely new—that what they had done in the past was all wrong—and felt rejected. This was the reason why people resisted change. Improvement is a continuous changing process . . . it means to *learn again*. Continuously learning and continuously improving—that is what we are doing.

Beseler also learned that *kaizen* was not a one-shot deal. In the past, management tended to seek short-term, flavor-of-the-month approaches. Management would say to employees, "Now you start quality circles, total quality management, or whatever," and expect quality to improve. Nothing happened, of course, because management did nothing afterwards.

Beseler further realized that his previous conceptions of the learning process had been wrong: "Learning cannot be done by a slogan of the month. To move 1800 people, you need to do a lot more than just a slogan. We used to give orders and that was it! We were too impatient. Now we know it is a slow, systematic process. *Kaizen* does not mean jumping from A to Z. It means going from A to B and then from B to C."

The starting point for *kaizen,* Beseler says, is to become problem-conscious: "Once you recognize a problem, there will be a solution." However, Beseler found that his biggest initial obstacle was difficulty in recognizing the problem. He knew things were not quite right, but could not pinpoint the trouble. Through various *gemba kaizen* activities, however, he has come to identify key problems and has started addressing those problems in a systematic manner.

Beseler has realized that a good manufacturing company is made up of building blocks such as total quality management, just-in-time production, total productive maintenance, *gemba kaizen* activities, *muda* elimination, and teamwork. Says Beseler, "What we did not realize from the beginning was how strongly these building blocks interrelate and depend on each other."

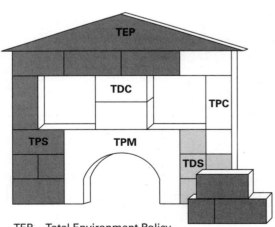

TEP - Total Environment Policy
TPM - Total Productive Maintenance
TDS - Total Delivery System
TDC - Total Design Control
TPS - Total Production System
TPC - Total Purchase Control

FIGURE I. The six building blocks of a total quality culture.

As Figure I shows, the Löbro TQC House is made of six major bricks: total environment policy (TEP), total productive maintenance (TPM), total delivery system (TDS), total design control (TDC), total production system (TPS), and total purchase control (TPC). While each of these "bricks" is important, the "mortar" cementing them together is just as important. This mortar consists of *kaizen* activities (continuous improvement), people's involvement, teamwork, training and education, communication, and policy deployment. In particular, top management must play a leading role in making quality happen, and middle managers must be involved as well.

LOOKING TO THE FUTURE

While *kaizen* at Löbro is currently focused on TPM, the company has already set its sights on the next set of challenges. The first of these goals is zero defects:

- To customers
- In the factory
- From suppliers

The second set of challenges is intercompany process development and improvement:

- Group activities
- Out/in-sourcing
- Added value chain

Referring to these challenges, Beseler notes that before the company began its *kaizen* efforts, employees used to say, "The rest of us are our enemies," but now they say, "Let's work together to satisfy the customer."

The company's ultimate goal is a JIT manufacturing system that is completely defect-free, both supplying products to the customer and receiving materials from suppliers just in time. Löbro management recognizes that TPM, with all its benefits, does not by itself guarantee success. If a well-maintained machine produces a mountain of surplus work-in-process or finished products, it will be impossible to make a profit. Thus Löbro management sees TPM as a foundation upon which to build a just-in-time production system.

ADAPTING TO MARKET CHANGES: SIEMENS OOSTKAMP

Siemens Oostkamp Belgium, which belongs to Siemens Electromechanical Components group, produces such electronic components as relays, connectors, and coils. Siemens Oostkamp is an internal supplier to the Siemens Telecommunications group, and at one time its products were sold almost entirely to Siemens companies. Since Siemens has adopted an outsourcing policy, however, the ratio of Oostkamp products delivered to Siemens has plunged to 44 percent. Meanwhile, international competition in the electronic components market has also intensified. These changes have forced Oostkamp's management to seek new markets.

That is what prompted the company to bring *kaizen* into its plant in 1992. The company held a series of *kaizen* seminars to familiarize top and middle management as well as union leaders with the concepts and tools of *kaizen*. From this case we can learn a pragmatic step to do *kaizen*. *Kaizen* at Siemens Oostkamp followed four stages: (1) collection of data on the current situations, (2) recognition of problems, (3) establishment of challenging targets for *kaizen* by management, and (4) empowerment of people to solve the problems with the use of proper tools. Siemens Oostkamp began actual *gemba kaizen* in 1993, with a combination of activities such as 5S and just-in-time.

In the same year, the department plant manager instituted policy deployment to set targets for improvement at the plant level. The plant manager established numerical targets for improvements in such areas as inventory reduction, ratio of indirect labor, number of product types, lead time reduction, and improved reliability of delivery. Monthly *kaizen* audits also began at the plant.

To provide a vehicle for these *kaizen* activities, self-managed work teams were formed. The work teams, in which every *gemba* employee was required to participate, emphasized teamwork and partnership, carried out the plant manager's policy by means of objectives they had set themselves, and employed problem-solving techniques. Figure J shows Siemen's Oostkamp's vision of the relationship between management and labor in a *kaizen* context.

As a result of these *kaizen* activities, Siemens Oostkamp was able to reduce inventory from 53.2 million deutsche marks in 1992 to 37.2 million deutsche marks in 1995. The storage area was reduced by 10 percent between 1993 and 1994, and the ratio of indirect labor overhead was reduced from 25.1 percent in 1992 to 24.8 percent in 1995. The number of product

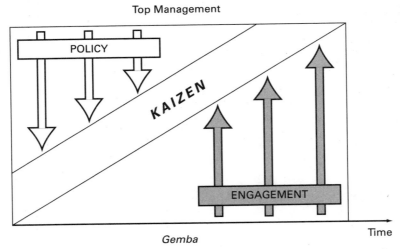

FIGURE J.   The policy of management is turned into engagement by the workers.

types has been reduced by 33 percent in the past five years. The delivery reliability has improved from 78 percent in 1992–1993 to 83 percent in 1994–1995.

OVERCOMING INITIAL DIFFICULTIES

COLLECTING DATA

Reinhard Straihammer, general manager, initially encountered difficulty in collecting information in *gemba*. On his first *gemba* walk through the plant, Straihammer was accompanied by Peter Teufel of the Kaizen Institute. When they asked supervisors whether specific information—such as the failure rate or the time required for machine setup changes—was available, the answer was always affirmative. When they said, "Show us the data," the answer was always, "It's in the computer." But when they asked the supervisors to retrieve the data from the computer, they got nowhere. The reality was that, in those days, no data was available. Even if it had been, it would not have been collected in a way that allowed it to be used for analytical purposes.

Thus the first challenge for Straihammer was to get the managers to understand the need to collect data—on machine breakdowns, rejects, changeover time, rework, number of suggestions, etc.—and make this information readily visible and accessible. More than six months passed before a new data collection system was in place. During this period, Straihammer had to go to *gemba* often to see to it that employees collected data and reviewed their work in an objective way. This helped the employees recognize where the problems lay.

The next task was to set targets for improvement by policy deployment. Simply assigning targets was not enough; management had to show how to achieve them. The Kaizen Institute provided training and other assistance in single-minute exchange of dies (SMED), just-in-time technologies (one-piece flow, U-shaped line, etc.), and in various problem-solving techniques.

Thus *kaizen* at Siemens Oostkamp occurred in four stages:

1. Data on the current situation were made available.

2. *Gemba* people were helped to recognize the problems.

3. Targets for improvement were established.

4. The tools for problem solving were provided.

Thereafter, *kaizen* proceeded smoothly.

ORGANIZATIONAL PROBLEMS

Another problem that confronted Straihammer concerned the organization itself. Siemens Oostkamp was organized on a functional basis—stamping, plastic molding, assembly, etc.—with a manager responsible for each function. In an effort to optimize operations in his or her own area, each manager typically bought the most expensive equipment. This arrangement resulted in redundant equipment and excess inventory.

Straihammer saw the need to question this functionally based organization. This need became all the more apparent when the company instituted just-in-time, made a flow line, and used *kanban* (production order slips) between the processes. Under the new procedures, only a minimum number of boxes of work-in-process—say, four—was allowed between the assembly and plastic molding processes for a particular product. Minimizing the batch size in this way made it obvious that the changeover time at the molding department was too long.

Before commencing *kaizen*, the company had had no data, so it had no clue where to start. Now, with information readily

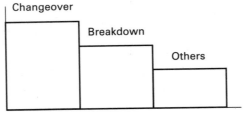

Causes of Machine Downtime

FIGURE K. Causes of machine downtime at Siemens Oostkamp.

available, it was easy to decide. (See Figure K.) Thus one *kaizen* effort led to another.

KEEPING UP THE *KAIZEN* MOMENTUM

Now that the policy deployment and *kaizen* audit are in place, says Straihammer, his next challenge will be keeping up the momentum, since only 70 percent of the company's workers have been involved in *kaizen* so far.

When I visited Oostkamp's *gemba* in January 1996, it was evident that the plant was undergoing many changes. In the areas where 5S has been introduced, the machines and floors were spotlessly clean, and potted plants had been placed in the corners and hallways. I was told that the plants had been the workers' idea. Machine layouts had been changed for a more efficient process flow, and isolated islands had been brought to the main line whenever possible. A warehouse once needed to store supplies and finished products is gone, and a new production process has been brought in. Many machines have been moved to eliminate transport *muda*. In the tool-and die-making section, the time to design and produce molds has been reduced from 120 days to 49 days.

I also observed signs of visual management everywhere. In fact, the three most conspicuous items in *gemba* were visual management, standardization, and policy deployment. Large charts on the walls display the plant manager's annual policy, including numerical data and trend charts for each item. The general objectives are broken down into tasks for *kaizen* teams and individual employees. The tools are placed in the areas designated for maximum efficiency and convenience, and markings on the floor indicate the placement of supply carts and finished products. As soon as a finished product rolls off the assembly line, it is placed on a cart in a designated area and shipped straight from there to the customer.

At Siemens, a number of operators told me that:

• Before *kaizen* began, they had had a strong resistance to it, and had found it difficult to accept change.

- Now that they have gone through the process of *kaizen*, however, they are happy with the results and have become much more problem-conscious; they have gained the ability to identify and solve problems themselves. Thanks to a change in the processing layout, they can identify a problem in the previous process right away and feed the defective item back to that process. Identifying a problem used to take days—and often the problem was discovered too late.

- They found that often it was not necessary to put a suggestion in the suggestion box because the moment a problem was found, they worked on it and devised a solution. Whereas they once viewed fixing problems as somebody else's job, they now regard it as their own. They have become much more committed to problem solving.

- The lead time required to produce coils for antilock brake systems, once 12 days, has been reduced to half a day.

- Production of ribbon cable connectors now begins only after orders are received, and finished products are shipped directly to customers. This department once kept a three-month inventory of finished products; this is no longer necessary, since the lead time has been reduced to three hours.

- At the tools and molds sector, home to a very aggressive 5S program, operators came to *gemba* on weekends to paint machines and floors.

SOLVING QUALITY PROBLEMS IN *GEMBA:* SAFETY AT TRES CRUCES

Most problems in *gemba* can be solved if (1) the five *gemba* principles are followed; or (2) data are systematically collected and analyzed. Some problems can be readily identified and solved if one takes the trouble of going to *gemba* right away, stays there for five minutes, and keeps asking "Why?" until reaching the root causes of the problem. In such cases, observation is the key and solutions can be reached on the spot in real time. Most problems in *gemba* can be solved in this way. However, other types of problems require collection of data in *gemba* and take some time to solve.

The following case describes how safety problems were solved at Tres Cruces Cold Storage Plant, a company in Argentina that manufactures such products as skinless sausages, hams, and salamis. Between January 1993 and May 1994, 27 accidents occurred at the company, costing it 78 man-days. The company organized a group made up of a supervisor and three workers at the raw materials receiving depot. They had to design a safety project to reduce accidents while meat was being unloaded and transported. (The company was handling about one hundred tons of meat per day.)

The group started its project by collecting information on the current status of accidents. Since no systematic means of

Scare Report

Name:_____

Supervisor:_____

1. When:

   Month _____ Date_____ Hour_____ Minute_____

   Where:

   What happened:

2. *Kaizen* Ideas

   If you have good ideas, please write them down

———————————————— ◆ ————————————————

1. This is how I dealt with the problem.   Date_____

   This is how I am going to deal with the problem.   Date_____

2. I cannot deal with the problem for the following reasons.   Date_____

FIGURE L(1).   A typical scare report form used in a Japanese *gemba*.

Scare Classification (Safety, Transport, Quality, Energy, Resources, TPM, Production, Others)

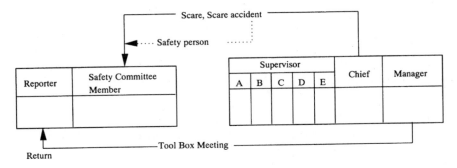

Scare Report
Toolbox Meeting Report

When	Date: _____ Before work During work After work During break		
Where			
Who & what			
What happened	(Major indication of trouble) 1. Almost got fingers caught 2. Almost got stuck 3. Almost got hit 4. Almost got cut 5. Almost got burnt 6. Other -		
Why	- -		
Superior opinions and instructions	- Countermeasures adopted Countermeasures not (People, *gembutsu*, or both) adopted yet (To be implemented by)		
Participants	Person in charge: Process: Leaders, etc.: Name:		

FIGURE L(2).   A typical scare report form used in a Japanese *gemba*.

collecting data existed at that time, only post-1993 data could be found. The group determined that 52 percent of accidents resulted in skin bruises, 33 percent in cutting injuries, and 15 percent in other types of injuries.

To gain a better understanding of the situation, the group members held brainstorming sessions aimed at defining the causes of the most frequent accidents. They designed a scare report for operators to submit during the following four weeks every time they were frightened by near accidents, creating a database for analysis.

Such scare reports are often used to report close calls in Japanese *gemba*. (See Figures L(1) and L(2) for typical examples.) The number and types of scare reports filed during the four weeks at Tres Cruces are shown in Figure M. Based on these findings, the *kaizen* group was able to identify major accidents and their frequencies and to plot them on the Pareto chart (Figure N).

Once the group became familiar with the nature and frequency of accidents, it was able to analyze possible causes. The team developed a cause-and-effect diagram, shown in Figure O.

KAIZEN ACTIONS

As a result of the findings, the *kaizen* team at Tres Cruces took the following ten actions:

1. Repair the electric hoist.
2. Ask supplier to quarter carcasses before shipment instead of doing so inside the truck.
3. Ask supplier to send pork after cutting the heads off the carcasses.
4. Shut the pork chamber's door while unloading beef carcasses.
5. Give operators safety devices such as shock-absorbing safety helmets.
6. Replace electric hoist's hook.

SCARE REPORT

PERIOD / SCARE	1st Week	2nd Week	3rd Week	4th Week	Total	%
Pork carcasses fall	///	////	/	‖‖‖	14	9
Cutting injuries	‖‖‖ //	‖‖‖ ////	‖‖‖ ‖‖‖	‖‖‖ ‖‖‖	36	24
Beef carcasses fall	‖‖‖ ‖‖‖ /	‖‖‖ ////	‖‖‖ ‖‖‖ /	‖‖‖ ‖‖‖ /	42	27
Frozen raw material falls	///	‖‖‖	‖‖‖	‖‖‖	18	12
Slide on truck floor	///	////	//	‖‖‖	14	9
Beef carcasses hit	//	//	///	/	9	6
Beef carcasses displaced	////	///	//	///	12	8
Other	///	/	//	//	8	5
Total					153	

FIGURE M. The number and types of scare reports filed at Tres Cruces over a four-week period.

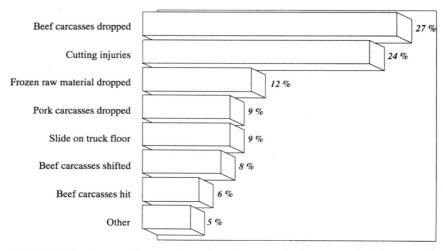

FIGURE N.   Pareto diagram identifying the types of major accidents at Tres Cruces over a four-week period according to frequency.

7. Attach protective cover to the unloading dock.
8. Improve method of cleaning floors.
9. Eliminate carcass-cleaning operations inside the refrigerated truck.
10. Use a portable conveyor belt to unload fat, muscle, and boned beef from the refrigerated truck.

The drop in the number of scare reports submitted since May 1994 has been a good indicator of the success of this project. (See Figure P.)

STANDARDIZATION

As part of the *kaizen* effort, the following items or procedures at Tres Cruces were standardized:

- The scare report
- Quartering of carcasses by the supplier
- The procedure for cleaning the sector's floor
- The use of the conveyor belt

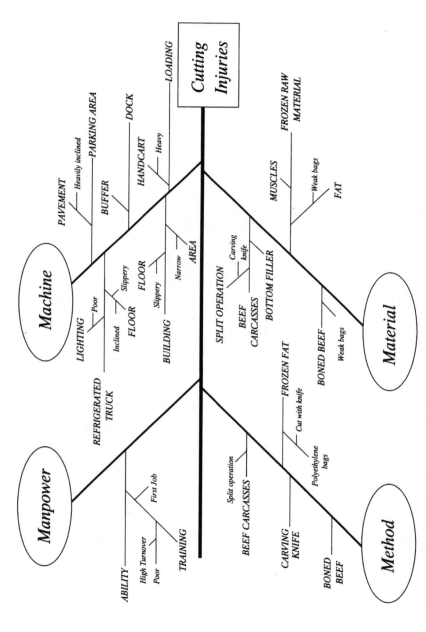

FIGURE O. "Fishbone" cause-and-effect diagram showing the nature of and relationship between accidents at Tres Cruces.

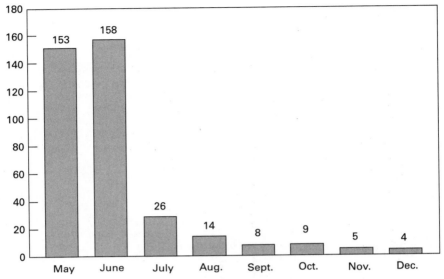

FIGURE P.   This chart illustrates the dramatic drop in scare reports at Tres Cruces.

SUBSEQUENT STEPS

The *kaizen* project was followed up by the following actions:

- Study of the feasibility of an overhead conveyor system.
- Study of the feasibility of unloading frozen fat directly into the cold storage chamber.
- Modification of the layout in order to improve reception of beef at the chamber

FINDING THE ANSWERS WITHIN *GEMBA*

Managers tend to look to outside sources for solutions. For instance, when faced with safety problems like those at Tres Cruces, management tends to turn to an outside safety expert for remedies.

However, the managers at Tres Cruces were able to solve

their company's safety problems almost entirely on their own by following *gemba-gembutsu* principles and collecting data. I firmly believe that managers can find the answers to most of the problems facing them—and in fact already have solutions at their fingertips—if only they take the trouble to collect the necessary data by involving *gemba* people and asking "Why?" until they reach the root causes of the problem. They can then come up with countermeasures for each cause and implement them.

As the Tres Cruces example demonstrates so clearly, once management becomes serious about making improvements, starts collecting data, and commits itself to continual follow-up, the employees themselves gain an enhanced recognition of the problem and become enthusiastic about finding solutions and doing a better job. At Tres Cruces, this was evidenced by the sudden drop in the number of scare reports.

Kaizen is contagious. The improvement registered by the team at Tres Cruces' raw material receiving depot, which reduced accidents by 79 percent in 1994, had an immediate impact on another group, the meat deboning department, which reduced accidents by 60 percent during the first half of 1995.

In the course of these *kaizen* activities, people at Tres Cruces gained many valuable insights:

- Priority should be assigned in selecting *kaizen* projects; the receiving depot and the deboning department had the worst records in the plant and the highest occurrences of accidents.

- Employees worked hard on the project continuously throughout the year and realized that continuity was one of the conditions for their success.

- Employees realized that lack of data and the unreliability of existing data were the major barriers to embarking on *kaizen*. All accidents that had occurred in the previous year had to be checked, one by one, and a system to collect data by tracking every future accident had to be developed.

- All workers were involved, trained, and motivated to work on the project.

- The team started to work on the problems closest to its heart (accidents), creating expectations and concerns that were fortunately resolved early in the game.
- Seeing how seriously management dealt with industrial safety instilled a sense of trust in workers.
- Management realized the importance of scare reports and taught employees how to use them to preempt problems.
- Having employees fully involved is very important in building initiatives; at Tres Cruces, workers were involved in naming major scares.
- Based on the findings at Tres Cruces, a new form was prepared for workers to refer to whenever they experienced a scare.
- The reports were checked weekly and the main causes of scares and accidents were identified, using Pareto diagrams.
- Accident-free periods of record length (167 days) were registered twice, once in 1994 and once in 1995.
- Better working conditions, accident reduction, and various other improvements registered during this period resulted in productivity improvements.

QUALITY IN
A MEDICAL CONTEXT:
INOUE HOSPITAL

Inoue Hospital in Osaka, Japan, specializes in hemodialysis. It has 22 doctors and 420 staff. Its hemodialysis division has 127 beds for hospitalized patients and 180 beds for visiting patients.

This is another case in which the collection of data (scare reports) has proved to be a crucial step toward improvement in the hospital environment.

SCARE REPORTS AS A QUALITY TOOL

In 1985, the hospital's director, Dr. Takashi Inoue, learned about scare reports being used in the manufacturing industry. The system requires that every time an operator in *gemba* witnesses a potentially hazardous situation, he or she must submit a scare report, which is then used as a basis for correcting the conditions that allowed the situation to arise. As the hospital was not immune to accidents, Inoue liked the idea of collecting data on scares to prevent an accident from actually taking place.

Often, scares happen as a result of somebody else's careless handling of the preceding tasks, and filing a scare report is tantamount to pointing the finger at someone else's mistakes. In introducing scare reports at the hospital, Inoue made it clear to everybody that the purpose of the report was to

273

assure the safety of the customers (patients), not to accuse colleagues who had made mistakes. Improvement of quality assurance was the main goal, and to do it, he said, everybody must be frank enough to admit mistakes. Otherwise, there would be no hope for improvement.

The hospital staff learned Heinrich's Law on Safety. Heinrich found that out of every 330 industrial accidents, 300 are accidents causing no damage, 29 are accidents causing minor damage, and 1 is an accident of grave consequences. (See Figure Q.) In order to avoid that one serious accident, Heinrich argued, both the total number of minor accidents and the total number of accidents causing no damage should be reduced.

Inoue Hospital classified its scare reports according to the categories in Heinrich's model, and standards were established. Scare reports at the hospital are now required in the following instances:

1. *Air:* If air has entered a patient's body during dialysis
2. *Hemorrhage:* If any hemorrhage over 10 ml has occurred
3. *Blood coagulation:* If the dialyzer circuit has had to be exchanged
4. *Leakage:* If any rupture has taken place

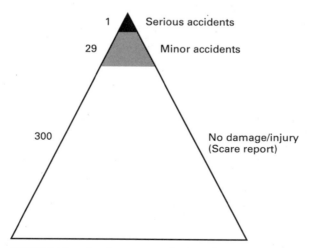

FIGURE Q.   An illustration of Heinrich's Law on Safety.

5. *Wrong medicine or wrong shots:* If any incident in which the wrong medicine or solution has entered a patient's body has occurred, even if it has not caused any harm

6. *Wrong sequence in withdrawing the needles:* If the needle has been withdrawn completely from the body, even when hemorrhage has not resulted

7. *Circuit malfunction:* If the dialyzer has needed to be replaced

8. *Water release:* If water has been released in any amount 500 grams more or less than the stipulated amount, or if it has taken 30 minutes longer than expected

Scare reports must be submitted every day, and this tool has greatly enhanced the safety awareness of the nurses and paramedical staff.

In the early days, the people responsible for causing the scare would ask, "Who reported it?" Sometimes doctors themselves were heard asking this question. But over time, everybody at the hospital has come to accept the scare report as a daily routine and a way to review and improve everyday work processes. Most problems arise from a failure to follow the correct procedures. Scare reports therefore help staff to review their own working procedures.

For instance, a nurse once tried to give a *hemo*static shot to a patient. The patient said, "I don't usually get any shots." When the nurse checked the record, she found that the patient was right. This scare happened because this was the first time the nurse had worked on this particular patient, and she did not get all the pertinent information from the previous nurse. Normally, mistakenly giving a shot of hemostatic agent does not constitute a serious accident, but at Inoue Hospital, it must be classified as an accident. A scare report must be submitted, and a measure to prevent recurrence must be devised.

The reports are assembled at each nurses' station and submitted to management every day. Every month, management compiles the reports and sends a summary to the staff. Each department must implement countermeasures right away and report them. If the solution is more complicated and will require more time, the subject must be taken up by the hospital's quality circles as a joint task.

Other examples of scares reported at the hospital have included the following:

- At the time of starting the dialysis, the artery chamber was found empty. This was due to the failure of the priming.
- The heparin switch was not turned on; this problem was discovered on the second check. Fortunately, no blood coagulation had taken place.
- After the hemodialysis, the needle was pulled out in incorrect sequence and a slight hemorrhage occurred.
- The wrong solution for continual injection was delivered, but this mistake was discovered before the solution was used.

The following table shows the incidence of dialysis problems at the hospital.

YEAR	NUMBER OF DIALYSIS PROCEDURES	WATER RELEASE MARGIN OF ERROR	BLOOD COAGULATION ACCIDENTS	HEMORRHAGES
1991	63,522	88 (0.14%)	21 (0.03%)	27 (0.04%)
1992	72,082	109 (0.15%)	55 (0.08%)	34 (0.05%)
1993	73,240	147 (0.20%)	75 (0.10%)	14 (0.02%)
1994	71,792	105 (0.15%)	49 (0.07%)	17 (0.02%)

In 1993, the hospital had a total of 839 scare reports in the following categories:

Wrong medicine or injection	41%
Water release	23%
Blood coagulation	17%
Air inclusion	10%
Hemorrhage	9%

QUALITY CIRCLES

Another feature of *kaizen* activities at Inoue Hospital is active quality circles, which were begun in 1983. This table shows how the number of quality circles at the hospital has grown over the years.

YEAR	NUMBER OF CIRCLES	NUMBER OF STAFF INVOLVED
1983	10	127
1985	18	132
1990	23	282
1995	41	429

The main subject areas addressed by quality circles are, in order of the number of projects: quality, efficiency, safety, and cost. A total of 189 projects have been completed since the first quality circle was organized.

Other topics addressed by the quality circles of the hospital have included the following:

- Improvement of clinical diagnosis forms
- Improvement of fail-safe switch for blood pump to catch abnormalities in dialysis apparatus
- Elimination of dosage mistakes
- Reduction of waiting time for dialysis
- Elimination of switching mistakes in the air-detection apparatus
- Optimum inventory of drugs
- Reduction of X-ray film loss
- Reduction of mistakes in serving special dietary meals

In order to evaluate the hospital's effectiveness, management always works hard to collect information from the following sources:

- Patients' claims
- Patients' remarks at the time of leaving hospital
- Review by a third party
- Countermeasures against an accident
- Cases in which death was involved
- Specific patients' symptoms
- "Hot mail" from patients to the hospital director

The hospital encourages its staff to experience medical treatment from the patient's perspective. In 1994, 16 nurses underwent hemodialysis, one administrative staff used a wheelchair, two secretaries tried laxatives, and one clerk underwent an examination by stomachic camera. The following remarks are from employees who underwent such experiences in 1995:

- Nurse A: "I underwent the experience of getting hemodialysis as a patient. I was expecting the pain of having the needle in the vein, but when I had to stretch my arm for three and a half hours, the muscles around my shoulder and elbow ached badly, and this was the hardest part. As I couldn't use my right arm, it was not easy to have a cup of tea and lunch lying on the bed."

- Nurse B: "I am right-handed, and as the needle was attached to my right hand, I had to eat with my left hand. I was unable to eat the Chinese food and could only eat rice dumplings, and I was very hungry. I was anxious to know who would be attending me as my nurse and hoped that it would be someone good at injecting the needle painlessly. Normally, when I am acting as a nurse and I hear the patient say something like that, I feel upset as I am always trying to do my best."

- Nurse C: "When I was lying down on the bed, I felt very uneasy. I suppose the patient feels the same way. I was very relieved when the nurse came to me and said, "Are you OK?" When you take off your white uniform and lie down on the bed, you feel very feeble. From the bed, people standing by you look very tall, and the doctor looks really great! It's a different feeling from what you get as a nurse. Everyone looks great from the bed. So, I think we shouldn't talk to them as if we are looking down upon the patients."

- Nurse D: "It seems that some patients hesitate to call a nurse even if they know the nurse well enough. It will be better if we can anticipate such needs and go to patients' beds without being called. I feel that they should not hesitate to call us but think we should take the initiative of calling them."

- Administrative staff member: "I have experienced sitting in the wheelchair. I found that the button on the side of the elevator was too high and inconvenient to push. We never had such a complaint from the patients, but when unattended, the patient will have to ask someone else to help."

In addition to gaining firsthand experience as patients, staff members are encouraged to experience working in areas outside their usual jobs. This helps them to better understand how business is conducted in other departments and assists them in building cross-functional teamwork.

TIGHTENING
LOGISTICS AT
MATARAZZO

Matarazzo of Molinos Rio de la Plata Company, a member of the Bunge & Born group in Argentina, is a manufacturer of fresh and dry pasta and other products. The company delivers its finished products to the group's distribution center, located five kilometers from the plant.

This case shows that a great improvement in the logistics management was registered by collecting data, observing operations in *gemba,* and using a commonsense approach to solve problems.

Before the company embarked on its *kaizen* project, deliveries took place between 6 a.m. and 6 p.m. every day; total time for each delivery (including loading at the plant, transport on the road, unloading at the distribution center, and returning to the plant) averaged about three hours. Six or seven trucks made a total of 10 to 14 journeys per day. Moreover, delivery personnel were usually required to work on Saturdays, as they could not meet all the daily requirements between Monday and Friday.

As the loading and unloading operations required the driver to step on the product in order to cover and uncover the pallets containing the product, goods were often damaged. Creating another bottleneck was the fact that the trucks had to be weighed four times—twice at the plant and twice at the distribution center (once when empty, once when full). To eliminate such logistical inefficiencies and optimize the operation, a *kaizen* group was organized.

Six months after the *kaizen* project began, the company found it needed only two trucks and four to six trailers, and daily working time was reduced by seven hours, to 11 hours. The operation time per truck was reduced by 22 minutes (an 88 percent improvement) and the cost per load was reduced by 35 percent.

The company achieved these results through the following *kaizen* activities:

- In the new procedures, a truck picks up a loaded trailer at the plant, travels to the distribution center, leaves the loaded trailer there (to be unloaded), picks up an empty trailer, drives back to the plant, and leaves the empty trailer there. The driver then picks up a loaded trailer and returns to the distribution center.

- The distribution center has designated two unloading docks for Matarazzo's exclusive use.

- Trailers have been fitted with structural roofs and sliding curtains, eliminating the need for the drivers to step on the product.

- A display board has been installed to show the weight of each truck and trailer. It includes all possible combinations, so that the loads only need to be weighed once, rather than twice, at each location.

The time saved by these improvements has made it possible to increase the daily number of trips per driver from one to five. And employees no longer have to work on Saturdays.

THE NEXT STEP: *KAIZEN* ON THE SUPPLIER SIDE

Shortly after the new procedures were in place, employees from the logistics and operations departments formed a group that included quality control and production people from each department. As the subject for *kaizen,* the group chose lead-time reduction of supplier service. Because of inadequate preparations at the plant to receive deliveries, the loading and unloading lot was perennially congested, resulting in an average service time of 3.5 hours. The *kaizen* team set out to bring the time down to under two hours. Toward this end, the group focused its work on the following items:

- Designing a schedule for receiving supplies in order to eliminate bottlenecks and allocate support personnel efficiently.
- Advising suppliers on how to improve delivery scheduling.
- Prioritizing suppliers by grouping them into critical and noncritical categories based on business requirements.
- Setting time targets for completing the unloading task and giving prompt service to suppliers who complied with those targets.
- Monitoring the time expended for each task and the suppliers' time inside and outside the plant.

Six months after the project began, and after 18 group meetings, supplier service time came down to an average of 70 minutes. Encouraged by this achievement, the group set a new goal: to reduce service time to less than an hour.

Stepping up their cooperation, several sections of the company produced a report on the time expended for each event (supplier arrival, waiting time outside the plant, unloading attention time, and time of departure from the plant). The suppliers welcomed this information because it enabled them to exercise precise control over their own transport, especially the contracted freights. The data also encouraged suppliers to abide by the agreed-upon scheduling.

Two months later, supplier service time had dropped to 45 minutes. As soon as the second goal was achieved, the group devoted itself to standardizing tasks and collecting data in order to stabilize, control, and maintain the target values they had achieved. Finally, as an alternative to manual data gathering, with all the cross-checking that entailed, the group developed a database application that allowed instant access to information such as activities carried out, classification by input and supplier type, service time, comparison with programmed events, etc. The database allowed the group to produce different kinds of reports, summaries, and graphs, depending on its needs.

KAIZEN EXPERIENCE AT ALPARGATAS

The largest manufacturer of textiles and sports shoes in Argentina, Alpargatas is a joint venture partner of Nike, USA. The company's sport shoe division produces different lines at four plants with annual sales of $200 million. The Tuchman plant, where the *kaizen* effort was undertaken, is dedicated to producing Nike shoes (two million pairs per year).

This case illustrates two aspects of *kaizen*. First, the company's *kaizen* team chose one of the most serious quality problems in *gemba* as the focus for improvement and discovered that, in addressing the quality issue, they had also found the best way to reduce costs. Second, the team members strictly followed the eight steps of *kaizen* (known collectively as the *kaizen* story), as suggested by the *kaizen* consultants and found that following these eight steps helped them achieve their target.

The *kaizen* story is a standardized format to record *kaizen* activities conducted by small groups like quality circles. The same standardized format is employed to report *kaizen* activities conducted by staff and managers. The *kaizen* story includes the following steps:

Step 1: Selecting a theme. This step addresses the reason why a particular target has been chosen for improvement. Targets are often determined in line with management policies. Their selection is also based on the priority, importance, urgency, or economics of the circumstances.

Step 2: Defining the goal.

Step 3: Understanding the current status. The members of a *kaizen* team must understand and review current conditions before starting the process. Going to *gemba* and following the five *gemba* principles is one way to do this. Collecting data is another.

Step 4: Collecting and analyzing data to find the root cause.

Step 5: Establishing and implementing corrective countermeasures and actions.

Step 6: Evaluating.

Step 7: Establishing or revising standards to prevent recurrence.

Step 8: Reviewing the process and starting work on the next steps.

The *kaizen* story follows the plan-do-check-act (PDCA) cycle. Steps 1 through 5 relate to *P* (plan); Step 6 to *D* (do); Step 7 to *C* (check); and Step 8 to *A* (act). The story format helps anyone to solve problems based on data analysis and enhances visualization of the problem-solving process. It also provides a way to keep a record of *kaizen* activities. *Kaizen* stories based on data analysis use various problem-solving tools to help the participants understand the *kaizen* process.

Kaizen was first applied at Alpargatas in June 1994 by a pilot team made up of production, industrial engineering, and technical staff. Two operators were also assigned to the team to work on *kaizen* projects on a full-time basis. The team's target areas for improvement were related to raising the product quality of Nike shoes to meet the company's stringent quality standards.

The project posed two challenges. First, the issue of craftsmanship had to be addressed, since producing shoes involved many manual operations. Second, the failure of many previous quality-improvement efforts had produced a high level of employee skepticism, which had to be overcome.

The team, which was assigned to work on the project on a full-time basis for three months, met formally once a day, with informal meetings throughout the day as the flow of work demanded. The *kaizen* consultant joined the team for three full days per week, and, at the beginning, led and coordinated the whole process. After a few weeks, the company *kaizen* coordinator began to lead the group, while the consultants guided the team in the use of the *kaizen* story and *gemba* approach. During the three months, the team worked on solving two main problems: excessive glue and heel quality. The remainder of this case history focuses on their work in the latter area.

Step 1, Subject Definition. Assembly Quality at the Heel. Assembly quality at the heel is one of the most important determinations of footwear quality. During the most recent quality audit, an American shoe consultant has pointed to heel assembly quality as the most urgent problem to be solved. To accomplish the desired improvements, the *kaizen* team chose minifactory Number 1, which conducted cutting, stitching, and back-part molding operations.

Step 2, Goal Definition (see Figure R).

Step 3, Current Situation (see Figure S).

Step 4, Cause Analysis (see Figure T). When the analysis began, few members of the pilot team expected that their work would eventually involve activities in other departments, such as upstream processes (stitching, cutting, and

Indicator	Defects %		Improvement %
	Current value	Target value	by 7/18/94
1. Assembly margin	37	7.5	80
2. Counter position	19	4.0	80
3. Counter centering	27	5.5	80
4. Flatness	33	6.5	80
5. Opening	54	11.0	80
6. Heel centering	23	5.0	80
7. Neck Position	47	9.5	80
8. Average defects % at back-part molding exit	34	7.9	80

FIGURE R.   *Goal definition.*

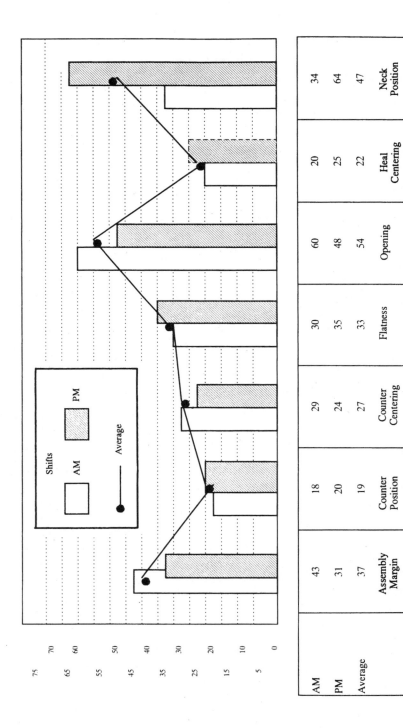

	Assembly Margin	Counter Position	Counter Centering	Flatness	Opening	Heal Centering	Neck Position
AM	43	18	29	30	60	20	34
PM	31	20	24	35	48	25	64
Average	37	19	27	33	54	22	47

FIGURE S. Current situation.

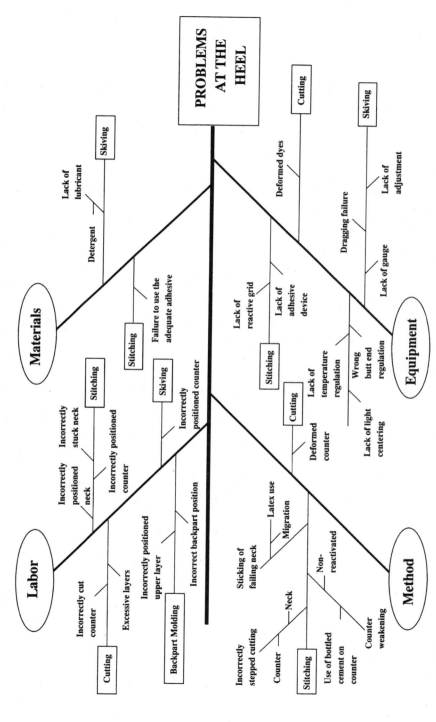

FIGURE T. Cause analysis.

289

counter-skiving) as well as maintenance, product development, and design. The analysis showed that the adhesive material that glued the counter to the heel actually deteriorated the counter material, causing inconsistency in the quality of the bond between the counter and the heel.

Step 5, Corrective Actions (see Figure U).

Step 6, Evaluation [see Figures V(1) and V(2)].

- To implement new methods, it was sometimes necessary to modify operator's working positions, build new tables, modify existing ones, and develop additional devices and tools.
- Throughout the project, the supervisor of the sector—a member of the pilot group—was consulted. He took part

PROBLEM	CAUSE	ACTION
Inadequate skiving	Lack of dragging at skiver	• Verify sharpness, speed-advance relation, belt tension
	No gauge for skiving width	• Verify original gauge
	Lack of detergent	• Establish minimum stock level
Inadequate cutting	Overlapped cutting	• Operation control - instruction manual
	Cutting greater number of layers than stipulated	• Operation control - instruction manual
	Deformed die	• Modify die height • Redesign not to allow sharp corners • Change to forged material
Inadequately positioned counter-stitching	Doesn't meet 6 mm. standard	• Train workers • Develop standard gauge
Inadequately positioned neck	Doesn't meet 9 mm. standard	• Train workers • Develop standard gauge
Inadequate blast counter	Heating temperature not meeting standard (maximum 80° C)	• Use adequate heating device • Discontinue use of additional glue • Reactivate glue on counter
Glue wasted at neck dumping	Inadequate mixture of glue in use	Define appropriate glue
Inadequately positioned heel in back-part molder	Heel is not centered Doesn't butt at back-part molding	• Place centering light • Regulate butt to between 12 & 15 mm. • Adjust centering faces to standards
Inadequate definition of heel border	Lack of temperature regulation	• Verify three times per shift
Inadequately positioned heel	Wrong reference points	• Redesign parts
	Wrong use of references points	• Train workers

FIGURE U. Corrective actions.

Indicators	Initial Value	Target Value	July Value
Assembly margin	37%	7.5%	7.6%
Counter position	19%	4.0%	5.6%
Counter centering	27%	5.5%	2.0%
Flatness	33%	6.5%	4.0%
Opening	54%	11.0%	9.5%
Heel centering	23%	5.0%	1.0%
Neck Position	47%	9.5%	8.1%
Average defects %	34%	7.0%	5.4%

Average values for July '94

FIGURE V(1).   Evaluation.

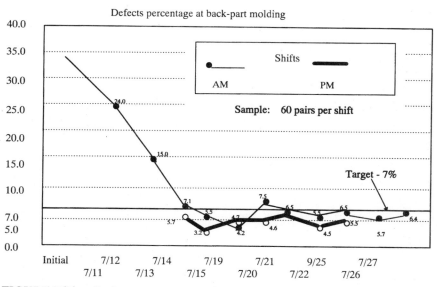

FIGURE V(2).   Evaluation.

in the *kaizen* process, followed up on the learning curves, and supported the implementation.

• The supervisor helped maintain close communication between the *gemba* workforce and the *kaizen* group, which allowed the workers to adapt to the new methods.

• The group prepared the instruction sheets as the basis for worker's training. This brought about consistent operations in both shifts.

- A checklist including points of adjustment was placed at the back-part molder machine, which shapes the shoe heel. This enabled workers to adjust the machine when deviations were observed.

Step 7, Addressing Problems and Preventing Recurrence. The team installed a control chart for indicators, and workers prepared instruction manuals. The team then introduced checklists for product quality and failures and management disseminated the new standards throughout other affected sectors.

Step 8, Follow-Up. Transfer these experiences to the remaining areas of the plant and contact other glue suppliers.

GENERAL OBSERVATIONS AND REFLECTIONS

The team members methodically followed the eight-step *kaizen* cycle and *found* that these steps helped them to undertake the problem-solving process in the right sequence. They also learned that using such tools as fishbone diagrams and Pareto diagrams helped them to work on the project in a systematic and orderly manner and to find solutions more readily. Furthermore, the eight steps helped them detect opportunities for future *kaizen*.

- The new work method paved the way for a subsequent project: implementing the one-piece flow of just-in-time production in the neck-dumping operations.
- This project identified many additional checkpoints.
- Team members found that having data greatly facilitated communication between supervisors and workers.
- The new method minimized glue waste.
- Along with quality improvement, productivity improved in the neck-dumping and counter-placing operations.
- Standardizing operators' tasks provided a standard for doing the job and facilitating training.

- Initially, the outside shoe consultant suggested that the back-part molding machine currently in use was obsolete and unfit for use. The completion of the project revealed that that machine was reliable with adjustments and maintenance.

Savings

The *kaizen* activity in the pilot area saved 34,000 Argentine pesos per year. Applying the same procedures to other areas engaged in footwear heel assembly forecasts total savings of 225,000 pesos per year. (The Argentine peso maintains a one-to-one exchange ratio with the U.S. dollar.)

Senior Management Support

The success of this project owes much to the support of senior management in several ways:

- Holding the initial training course and meeting
- Participating in group work meetings and getting involved in the details of the discussion
- Participating in formal presentations of the work done by the team and encouraging its members to keep up their good work

KEEPING AN EYE ON THE DATA: INFOTEC

The business of Infotec in Italy is to distribute copier and telefax equipment and supply consumable and technical services. While the company already had measures in place to check the performance of its service representatives before 1993, it was not until that year that management became serious about collecting and analyzing data on the company's servicing activities as a basis for improvement.

This is a case where data collection plays a key role in managing the behaviors of employees in the business of distributing copier and fax equipment and supplying consumable and technical services.

Infotec headquarters in Milan developed several control points as major criteria to check the quality of its services:

1. *Number of service calls* (the total number of service calls each service representative makes to customers on a daily basis)

2. *Number of callbacks* (the number of daily cases in which the service rendered by a service representative was not adequate and the service representative had to go back for rework)

3. *Number of returns to fit* (*RTFs*) (the number of daily cases in which the equipment broke down or the service rep could not complete the task at the first call, due to lack of spare parts or insufficient knowledge to fix the problem, and had to return to the customer's site later)

4. *Response time* (the interval between the time the customer called for help and the time of a service representative's arrival)

5. *Productivity* (the number of "good calls"—calls completed each day on the first visit without either callbacks or RTFs)

A supervisor, overseeing about ten service reps, reviews each representative's performance based on the above criteria and carefully coordinates their activities for maximum productivity.

Every year, management sets a target to be achieved by the service representatives for each item. The targets differ from area to area, reflecting the different sizes of the area to be covered, the amount and kind of equipment installed, and the number of service engineers assigned in each area. For instance, the target response time for the Milan branch for 1996 ranged from eight to ten hours. The target for callbacks and RTFs as a percentage of total service calls was 15 percent for 1995.

A good measure of a service representative's productivity is good daily service calls. For instance, when a service representative makes eight calls a day but half of the calls require follow-up for such purposes as readjustment, the number of good calls is actually only four. Currently, at all of Infotec's operations in Europe, the daily target for good calls is set at 4.5.

Since the company began collecting data on service activities, the response time of service representatives has been as follows:

1993	13 hours
1994	14 hours
1995	12 hours

The fluctuations in response time do not necessarily reflect the productivity of the service representatives. In 1994, for example, the number of service representatives was reduced, while more machines were installed. Nonetheless, every service representative is aware of the existence of targets, and makes every effort to become more efficient. For instance, in the early 1990s one representative used to be responsible for servicing an average of 100 copying machines; today, each representative takes care of 150 machines.

Various systems have been developed to collect data. Supervisors have the crucial role of collecting and analyzing data for better productivity and customer satisfaction. For instance, thanks to information on used parts, the stock of parts carried in the service person's car has been greatly reduced. Grid charts used by the supervisor have made it possible to keep track of the stock of parts down to the level of the individual service representative. Following are some examples of supervisors' involvement in collecting data. The supervisor must:

- Accompany service representatives on customer calls at least five times a year with a checklist in hand.
- Analyze monthly the RTFs caused by parts that were not available and adjust the stock of the parts kit carried in cars. For good parts returned, the supervisor must identify causes and prepare training programs.
- Review the service representatives' zones quarterly in order to optimize travel time.

A supervisor's performance is assessed in light of the targets achieved as well as inventories and the stocking of the representatives' cars. An incentive plan for supervisors has been introduced.

Vittorio Neri, Infotec's technical service manager, says that the various data Infotec has been able to obtain have helped the company establish a clear vision for better resource allocation and decision making. He says that converting numerical data into visual form—for example, into trend graphs and bar graphs—helps to improve understanding by everyone concerned.

Figures W and X demonstrate the difference between showing numerical data in tabular and visual formats. Figure W shows the number of daily calls, callbacks, and RTFs and the percentages for each service person in the branch, for example. While looking at the table of the original data did not yield much insight into what was happening, it became apparent,

NAME	Giorni tec.	Ore field %	Tot. interv.	Tot. att.	att. ripa.	Richiamate	Rimandate	Rich. ripa.	Rimand. ripa.	nette gg.	Rich. %	Rimand. %	Rich. & rimand.	T. risp.	Costo per int.
1	198.80	78.56	843	1,177	1,115.30	142	31	124.40	30.70	5.67	11.15	2.75	13.91	11.70	11.887
2	174.09	75.86	775	967	1,011.40	161	73	173.40	77.70	5.24	17.14	7.68	24.83	13.61	15.791
3	198.88	79.66	650	936	1,103.30	144	67	180.30	86.30	5.04	16.34	7.82	24.16	12.47	31.579
4	192.48	84.96	882	1,007	1,000.50	173	37	163.80	35.10	4.94	16.37	3.51	19.88	16.42	17.970
5	189.19	74.75	953	1,157	1,242.30	335	115	370.40	128.90	4.91	29.82	10.38	40.19	6.47	25.691
6	53.74	28.39	220	261	274.25	46	6	53.00	6.40	4.76	19.33	2.33	21.66	14.23	17.864
7	181.00	80.98	676	882	967.00	171	67	189.50	78.70	4.66	19.60	8.14	17.74	11.80	24.915
8	187.76	81.35	700	974	911.10	108	77	97.10	75.40	4.66	10.66	8.28	18.93	15.43	18.076
9	205.19	77.28	629	1,053	999.10	175	55	167.70	55.50	4.51	16.79	5.55	22.34	0.82	8.071
10	191.63	78.75	755	987	980.20	150	116	151.80	125.70	4.43	15.49	12.82	28.31	11.56	19.642
11	183.26	72.57	880	1,093	995.40	287	65	278.40	61.20	4.39	27.97	6.15	34.12	7.99	16.291
12	192.31	84.84	736	900	983.30	178	81	198.60	92.40	4.37	20.20	9.40	29.59	10.61	16.712
13	164.38	52.87	433	698	781.10	118	46	134.00	54.70	4.32	17.16	7.00	24.16	11.54	21.033
14	139.35	71.41	595	718	725.90	163	66	166.50	71.90	4.28	22.94	9.90	32.84	6.35	21.897
15	205.31	90.91	736	941	974.05	149	77	160.10	82.00	4.28	16.44	8.42	24.85	13.81	25.186
16	181.41	82.50	725	881	955.40	199	97	218.50	111.90	4.24	22.87	11.71	34.58	11.24	24.485
17	197.20	77.84	744	1,028	942.30	206	80	202.70	83.70	4.04	21.51	8.88	30.39	18.10	20.359
18	195.75	80.82	571	765	901.00	127	79	150.60	96.70	4.03	16.71	10.73	27.45	10.39	23.887
19	181.88	76.27	684	905	858.30	189	63	194.50	63.40	4.01	22.66	7.39	30.03	11.40	29.213
20	157.06	67.63	524	751	728.50	140	72	136.90	74.70	3.99	18.79	10.25	29.05	9.50	14.438
21	194.44	83.64	626	908	965.90	174	169	187.30	183.20	3.81	19.39	18.97	38.36	13.97	22.172
22	192.38	86.38	724	857	840.83	182	55	183.10	53.20	3.80	21.78	6.33	28.10	11.76	19.818
23	55.13	32.43	202	256	256.90	63	21	65.20	21.40	3.79	25.38	8.33	33.71	14.07	19.426
24	199.69	77.24	765	932	924.20	225	91	224.50	91.20	3.74	24.29	9.87	34.16	10.43	21.150
25	183.86	61.67	656	934	874.40	202	133	190.70	131.90	3.71	21.81	15.08	36.89	9.60	23.188
26	204.63	82.21	728	888	888.20	191	76	192.20	75.40	3.68	21.64	8.49	30.13	11.82	20.577
27	204.66	80.68	740	896	931.30	206	91	221.00	97.60	3.68	23.73	10.48	34.21	9.48	15.350
28	176.50	78.38	632	842	805.70	203	110	195.10	105.40	3.55	24.21	13.08	37.30	12.51	28.046
29	193.66	77.12	687	929	763.70	184	57	154.40	51.40	3.47	20.22	6.73	26.95	14.35	10.333
30	191.31	81.28	613	788	793.00	136	113	136.60	124.20	3.40	17.23	15.66	32.89	11.19	27.372
31	141.41	57.22	469	570	596.50	112	80	118.90	86.90	3.40	19.93	14.57	34.50	12.05	21.420
32	186.76	73.22	641	827	681.70	122	75	104.30	68.40	3.27	15.30	10.03	25.33	9.74	21.356
33	206.34	79.61	675	881	792.10	189	84	171.20	75.30	3.22	21.61	9.51	31.12	11.78	17.134
34	176.50	65.84	610	827	665.80	195	60	164.20	51.20	3.12	24.66	7.69	32.35	10.24	13.413
35	194.90	77.12	698	999	704.40	184	80	140.00	62.80	3.12	19.88	8.92	28.79	8.00	16.069
36	174.90	76.43	804	1,035	713.40	276	100	205.00	72.80	3.10	28.74	10.20	38.94	9.89	24.897
37	35.75	58.73	106	130	137.80	31	14	33.00	14.60	3.10	23.95	10.60	34.54	8.26	15.574
38	197.19	74.09	656	982	705.00	194	67	151.20	50.40	3.09	21.45	7.15	28.60	9.91	21.688
39	169.76	74.73	659	851	620.60	190	63	156.80	47.40	3.00	25.27	7.64	32.90	9.82	34.445
40	196.36	77.05	592	861	608.40	199	110	152.00	82.40	2.37	24.98	13.54	38.53	13.26	25.780

FIGURE W. Tabular presentation of Infotec data.

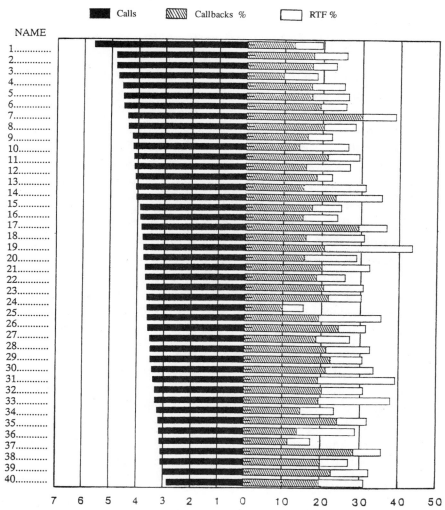

FIGURE X.   The tabular presentation of Infotec data converted into a bar graph.

when the data were converted into a bar graph (Figure X), that those with a high ratio of good daily calls are the ones who had low percentages of both callbacks and RTFs. This is why management added the combined percentages of both callbacks and RTFs as one of the control points.

Says Vittorio Neri:

One of the lessons learned from the *kaizen* seminars within Infotec was the value of collecting and making good use of data. We learned that merely storing and computing data was not enough, and that we had to analyze and put data to use. However, data must be converted into visual forms; otherwise, not everyone can understand them by merely looking at the numbers. So, we had to make the data as visible as possible. We asked our EDP people to submit data in graphs as much as possible. It is not an easy job, but we keep trying it.

Kaizen stresses personal involvement and continuous improvement. After *kaizen,* we introduced Bill Conway's statistical approach, and learned how to make good use of statistics. All these activities require commitment, extra work, and unending effort for continuous improvement. However, Italians are not the same as the Japanese. We are not so self-disciplined. Since we have other priorities as well, often we forget *kaizen* and lose momentum.

For these reasons, the fact that we obtained the ISO 9000 certification in July 1995 has been very beneficial, since it calls for an official review of the standards every six months, a reminder that we have to keep trying to do a better job all the time. You might call it an external pressure. I believe we need the three of them—the *kaizen* way of thinking, the statistical approach, and the constant external pressure—to review the standards.

SUPPORT FROM TOP MANAGEMENT: FIDELITY INVESTMENTS

One of the most difficult aspects of introducing and implementing *kaizen* strategy is assuring its continuity. In my public seminars I often ask the audience, "Why is it that when a company introduces something new, such as quality circles, a suggestion system, or total quality management, it experiences some initial successes, but soon such successes disappear like fireworks on a summer night and after a while nothing is left, and management keeps looking for a new flavor of the month?" And I answer my own question by saying, "This is because the company lacks the three most important conditions for the successful introduction of *kaizen* strategy. The first condition is top management commitment. Unless top management is committed, and renders full support, nothing will succeed." "The second," I begin, then pause a moment and watch out of the corner of my eye as members of the audience pick up their pens to write down my words in their notebooks. I finish my sentence by saying, "is top management commitment." By then, they stop writing and begin to smile. When I end by saying that the third condition, too, is top management commitment, the room fills with laughter.

When I mention these three most important conditions, I am in fact serious, as I know that nothing gets done without top management commitment, particularly when a corporate culture change is at issue. The successful introduction of *kaizen* strategy involves setting up an organization dedicated to promote *kaizen,* appointing the best available personnel to manage the *kaizen* process, conducting training and education, and establishing a step-by-step process for *kaizen* introduction. However, without top management supporting every move, the trial will be short-lived regardless of other preconditions. Time after time I have seen middle managers take enthusiastic initiatives to introduce changes, only to fail in the long run because of lack of top management support.

Top management may express commitment in many different ways, and it must take every opportunity to preach the message, allocate resources for successful implementation, and become personally involved in following up the progress of *kaizen.* The case of Fidelity Investments shows how top management consistently played its role in bringing about this process of change.

Fidelity Investments, founded in 1946 to manage a single mutual fund named Fidelity, has created more than 220 other mutual funds over the years, becoming the largest and best-known mutual fund manager in the United States. Fidelity is also the leading provider of retirement plan services to corporations, and the nation's second-largest discount brokerage firm. The firm is privately owned by the founders' family and current employees.

Fidelity's practice of *kaizen* began with the company's chairman and CEO, Edward C. Johnson III. A long-time student of eastern philosophy and religion, Johnson became interested in Japanese management practices, and in the 1980s he discovered *kaizen.* "*Kaizen* means," he said, "that if you sweep the building, you always want to try to do a better job—and in a shorter time." But he had never before considered applying the philosophy to his company as a basic way of doing business. Johnson took every opportunity to communicate his belief in *kaizen* to Fidelity employees. Many leading newspapers and magazines such as *USA Today* and *Fortune* magazine reported his leadership in this area. The corporation's 1987 annual report contained the following message from the chairman:

> The idea of *kaizen* is interesting and useful. For example, it advocates gradualism. Revolutionary breakthroughs are rare, but everyone can make minor improvements in their work. If the effort to make these small improvements is sustained over time, great progress will result. Those who wait for thunderbolts from heaven may never progress at all.
>
> *Kaizen* also suggests that every aspect of a business needs to be improved. No area is unessential. Each can be a competitive strength—or a competitive liability.
>
> This is how Fidelity has been built. It is the product of years of effort spent developing many skills, incorporating many professions. We are the market leader because of this long-standing and comprehensive diligence.
>
> We cannot lose sight of this process. If gradually, little by little, you and I continue to pile improvement upon improvement, we will develop an overwhelming collective strength. The sustained force of your talents, constantly evolving, can help Fidelity purge inefficiencies, hold on to our gains, and build on our very considerable strength.

The cover of the annual report included the two Chinese characters for *kaizen*. And in the annual report for the next year, the chairman wrote the following message:

> You may have heard people speak of an idea that the Japanese call *kaizen*. *Kaizen* is a practical way for us to go about achieving our corporate goal.
>
> The idea is sometimes described as "making small, incremental improvements in all areas of the company over an extended period of time." That's part of it, but there's a good deal more. *Kaizen* involves:
>
> • Identifying our corporate goal and the standards that define it
>
> • Measuring progress toward the goal
>
> • Raising standards after old standards are routinely met

- Recognizing problems and needs, rather than denying them, so they can be addressed
- Listening closely to customers and treating our fellow employees like customers
- Gradually improving all processes, operations, departments, and professional areas
- Working together, across department and company lines, to ensure that quality and service goals are met
- Developing employees and helping them to develop themselves, so they can help meet our gradually rising standards

These principles made Fidelity the company that it is. Our past is a record of gradual building and improvement in many areas, each and every one making a vital contribution to the collective effort.

Our future is being built now, in departments throughout the company, by people with the energy and honesty to try to improve their own performance. Executives, managers, and individual contributors are all involved. They display the Fidelity spirit, they keep alive our tradition of progress.

Fidelity fundamentally believes that employees practice *kaizen* most enthusiastically when they feel a deep sense of ownership in their work. Fidelity fosters this feeling of ownership by dividing power in the company among small divisions (each called a company) with aggressive, entrepreneurial leadership. Each of these Fidelity companies is responsible for its own management systems, its own strategies and activities—and its own results.

This focus on results is far more important inside Fidelity than any concern for corporate rules or organizational bureaucracy. "Anybody at Fidelity who has discovered a way to improve the business gets the same level of support and respect—whether they're a company president or a frontline representative," says Johnson. "We value good ideas and constant forward momentum here—not titles and ranks."

Fidelity works hard to create an environment of continuous improvement as a normal and accepted part of everyday life.

Beginning with corporate orientation sessions on their first day at Fidelity, employees receive the clear message that they are responsible for continuously improving their daily work performance. They see a videotape that explains the origins and meaning of the *kaizen* philosophy at Fidelity, and they hear senior managers talk about how their future success within the corporation depends on being creative and proactive in making Fidelity's business better overall. One part of many orientation segments is a game in which new employees can begin to practice *kaizen* in an easy, entertaining way, and start to understand how to apply the philosophy to their own new jobs.

In 1995 Fidelity began to publish a corporate newspaper, called *The Fidelity Exchange* that often features articles and photographs about people who have made improvements in their work. A recent newspaper article contained this request:

> You probably know of many times when the practice of *kaizen* resulted in noticeable improvements at Fidelity. We'd like to hear your stories and plan to publish parts of them in future issues of *The Fidelity Exchange*. Mr. Johnson will host a special lunch for six storytellers later this year.

Fidelity's commitment to *kaizen* is reflected in its performance management and compensation systems. Each fall, Fidelity companies establish business goals for the coming business year. These goals are tiered through the company's various divisions and departments down to the individual manager level. Although Fidelity has no corporate requirements about the format and content of these goals, at least half of them tend to focus on improvements in existing products or processes, rather than on the creation of new ones. Progress toward goals is evaluated and adjusted on a monthly and quarterly basis. At year-end, employees receive bonuses that—depending on their compensation package and their success in implementing *kaizen*—could range from 10 percent to over 100 percent of their base salary.

Fidelity defines *quality* as "How we organize, operate, evaluate, and continuously improve all aspects of our business to maximize customer satisfaction and profitability over the long term." Corporate management promotes *kaizen* by a small staff of people who work full time to assure that employees hear the continuous improvement message on a regular basis. This department, which Fidelity calls Corporate Quality, supports Fidelity's commitment to organizational learning. Fidelity actively benchmarks its competitors and continuously studies the best practices of many other companies in service and manufacturing industries. Fidelity has also made a major commitment to benchmark the best practices within its own divisions and business units and to ensure that information and learning is easily available to other groups.

In 1994, for example, Fidelity appointed a full-time vice-president-level executive to help the corporation's many telephone service centers learn from each other. This executive coordinates communications and airing of best practices for some 12 phone centers located in nine cities around the world (and representing six different Fidelity companies). Her role is to ensure that technology, training, measurement systems, and business processes that are improved at one site are immediately transferred to all other appropriate sites. The phone centers also work together to improve the quality of Fidelity's phone service overall.

The sharing of best practices happens in a number of other ways as well. An informal network of *kaizen* teachers from Fidelity's various business units—and collectively called the Quality Support Council—has been meeting monthly since 1989 to share information and experiences with one another. This group has been responsible on an informal basis, for guiding many of the cross-corporate improvements at Fidelity, including the development of a problem-solving model called STRIDES. This model provides employees in every part of the corporation with a common language and process for implementing *kaizen*. As stated in Fidelity's *Models for Quality Improvement*, STRIDES is the approach to use "when the problem is more complex. . . .":

S—*Situation:* "Where are we now?"

T—*Target:* "Where do we want to be?"

R—*Research:* "What research do we need?"

I—*Implementation Plan*: "What is our plan?"
D—*Do it!*: "Let's do it!"
E—*Evaluate*: "What's working? What's not?"
S—*Standardize*: "How will we standardize?"

Fidelity also leverages the fact that it has thousands of representatives on the phone every day talking with customers—and getting good ideas from them. Through a system called the Value Network, Fidelity gives its phone representatives a tool for providing the organization with unsolicited customer feedback. Representatives are encouraged, but not required, to submit issues they recognize as relevant by recording customer suggestions and requests into a central voice-mailbox, using an autodial button on their phones. These comments are transcribed and passed along to the managers responsible for various aspects of Fidelity's service. The transcriptions are also analyzed by a central quality staff and discussed at monthly executive meetings to make decisions about improvements that cut across functional and organizational lines. The following table shows real-life examples of the Value Network in action.

When Representatives Reported That:	Fidelity Took This Action:
• Customers were having trouble understanding the format of brokerage trading confirmations.	• Redesigned the confirmation and provided guidance for representatives in explaining the new format to customers who called.
• Customers were concerned about a mutual fund's performance.	• Quickly (within three hours) distributed to all phone representatives an explanation of the ways in which market activity was affecting the fund's performance. Phone reps were thus able to provide customers with more complete and helpful information.
• Customers complimented Fidelity on an improvement in its telephone service.	• Sent a message to all telephone representatives thanking them for their participation in the improvement.

PROCESS MEASUREMENT AND IMPROVEMENT

One of the ways in which Fidelity practices the philosophy of *kaizen* is through process measurement and improvement (PMI). Using PMI, many of Fidelity's customer service and transaction processing areas have developed checklists of criteria to measure for each critical business process.

PMI is an ongoing program that measures work quality and looks for ways to improve Fidelity's business processes, supporting its efforts to continually improve the quality of products and services delivered to customers. The heart of PMI is team-based involvement and accountability for process improvement. The program focuses on improving work processes rather than on the quality of work done by individuals and is an adaptation of the statistical process control commonly used in manufacturing. PMI is an initiative that requires each operating department to:

- Identify its work processes
- Establish criteria for measuring accuracy, completeness, and consistency of work and/or the amount of time to complete work
- Train all staff to sample work
- Have staff, selected at random, take and evaluate random samples of work daily and record results weekly on departmental PMI process control charts
- Investigate root causes of abnormal performance
- Conduct other efforts to improve the work process on an ongoing basis.

PMI is as much a cultural change as a set of techniques. At its heart is a philosophy of promoting team-based involvement and accountability for quality. Some of the key elements of that philosophy are:

- No inspection/verification staff. Once they are trained in their jobs, all staff sample and measure work, because all staff are involved in the process of producing the work.

- Work is measured at the group or process level. We are looking at the work the way the customer sees it, and customers don't care who did the work.

- Any staff member can call a meeting if he or she has reason to believe that the group has crossed its action lines or if he or she spots a problem that is affecting the quality of the group's work.

- Fix the problem, not the blame. PMI data is used to identify problems and to improve group performance. We don't focus on who did it; we focus on what the problem is and how to fix it.

- Charts and data must be consequence-neutral. No individual feedback is tied to PMI and nobody is ever criticized or punished for reporting negative results.

- Improvement targets are not dictated by the corporate office. It is up to each group to: (1) set its own improvement goals; (2) use the data to identify its biggest problem areas; and (3) change its work process to address these areas.

The PMI checklist for customer correspondence is as follows:

1. Was the letter time-stamped?

2. Was the item entered into Fidelity's tracking system on the same day it was time-stamped?

3. Did a representative receive the letter within 24 hours of the first Fidelity time-stamp?

4. Did we call the customer the day we received the letter? How many days did it take for us to make initial contact with the customer?

5. Were all escalation procedures followed?

6. Did we provide our name, phone number, and expected time frame to the customer in our first communication to him or her?

7. If we did not meet the first expectation we gave to the customer, did we call the customer back and reset expectations?

8. Did we take appropriate action on behalf of the customer every day toward resolution of the customer's issue?

9. Did the core process take five days or less?

10. How many days did it take for us to complete the process?

11. Were all our actions documented in our tracking system?

12. Did we internally identify, address, and answer all of the corporate issues raised by the customer problem?

13. Were all the customer's questions or issues answered/ addressed?

14. Were all adjustments made to the customer's account correct?

15. Were regulatory compliance procedures followed by the representative?

16. Did we take advantage of all opportunities to dazzle this customer?

17. If appropriate, did we follow up with the customer and document action taken to complete this follow-up?

18. Was all documentation coded correctly?

PROCESS REDESIGN

Fidelity also employs the philosophy of *kaizen* to redesign its business processes. The following table shows Fidelity's process redesign model:

• Use customer feedback to identify top sources of dissatisfaction (or opportunities).	• Assign a team to each process that needs to be redesigned. Give the team special sponsorship and resources.	• Develop and implement improvements in an expedited time frame. • Use measurements to continually improve the process.

One notable success story is the redesign of the process through which customers transfer money from other financial institutions to Fidelity. Making this process quick and easy for customers is a big priority for the Fidelity. The transfer of money into Fidelity is the beginning of the customer's relationship with the firm, and any delays or cumbersome paperwork could create a very negative first impression. Customers regularly reported frustration with the transfer-of-assets process, so Fidelity put it on its priority list for process redesign.

The redesigning of the process began with gathering and analyzing the top sources of customer dissatisfaction. The data was gathered from comments made by customers via Fidelity's phone and branch representations (captured by Fidelity's Value Network), complaint letters, and face-to-face visits. The data revealed nine areas of dissatisfaction; these were dubbed "The Nifty Nine."

Fidelity assigned a team of senior managers to redesign the transfer-of-assets process. The team established the following objectives:

- To make Fidelity's transfer-of-assets process transparent to the customer, so that he or she may make purchase decisions based solely on Fidelity's products and services without being influenced negatively by a difficult or cumbersome transfer-of-assets process.

- To offer the best customer service and assistance in the industry during the transfer-of-assets process, so that the customer's experience with Fidelity is preferable to experiences with other firms.

The team began its work by benchmarking the best and worst practices of its competitors. It used this information—along with a lot of customer feedback—to establish new customer-focused service standards. It then began to measure performance against these standards, zeroing in on the areas where it discovered the biggest performance gaps.

The team undertook a variety of major improvement initiatives, including:

- Establishing better initial communications with customers to assure that their expectations matched current realities

- Developing relationships with the customer's previous custodian to help speed the transfer process along
- Improving the accuracy and timeliness of transfer requests initiated by customers in branch offices
- Ensuring accurate and consistent ongoing communication to customers and Fidelity representatives
- Increasing efficiency through the use of technology and streamlined processes and practices
- Establishing a process management team to ensure ongoing accountability for the continuous improvement of the transfer-of-assets process.

Within a year, the team had achieved spectacular results. General customer complaints about Fidelity's transfer-of-assets process had declined more than 75 percent. Customer letters to Fidelity's chairman complaining about the process had dropped from almost 15 percent of total volume to virtually nothing.

"Every person at Fidelity is responsible for continuously improving the quality of the service we provide our customers and the efficiency of our internal operations," says Ned Johnson. "If we are to maintain and improve our leadership position within the financial services industry, we must get better and better at finding opportunities to improve. The biggest threat to our success doesn't come from our competitors: it comes from us. We can never stop getting better. Complacency is our enemy."

A FOCUS ON TRAINING: *KAIZEN* AT LUCAS AUTOMOTIVE

This case shows detailed schedules of training programs and their subject matters as well as *gemba kaizen* seminars and workshops conducted within the first few years of the company's journey to *kaizen*.

Lucas Automotive GmbH, located in Koblenz, Germany, produces drums, disk brakes, boosters, ABS-systems, and other automotive components. As of 1995, the plant had 1800 employees, including part-timers. In September 1994, Dr. Günter Schiele, the company's managing director, decided to introduce *kaizen*. Accordingly, he developed a master plan to introduce basic knowledge of *kaizen* to the company during a four-month period in 1994, to provide in-house trainers with an in-depth education on the subject in 1995, to extend this education to general employees in 1996, and to keep up the momentum of continuous improvement thereafter. As Figure Y shows, a kickoff in September 1994 introduced *kaizen* to the company. In 1995, the company developed in-house *kaizen* trainers—employees with the know-how to lead the change process by themselves. It extended *kaizen* training to general employees in the latter half of 1995 and into 1996.

Ten *gemba kaizen* workshops and six seminars were given during the introduction period of four months in 1994. (See Figure Z.) The *Kaizen* workshops usually lasted three to five

LUCAS KOBLENZ | *KAIZEN* Master Plan | Date: Feb. '96
Name:

| 1994 | 1995 | 1996 |

Sep | Oct | Nov | Dec | Jan | Feb | Mar | Apr | May | Jun | Jul | Aug | Sep | Oct | Nov | Dec | Jan | Feb | Mar | Apr | May | Jun | Jul | Aug | Sep | Oct | Nov | Dec

Kickoff
19 Sep. '94

Introduction

Education of trainers

Education of employees

Continuous improvement

KAIZEN team

Aim: To teach basic knowledge of *KAIZEN*

- What does *KAIZEN* mean
- What kind of philosophy *KAIZEN* embodies
- How to work with *KAIZEN*

Aim: Education of LUCAS *KAIZEN* trainers

- The trainers are able to teach all kinds of seminars and workshops without any help from the outside consultant

Aim: Education of employees

- Realization of *KAIZEN* activities in different seminars and workshops

Aim: Concentration on continuous improvement in small steps

- Continuous improvement by our employees under the leadership of our supervisors
- Concentration: 5S and reduction of changeover time
- Introduction of audit system
- Activation of QC - groups

Aim: Support of our *KAIZEN* groups by a permanent *KAIZEN* team for quick realization of improvement

General Overview

Lucas

FIGURE Y.   A general overview of Lucas Automotive's *Kaizen* Master Plan.

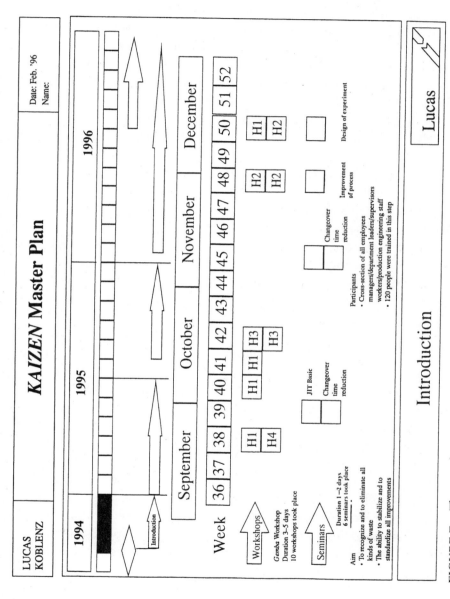

FIGURE Z. The introductory phase of Lucas Automotive's *Kaizen* Master Plan.

days at designated areas in *gemba*. After receiving introductory instruction on the first day in such subjects as the seven types of *muda*, *takt* time versus cycle time, pull production versus push production, and one-piece flow, the participants were assigned to do *kaizen* within the designated area. They often made dramatic changes in such ways as reducing the number of operators, inventories, and lead time, or changing the layout. These workshops helped participants see how much room for improvement existed in their workplace.

The seminars, meanwhile, set out to equip participants with the problem-solving tools they would need to cope with problems arising in the course of *gemba kaizen*. The subjects included how to recognize and eliminate all kinds of *muda*, how to stabilize and standardize improvements, and how to reduce changeover time. The last seminar, held for engineers in 1994, addressed the subject of design of experiments. About 120 people participated in the 1994 training sessions at Lucas Automotive.

In the first half of 1995, the company began educating internal *kaizen* trainers, to carry on the momentum even when the *kaizen* consultants had become less involved. (See Figure AA.) Eight people of various backgrounds (including *kaizen* coordinators, production support people, and employees from the logistics, quality, and maintenance support departments) were selected as internal trainers. Of the five workshops given in 1995, one concerned changeover time and another TPM. The subject matter covered in the seminars was also expanded to include 5S, JIT basics, *kaizen* basics, visual management, TPM, and problem solving.

Once the internal trainers had become familiar with *gemba kaizen*, they began leading seminars and *gemba kaizen* sessions themselves. During 1995, the newly trained *kaizen* experts gave fifty workshops and seminars; they also held a special seminar for sixty foremen and supervisors. In this manner, some four hundred employees of Lucas Automotive underwent *kaizen* training in 1995. During the same year, management also instituted monthly *gemba* audits.

In the latter half of 1995, various *kaizen* activities involving employees took place. (See Figure BB.) Some special topics were added to seminars, and the monthly *gemba* audits

KAIZEN Master Plan

LUCAS KOBLENZ				

1994 **1995** **1996**

Education of trainers

Week	1	2	3	4	5	6	7	8	9	10	11	12	13	14	15	16	17	18	19	20	21	22	23	24	25	26

January February March April May June

H1
H3
Gemba WS

H4
Gemba WS

H3
Gemba WS

Workshops
Duration 1–5 days
6 workshops took place

5S
JIT Basic
KAIZEN Basic
Visual Management

Changeover time reduction

Seminars
Duration 1–5 days
6 workshops took place

Preparation for workshops

T P M
T P M
Problem solving

Audits
Duration 1 day
7 audits took place
8 people were instructed
Duration of education: 40 days

- KAIZEN coordinator
- 4 production support people
- Logistic department
- Quality department
- Maintenance support department

During the instruction of the trainers, nearly 50 workshops and seminars (5S, TPM, changeover time reduction) took place under the leadership of our trainers
Duration of the workshops: 1–2 days

60 supervisors and foremen were trained in a separate KAIZEN basic seminar
Duration 1 day
6 seminars took place

Participants:
- Supervisors/foremen/workers
- 200 people were trained in this
- step

Education of trainers

Lucas

FIGURE AA. The education of trainers in Lucas Automotive's *Kaizen* Master Plan.

317

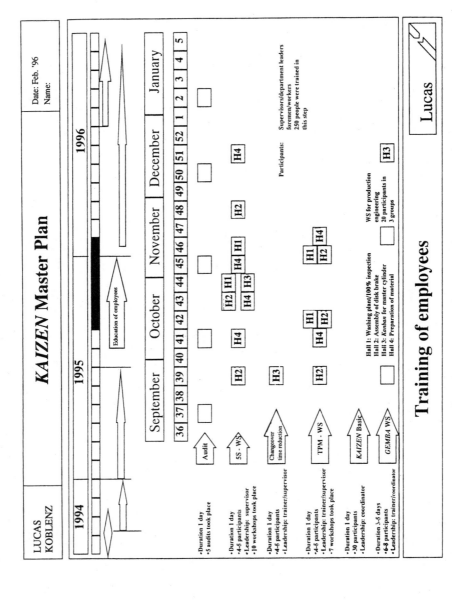

FIGURE BB. The training of employees in Lucas Automotive's *Kaizen* Master Plan.

continued. The targets for *gemba kaizen* became more specific to accommodate the specific needs of *gemba*. Examples of targets included 100 percent inspection in the washing plant and wheel cylinder assembly and effective use of *kanban* (production order slips) in the master cylinder area.

Figures CC, DD, and EE show the layout changes and

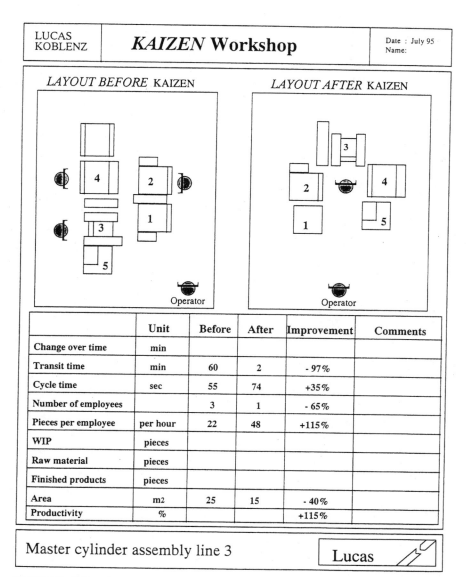

FIGURE CC. Layout changes and resulting improvements in the Master Cylinder Assembly Line 3 following the *kaizen* workshops at Lucas Automotive.

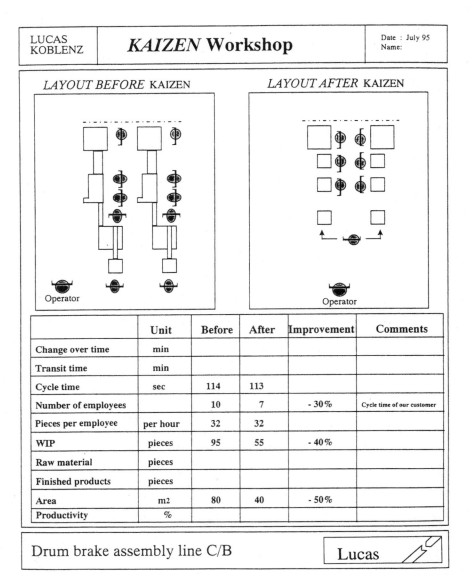

	Unit	Before	After	Improvement	Comments
Change over time	min				
Transit time	min				
Cycle time	sec	114	113		
Number of employees		10	7	- 30%	Cycle time of our customer
Pieces per employee	per hour	32	32		
WIP	pieces	95	55	- 40%	
Raw material	pieces				
Finished products	pieces				
Area	m2	80	40	- 50%	
Productivity	%				

Drum brake assembly line C/B   Lucas

FIGURE DD. Layout changes and resulting improvements in the Drum Brake Assembly Line C/B following the *kaizen* workshops at Lucas Automotive.

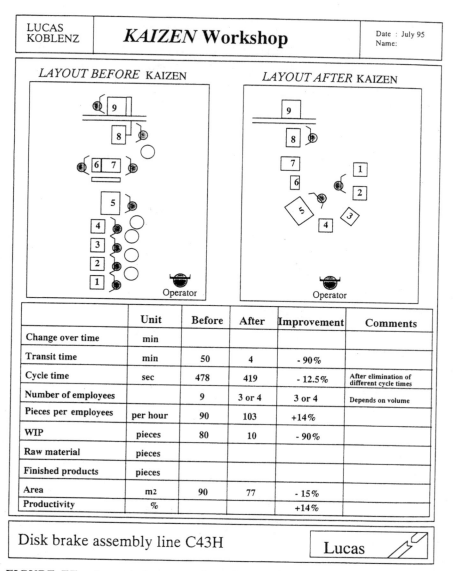

	Unit	Before	After	Improvement	Comments
Change over time	min				
Transit time	min	50	4	- 90%	
Cycle time	sec	478	419	- 12.5%	After elimination of different cycle times
Number of employees		9	3 or 4	3 or 4	Depends on volume
Pieces per employees	per hour	90	103	+14%	
WIP	pieces	80	10	- 90%	
Raw material	pieces				
Finished products	pieces				
Area	m2	90	77	- 15%	
Productivity	%			+14%	

FIGURE EE. Layout changes and resulting improvements in the Diskbrake Assembly Line C43H following the *kaizen* workshops at Lucas Automotive.

improvements made as a result of *kaizen* workshops at Lucas. At the disk brake assembly line C43H, for example, the number of operators was reduced from nine to three or four. This was due to the fact that the layout of the previous line was designed to meet the highest volume of demand. The new line shows that the number of operators can fluctuate between three and four to meet changing orders from the customer.

KAIZEN AT AN INSURANCE COMPANY: LA BUENOS AIRES

In this case a strategic goal was established by management first, and then various *kaizen* activities followed to achieve the goal. When a companywide strategic goal is established, it helps everyone to recognize the need to do *kaizen* in his or her own area.

La Buenos Aires (LBA), a leading Argentine insurance company, defines its business as offering services to the customers—not selling insurance to them. LBA's mission is "always to be with the customers in the moments they need us most."

To realize its mission and enhance its competitive edge, LBA adopted a strategy in 1987 called 24-Hour Service. This service calls for LBA to be with its customers in their moments of crisis, when they most need help. Depending on the circumstances, the 24-Hour Service may provide firefighters, private guards, medical care, towing or mechanical assistance, legal council, or other help to clients.

A second strategy, launched by LBA in 1988, is known as Jet-Claim, because it offers payment of claims on the same day. People who have incurred losses—even well-insured people—are always uncertain as to whether they will receive sufficient compensation to cover their losses. Jet-Claim brings the customer peace of mind by paying up to 70 percent of the total amount of a claim on the day the claim is filed. LBA was a pioneer among Argentine organizations in introducing these two features. The company's management believes that, even to this day, no other insurance company offers payment within 24 hours, and that LBA is probably the only company that cuts its checks before a claim has been processed.

FROM SERVICE IMPROVEMENTS TO *KAIZEN*

After adopting these groundbreaking strategies, LBA embarked on various other *kaizen* activities. LBA thus offers an interesting case of a company that first introduced corporate strategies and *then* carried out *kaizen* activities to achieve the strategies. In the process, LBA became one of the most successful companies in Argentina.

PAVING THE WAY FOR SAME-DAY PAYMENT

When the company's management agreed upon the idea of offering same-day payment in 1987, one of the managers asked if any obstacles existed to implementing this strategy. One of the members of the automobile claim department answered, "Our problem is that it takes 48 hours for the authorization department to tell us if we can pay or not." The manager then asked a person from the authorization department how long it actually took to verify this procedure. The answer? "No more than 15 minutes."

As a result, the authorization department agreed to verify every document in 15 minutes. In the past, claim documents had piled up in the in-basket for needlessly long periods of time. To make this and other new strategies work, a series of reorganizations and transformations changed LBA from a conservative and traditional organization to a modern one. This included such things as the latest data-processing system. The company set out to achieve zero defects and dramatically reduce time in the operating processes. For LBA, doing *kaizen* to realize the corporate strategies turned out to be a very exciting experience.

WHEN TRAGEDY STRIKES: LBA IN ACTION

On March 17, 1992, a bomb exploded at the Israeli Embassy in Buenos Aires, causing damage to five city blocks and resulting in a claim that amounted to nearly $50 million. That very night, LBA offered emergency services (providing rooms in hotels or private homes) to its clients via its 24-Hour Service. On the following day, employees in charge of claims and liquidation organized a task force and set up an office near the site to offer such services as debris clearing. Estimates of losses were made immediately after the incident, and the claims on fixed amounts were paid promptly on the same date. Where on-the-spot appraisal was difficult, advance payments were made.

THE COMPETITION HEATS UP

Due to the liberalization of the Argentine economy in 1993 and the ensuing entry of international companies, LBA's competitive environment, in terms of both price and commission, became very intense. Even in the face of this increased competition, however, LBA's performance remained outstanding in all key areas such as liquidity, property solvency, public image, innovative business policies, and constant improvement of products and services.

To remain competitive and maintain its leadership position, LBA set out to reduce fixed costs. To do so, it consolidated its Buenos Aires operations, brought in a new computer system, and imposed strict controls on operating costs. The company thus reduced its staff by nearly 15 percent, resulting in a productivity increase of 35 percent per person.

The company's 24-Hour Service proved to be a major customer draw. During the space of one year, the company settled 20,000 claims, amounting to over $69 million. And by continuing to focus on client service, diversifying into different client segments, and establishing offices throughout the country, LBA maintained its standing as a leading insurance company in Argentina in 1994. As a result, LBA—working jointly with the main insurance producers of the country and international brokers—offered insurance to more than two dozen newly privatized companies.

Establishing a computer network enabled the company to better communicate with its offices all over the country. This, together with a revamping of management procedures, cut management costs by 13 percent—one of the largest reductions ever achieved in the market. In this way, LBA achieved not only a per-employee productivity increase of 33 percent, but also an efficiency level compatible with the international standard. For its claims-paying ability, for instance, LBA achieved ranking in Category A by the country's rating service.

A *KAIZEN* SUCCESS STORY

On July 18, 1994, tragedy struck another of LBA's customers. The building occupied by AMIA (Asoc Mutual Israelita Argentina) was destroyed, killing 94 people and injuring 190. LBA responded as quickly as possible, not only with respect to the damage covered by the policy, but also in other areas that needed service. As it had done after the Israeli Embassy bombing, the company set up a service office at the site. The company covered 22 claims—many of which were anticipated thanks to the information provided by the systems department—that amounted to a total of between $1.3 and $1.6 million.

For an insurance company to set out to do something so ambitious as to make payment on the day a claim is filed requires tremendous internal discipline and *kaizen*. The following report by Fernando Coletti, quality and customer service project leader at LBA, illustrates some of the improvements that have taken place since the company began its ambitious program of changes:

In 1991, we analyzed customers' complaints (both internal and external) and identified specific areas of our operations that needed improvement most.

We formed improvement and follow-up teams and introduced an inspection system based on self-control, in which every employee was obliged to inspect 50 percent of his/her own work, such as preparation of documents. It encouraged competition in the quantity and quality of the task among the teams.

We realized that self-control was one of the most important parts of our staff's operations and redefined the role of our employee as a responsible holder of the task—no one knows the task better than the person himself/herself in charge of the task.

The items that we highlighted were:
• Delivery time of policies
• Mistakes in issuing policies
• Time of liquidation and payment of claims
• Low standard in telephone attention

We changed our perception of our business structure from that of an insurance company to one of a company that provides service to customers by selling and managing insurance. We had to understand that the customers, whether internal or external, determine whether we are providing the quality and improvement that they need. All this helped us to realize the problems that our clients faced.

Therefore, all we needed to do was to listen to the customers and identify the causes and processes which produced complaints or problems.

We realized that our employees had been carrying out their tasks as a daily routine, in an unstructured manner, with no standard and inspection of each process of their work.

One example was the policy-issuance department, which issues policies and assists in claims. The department was engaged only in the production and issuance of policies and could not provide any counseling on claims. Therefore, a new department, a client's service-management department, was created. This change was necessitated to focus on the client's various needs, not only with respect to the payment of the claims, but also rendering mechanical, legal counseling, towing, and counseling services to the insured.

As a result of a profound change that took place, we were able to break the preconception that job and quality are two different things.

The new inspection mechanism allowed us to correct, through constant self-inspection, the defects in the operation. This meant that each employee must be his or her own inspector.

We redesigned products that not only improved our business but were considered revolutionary in the Argentine traditional insurance market. Consequently, LBA has come to hold a preferred position since it is, in our country, the pioneer in the payment of claims in 24 hours.

This could only be achieved through self-inspection, solution of the problems, and continuous and steady improvements in results and introduction of new standards.

At first, it was difficult for LBA's employees to accept the idea of self-inspection since they considered it as an additional duty, and they already had many duties to fulfill. Initially, they felt that they were being watched over their shoulder but they became aware of the rule: *self*-control. Gradually, LBA's employees accepted the change and a spirit of competition in quantity and quality within the same team.

In order to standardize the operation, we incorporated "Duty Cards," and a culture of continuous improvement and productivity was imposed.

We could gradually reduce conflict areas and complaints, not only from the insured but also from producers and brokers. The producers and brokers were supplied with standardized information in order to sell our products. By this means, the middlemen became independent with respect to the sales operation, and consequently they had less doubt and required less advice. This allowed our staff to answer fewer inquiries and to increase and improve the production without interruption.

We achieved an outstanding result in the first internal audit carried out without advance warning in an issuance department, which showed an 83 percent improvement in the issuance and making of policies.

The second internal audit was conducted with advance notice and in this case showed a 92 percent improvement. By this means, the standards previously set were upgraded, improving the quantity and quality of the job as well.

Our staff are becoming aware of the important processes of our business, and are getting more involved in their contribution to the business and its results, because they are an important part of LBA. As central part of the operation, they are rewarded by a quarterly bonus which is granted by management to the responsible persons fulfilling their goal.

This involvement allows each member of LBA to present daily quality control suggestions.

Cooperative spirit, initiatives, anticipation of future problems, and control have become household words in LBA.

In the wake of these successes, LBA invited me to give an overview of *kaizen* to its executives. The subject was how to assure continuous improvement and how to build a coherent system for that purpose.

When I visited LBA in 1993 and was shown around the office, I noticed that display boards were erected behind each working group, showing the daily and monthly individual production of insurance policies, quality levels, including mistakes and complaints from customers, etc., on the graph. The telephone operators also had a chart on the wall showing percentages of unfulfilled telephone calls from customers on the monthly basis. This was visible management of administration.

KAIZEN AT "COMPANY A" IN EUROPE

By Jean Labadie

Company A has a global strategy known as the Five Core Strategies. One of these Five Core Strategies is its production system, which includes production systems such as just-in-time (JIT) and total productive maintenance (TPM) based on the *kaizen* philosophy. During the last several years, Company A conducted many *kaizen* activities at its factory. Two cases illustrate its progress and learning experiences.

Kaizen at Company A is a vivid reproduction of the personal experiences of a manager when *kaizen* was first introduced into a company. These two cases give many insights as to why it is not easy to successfully introduce *kaizen*, and they describe a profound transformation of personal values that have taken place.

IMPROVING THE SCREWING OPERATION

The company builds cooling modules consisting of a radiator and fan for cars. One operation affixes fans to radiators with self-tapping screws. Three people perform this operation: two by manually feeding the screws and the third by using an automatic feeding machine. Before we improved this operation, many screws dropped on the floor around the workstations and even on the product itself. We began our 5S workshop with a simple target: to achieve and maintain zero dropped screws at the workstation at all times.

During the workshop we asked operators to collect all items on the floor and put them in a plastic bag. At first the operators were skeptical as to the usefulness of this exercise. As one said, "It's obvious that we're going to collect many screws!" However, we next asked the operators to count and sort the objects they had picked up. They found 145 screws. After a "five-times-why" session, in which the operators discussed the reasons these items had fallen on the floor and on the product, the situation began to improve.

As the result of a week-long *kaizen* project, no more screws were found lying around the workstations. But improvements went even further than that. The operators redesigned the box used to dispense screws for the manual feeding operation. The existing box made it difficult to grab the correct number of screws. Operators would therefore take out six screws when only four were required and place the extras on the surface of the radiator. After fitting the four required screws, the operator would return the extras to the box. This back-and-forth operation had been taking place one out of every three times.

To address this problem, the operators designed a cardboard box that made it easier to take out the correct number of screws. A week later, the cardboard box was replaced by a metal one. While the system was not perfect, the spirit of improvement had been sparked. The following Monday, an operator arrived with a prototype he had made from a matchbox that showed how he would like to receive the screws. A week later the prototype became reality, and the metal feeder was installed. This newly designed feeder box allowed employees to take out only the number of screws required. For the first time, everyone approved of the system, and as a result of this improvement:

- Quality improved because operators no longer had to place screws on top of the radiators
- Cost (i.e., productivity) improved because operators no longer had to pick up unnecessary screws

Another improvement concerned the automatic feeder. The operator was tired of collecting dropped screws at the end of the day; this spurred the process of improvement. One day in a 5S workshop, when the operators were sorting the screws and attempting to determine which ones were creating problems, they found that those with a wider diameter (out of tolerance) were blocking the feeding machine. So they fashioned a sifter by drilling holes in a plate. The result was breathtaking: stoppages of the automatic feeder dropped from 26 per shift to none, and productivity increased by 6 percent.

The purchasing department was called in and asked to have the supplier perform the sorting operations. The enthusiasm of the *kaizen* group exerted pressure on the purchasing department to tackle the problem immediately. Two weeks later, the improvement was stabilized, and three months later, it persists. In this area of our factory, management and operators alike keep gaining confidence, and we continue to initiate improvements every time we encounter a problem. The most important improvement, though, is the fact that our operators have become involved in *kaizen* activities.

In order to portray our *kaizen* process fairly, however, we must add that we appointed a full-time person to support this process. This person conducts *kaizen* sessions and helps operators generate ideas when they have difficulties. When there are specific problems to be addressed, we also allocate a three-hour session to *kaizen* activities every two weeks.

REMEDYING A LEAK ON THE QUARTER-TURN TAP

Our customers require a tap called a quarter-turn tap to purge the radiator. The tap consists of a seal fitted onto a screw which goes inside a molded form. Since 1987, our radiator tests have detected leakage problems accounting for a loss of 6 percent in the overall efficiency rate (OER) on the assembly lines. In March 1993, when we began a TPM workshop on the manufacturing line and asked operators to list major problems in performing their work, workers on all three shifts ranked the quarter-turn problem number one.

The engineering department claimed that this problem had been solved, yet the operators continued to encounter leaks. The quality department was also convinced that the quarter-turn tap was not causing the leaks and forbade the operators to manipulate the tap. Fixing the quarter-turn tap thus became a covert operation on the factory floor.

In January 1994, I spent a full week with the night shift. I happened to be present as an operator was fixing a leak. "When it is difficult to unscrew it," the employee told me, "the seal is generally pinched." About ten problems of a similar nature occurred that same night. By the end of the evening, I was convinced that there was a real problem with the quarter-turn tap.

I decided to bring the problem to the fore by quantifying it. We measured the unscrewing torque of all radiators coming out, whether they were good or not. The result showed a positive correlation of 86 percent between the unscrewing torque and the leak. But with the torque above a certain level, we could predict the leak 100 percent. In March 1994, the operators reported these findings to the shop floor that was producing the quarter-turn tap, the engineering department, the quality department, and the plant management. After three months, nothing had happened. To trigger action, we organized an observation meeting in which members of all concerned parties were invited to observe ten leaking radiators. The result was so obvious that all parties agreed to address the problem. Again, however, no one took the initiative to solve it because no one had the slightest idea how to do so.

At the end of June 1994, I investigated the problem further in the workshop that produced the quarter-turn tap. In my investigations I followed the simple axiom, "To understand the problem, create it." By producing the quarter-turn tap at an accelerated speed, we were finally able to reproduce the defects and thereby understand the underlying cause. It was only then that the organization took remedial steps.

In September 1994, a *kaizen* group was created. It started

with a reject rate of 7200 PPM and set an objective of 20 PPM. The group uncovered five major problems:

1. *Problems linked to process.* Dirt created leaks, and misalignment of the tools pinched the seal. These problems were solved within a month and at a cost of no more than $500. The defect rate dropped to 4500 PPM.

2. *Problems with some of the taps received from the supplier.* We were receiving taps with missing seals because the supplier was shipping assembled taps to us in the same cartons that had been used to ship nonassembled taps to the supplier. Unknown to the supplier, nonassembled taps were sometimes hidden in the corners of the boxes. We solved this problem by having the supplier use a separate box for each process, at a cost to the supplier of $50. The defect rate dropped to 2000 PPM.

3. *Problems linked to the size of the molded part,* both on our premises and at the supplier site. The supplier had two prints completely out of tolerance for every eight prints on the mold. Fixing this problem cut the defect rate to 700 PPM.

4. *Problems linked to the seal.* As the defect rate dropped, operators and technicians started to concentrate on new problems; for example, the seal was found to be scratched in some cases. Our supplier, who by that time was lending his full support to our improvement process, went to his own supplier. Our supplier is currently improving the process to guarantee a seal surface of a certain level of quality.

5. *Problems linked to design of the system.* We addressed these problems only after making improvements in the other areas. This was in line with the *kaizen* spirit of forcing the organization to improve its process *before* looking for new innovations that might require more time and money. We determined that the seal was in fact loose on the shaft, and a slight misalignment pinched the seal. In response, we changed the seal dimensions to be centered during the fitting of the quarter-tap turn. The defect rate dropped to 75 ppm on September 1995.

One of the causes for these problems had been a lack of information feedback. Leaks are identified only on the last operation of the assembly line, for instance, and the internal supplier of the line who fits the tap is not aware of his mistakes. One of the operators' first remedial actions, therefore, was to keep the operator constantly informed of the leaks. Although this helped reduce the defect rate, it was not enough. We have considered performing the tap-fitting operation on our direct assembly line (thus putting into practice the *kaizen* concept of customer-supplier relations) and have tested this concept. At this time, however, modifications are still in progress and no solution has yet been implemented, but we feel confident that our plans will help us achieve 20 PPM before December 1995.

This experience, although still in progress, has taught us many things, including:

- Operators on the floor can provide information and lead the organization to work on the real problems, enhancing overall quality and productivity.
- At least half the improvements can be made within our factory and virtually cost-free.

PERSONAL EXPERIENCES AND OBSERVATIONS

Typically when I meet with technical people to solve a particular problem, they start right away to talk about solutions. The moment the discussion becomes a vicious circle (usually about ten minutes into the meeting), I force myself to change the group's approach. This is often difficult, as our people are reluctant to spend time understanding the problem. This is where my determination and commitment are important. During my last two years of *kaizen* work, I have developed a personal approach to this problem.

Our people love new ideas; we often reinvent what others have done. So instead of stopping the employees in their tracks, I use *their* ideas, asking them, "What problems made you think of this solution?" or "What do you intend to improve with this solution?" From there, we go back to the problem, which we then analyze with "five-times-why" and classify using the Ishikawa diagram. We then proceed with the *kaizen* methodology. People always find it interesting to work this way. I think that is because everybody is given a chance to participate and build. Offering ideas is usually a privilege reserved for a few people, but in this case everyone is encouraged to participate.

Every time I work in a group—whether as a leader, a trainer, or a participant—I draw people in using the *kaizen* way. As I said before, it does not always go smoothly. The commitment of our CEO and his staff to implementing the Five Core Strategies has been the key to the success of our *kaizen* activities. Sometimes I have had to adopt a position differing from the plant management's. I have done so only because I knew my position was in line with the Five Core Strategies.

The most difficult part has been getting the plant management to practice the *kaizen* tools. My notes of March 1993 showed that one of the main reasons why *kaizen* took place so infrequently in our plant was management's failure to practice the *kaizen* tools. I believe that the underlying cause is social. *Kaizen* is first and foremost a group activity, and our school system places little emphasis on group activities. Performance usually relates to individual achievement. When managers here meet to discuss problems, therefore, they often exchange ideas on solutions rather than work together to determine the root causes. Today at our company, however, management is using these *kaizen* tools and finds them surprisingly effective, even in areas not related to production.

HOW DEVIATING FROM THE *KAIZEN* APPROACH HAMPERS PROBLEM SOLVING

As an aid to the process of *kaizen,* we use problem follow-up sheets provided by the Kaizen® Institute. The forms contain the date, the problem, the solution, the name of the person in charge of implementing it, the schedule, the due date, and the plan-do-check-act (PDCA) wheel. One day I received a revised version of this sheet showing the PDCA wheel with a big R in the middle. According to the explanatory key at the bottom of the page, this meant "Abandoned solution." This incident clearly illustrates a mind-set that focuses too much on producing solutions and too little on understanding the root causes of the problem. Even if we find that a solution is inadequate, simply abandoning it will not do because the fact remains that we have a problem. Before trying to find solutions, we must gain a better understanding of the problem.

I have participated in many Western-style problem-solving sessions. In these meetings, the usual method of choice is to find a quick fix to the problem. When a problem is identified, immediate action is taken. Analysis, and eventually the final solution, come only afterward. In the pamphlet used as a guide in such problem-solving sessions, action and follow-up typically constitute less than 20 percent of the diagram that depicts problem solving. As a result, people expend most of their energy in firefighting and forget about the aspect of the solution that emphasizes ensuring that the problem will not recur.

The PDCA approach, however, allows no firefighting; the root causes have to be addressed first. Addressing the root cause accounts for 75 percent of the PDCA problem-solving diagram. This has proven to be a key to success in our *kaizen* approach, although we believe we still have a long way to go on the A (act) of PDCA.

A SOCIOLOGICAL APPROACH TO PROBLEM SOLVING

In September 1993, during his effort to trigger attitudinal changes in the factory, our new plant manager reminded us of what a former supervisor had once said: "Weak people have problems; strong people have solutions." Discussing this comment with our plant manager, we realized that this idea was contrary to a sound *kaizen* approach. The old supervisor's approach encourages people to skip over analyzing a problem. It also heightens people's fear of problems. I once heard someone go so far as to say, "Unless I have a solution, I can't take up a problem." Now I tell our people, "So, you have a problem! That's a golden opportunity to improve!"

Some parts of our factory are improving more steadily than others; I believe this is because they practice improvement continuously. The section that assembles the cooling module is a prime example. This section is constantly improving on solutions. I believe that in order to enjoy sustained improvement in our operations, we need to practice the PDCA wheel every day. The PDCA wheel then behaves like a gyroscope, which maintains its equilibrium by turning steadily and rapidly.

HOW *KAIZEN* HAS CHANGED ME

The *kaizen* approach has changed me in many ways. The most visible change is the fact that I no longer have a desk. I have a filing cabinet on wheels. Two drawers hold my files, and two others hold my stationery and working files. My computer and printer sit on top of the cabinet. A ten-meter extension cord allows me to operate the computer and printer anywhere in the factory. This "desk," which moves with me to wherever problems exist, has many advantages. First, it allows me to view a situation firsthand, rather than having to rely on a verbal explanation. This cuts down on long, drawnout arguments. Second, it allows me to do things like type the minutes of a meeting in real time. People can read them with me, and when the workshop is finished, so are the minutes.

The room I share with my staff contains six small tables, each about one meter by one-half meter. We all have desks on wheels. When two or more employees need to discuss a topic, we meet in an adjacent room. Before each meeting, participants must write down the objectives and the amount of time they wish to take. This habit has forced us to be efficient and to consider the problem before doing anything else. This is how I have translated *kaizen* into an office environment.

The second visual change brought about by *kaizen* is the way I dress. I now wear the standard operator's uniform. This conveys two messages:

1. To the operators, it says, "Your problems and ideas are important."
2. To technical people, it says, "Reality lies in the worksite and not on our desks."

My way of speaking has also changed. I now ask "Why?" questions at least twenty times a day. Striving to understand *why* something is happening has become a reflex. In the past, I preferred simply to keep coming up with one new idea after another. This change has been profound. At first, I had to make a constant effort to refrain from considering solutions before I had fully understood the root causes of a problem.

The way I view problems has also changed. Since I started working in the industry, my intuition has told me that incremental improvement before innovation was the only way to foster sustained progress in a company. But until I heard about the *kaizen* approach, this was just a vague idea in my mind. *Kaizen* has made me aware that a problem is a golden opportunity to improve. No longer do I feel powerless in the face of a problem. Instead, I feel confident of my ability to improve the situation.

When I began implementing TPM in the *kaizen* spirit, I worked closely with one of the supervisors. He explained his problems to me in a straightforward manner. A typical Western manager would have viewed this man as a poor supervisor. (In fact, this supervisor is now recognized as one of the best in our plant.) The supervisor and I applied the "five-times-why" approach to each of his problems, and each time this approach yielded a good strategy for improving the organization. This experience brought me what I believe is the greatest attitudinal change I have ever experienced: *I no longer fear problems.*

MY COMMITMENT TO *KAIZEN*

My commitment to *kaizen* is natural. Since it has become the only way for me to improve, I do not have to force myself to work in this manner. However, I need to convince, if not to convert, my fellow workers. This is where a strong commitment is necessary. This commitment can be applied to a meeting at which people are seizing upon solutions without understanding the problem, or to an organization that stalls in the face of a setback such as the leak in the quarter-turn tap. Another aspect of commitment is sustaining continuous improvement even in a big new project.

Thus my commitment to *kaizen* is a daily one. It's my attitude both toward problems and toward people.

ABOUT THE AUTHOR

More than any other business authority in the world, Masaaki Imai has championed the concept of *kaizen* throughout the world in thought, word, and deed. Considered one of the leaders of the quality movement, Mr. Imai is an international lecturer, consultant, and chairman of the Kaizen Institute, which has offices worldwide.

Mr. Imai's first book, *Kaizen*—translated into 14 languages, with more than 179,000 copies sold—has become the "bible" of the quality/management movement. *Gemba Kaizen* picks up where *Kaizen* left off, introducing the latest quality-improvement methods and focusing on their application in making products and rendering services—the core activities of your business.

INDEX

KAIZEN® INSTITUTE

Founded by Masaaki Imai, the Kaizen Institute is a worldwide network of consultants from a wide variety of organizational, professional, and technical backgrounds with offices in Japan, Europe, and the United States. It also works through its licensees in South America and Mexico and has a plan to expand to other major industrial regions in the world.

Kaizen Institute's professionals share a common goal: to help their clients transform themselves into a world-class status in the global marketplace, able to sustain continual improvement in all technical, cultural, and leadership aspects of their enterprises. To do this, Kaizen Institute aims at transferring its expertise and technologies to its clients. Kaizen Institute places much emphasis in assisting its clients in building internal structures to assure continuity of companywide *kaizen* efforts.

The Kaizen consultants have visited and studied many of Japan's leading companies and have worked closely with their Japanese counterparts. They have led or been involved in significant change efforts, both as consultants and as executives in manufacturing and service companies. All are highly qualified by their experience, expertise, and ability to work with all management and employee levels, including union leadership.

Because of its close link with Japan, Kaizen Institute has access to the unique resource of Japanese experts in Just-in-Time, Total Productive Maintenance, Total Quality Management, Policy Deployment, and other systems that have made Japanese companies the leaders in quality and productivity. Kaizen Institute also arranges study tours for overseas managers to visit and observe Deming Prize, PM Prize, and other prize-winning companies as well as those companies that have successfully implemented just-in-time production systems in Japan.

The major services of Kaizen Institute include:

- Consulting for long-term *kaizen* implementation
- *Gemba Kaizen* workshops at the clients' sites
- In-house *Kaizen* seminars
- *Kaizen* Study Tours to Japan

The Kaizen Institute can be contacted at the following locations:

Kaizen® Institute (Japan)
MY Akasaka Bldg.,3F
2-11-15 Akasaka
Minato-ku, Tokyo 107
Tel: 81 3 5563 9391
Fax: 81 3 5563 9381
E-mail: gemba@kaizen.co.jp

Kaizen® Institute (Germany)
Königsberger Straße 2
60487 Frankfurt/Main
Tel: 49 69 953012 0
Fax: 49 69 953012 17
E-mail: 101553.3624@
  compuserve.com

Kaizen® Institute (France)
54 Boulevard Saint-Jacques
75014 Paris
Tel: 33 (0) 1 45 35 66 44
Fax: 33 (0) 1 45 35 65 64
E-mail: 101623.710@
  compuserve.com

Kaizen® Institute (UK)
4 Tavistock Place
London WC1H 9RA
Tel: 44 171 713 0407
Fax: 44 171 713 0403
E-mail: 100343.257@
  compuserve.com

Kaizen® Teaching International
  Coordination Office (Switzerland)
Zürcherstraße 4
8852 Altendorf
Tel: 41 55 451 19 40

Fax: 41 55 451 19 49
E-mail: 101553.3626@
  compuserve.com

Kaizen® Institute (USA)
930 South Mopac
Barton Oaks Plaza
Building II, Suite 530
Austin, TX 78746
Tel: 1 512 261 4900
Fax: 1 512 328 5749
E-mail: kmkad@mailaustin.
  computize.com

Kaizen® Support AB (Sweden)
Bredgränd 2
S-111 30 Stockholm
Tel: 46 8 790 50 35
Fax: 46 8 790 50 45

Kaizen® Institute (Spain)
C/Provenza, 288 Pral.
08008 Barcelona
Tel: 34 3 487 23 42
Fax: 34 3 487 96 76

STRAT (Argentina)
Av. Córdoba 1255-Piso 4
1055 Buenos Aires
Tel: 54 1 815 9652
Fax: 54 1 815 9658

ABG Internacional (Mexico)
A. De Cossio #105-90 Piso A
Col. Tangamanga, S.L.P. 78269
Tel: 52 48 17 94 81
Fax: 52 48 17 94 27